THE JORDANAIRES

THE JORDANAIRES

The Story of the World's Greatest Backup Vocal Group

AS TOLD BY GORDON STOKER

WITH MICHAEL KOSSER AND ALAN STOKER

Backbeat
Books

Essex, Connecticut

Backbeat Books

An imprint of Globe Pequot, the trade division of
The Rowman & Littlefield Publishing Group, Inc.
4501 Forbes Blvd., Ste. 200
Lanham, MD 20706
www.rowman.com

Distributed by NATIONAL BOOK NETWORK

British Library Cataloguing in Publication Information available

Library of Congress Cataloging-in-Publication Data

Names: Stoker, Gordon, 1924-2013, author. | Kosser, Michael, author. |
    Stoker, Alan, 1954- author.
Title: The Jordanaires : the story of the world's greatest backup vocal
    group / as told by Gordon Stoker, with Michael Kosser and Alan Stoker.
Description: Essex, Connecticut : Backbeat Books, 2022. | Includes
    bibliographical references and index. | Summary: "The Jordanaires were
    the premier studio backup group of the 1950s, 1960s, and 1970s. From
    Elvis to Patsy Cline, to Perry Como, and to Neil Young, they were much
    more than oohs, aahs, and doo-wops. Easy-going, talented, and thoroughly
    decent, they were the beloved confidantes of many of the world's
    greatest singing stars"— Provided by publisher.
Identifiers: LCCN 2022016105 (print) | LCCN 2022016106 (ebook) | ISBN
    9781493064571 (paperback) | ISBN 9781493064588 (epub)
Subjects: LCSH: Jordanaires (Musical group) | Vocal groups—United States.
    | Singers—United States—Biography.
Classification: LCC ML421.J67 S76 2022 (print) | LCC ML421.J67 (ebook) |
    DDC 782.42164092/2 [B]—dc23/eng/20220405
LC record available at https://lccn.loc.gov/2022016105
LC ebook record available at https://lccn.loc.gov/2022016106

CONTENTS

ACKNOWLEDGMENTS

We, the authors of this book, would like to thank the following people for their contributions to this book: John Rumble, Douglas B. Green, Paul Kingsbury, Bill Lloyd, Brent Stoker, Jenna Stoker Wright, Barb and Greg Hall, Bergen White, John Cerullo, Chris Chappell, Barbara Claire, Laurel Myers, Bobby Braddock, Kathleen Campbell, Don McLean, Steven Gaydos, Cole, Greg Matthews, Stan Hitchcock, Hylton Hawkins, Gina Kosser, Curtis Young, Brenda Lee, Ronnie McDowell, Hargus (Pig) Robbins, Brenda Colladay, and Ron Oates.

ABOUT THIS BOOK

Michael Kosser

The Jordanaires were a force in American music for more than six decades. Their voices appeared on billions of sold records. They were the spirit and vocal sound behind the king of rock and roll.

They were also a prime force in bringing country music into the mainstream of American culture, and there were weeks when you could hear their voices on half the records in the country's Top 10. All told, they backed up more than 2,000 recording acts, including many of the greatest names in American pop and country music. And before all of this, they, more than any other group in southern gospel music, brought the power of black spirituals to the attention of white America.

I first met Gordon Stoker in 1973 when I was a young songwriter getting my first country cut by the queen of country music, Kitty Wells. The Jordanaires were on that session, and they treated me and my cowriter as if they were our lifelong friends. How strange to think that nearly 50 years later, I would be cowriting a book with Gordon, 8 years after his passing, and his son, Alan, who has been my friend more than 30 years.

In this book, I am the one who writes in italics. The characters, the stories, the action, the facts, and the joy of it all come primarily from Gordon, Alan, and Alan's brother Brent but also from a number of other people who worked with the Jordanaires over the years. It's my job to take all these bits and pieces—which come from interviews, e-mails, social media posts, and other sources—and make them go together in such a way that you may understand how a handful of heartland boys changed all our lives. (A full list of sources can be found on page 219.) Thank you for taking the time to read about the greatest vocal backup group of all time, the Jordanaires.

INTRODUCTION

Alan Stoker

In my mind, my dad, Gordon Stoker, was the heart and soul of the Jordanaires, the greatest vocal backing group in the history of recorded music. If you knew him, you knew that he loved to laugh and to make people laugh. Being around him as family, we all knew that. But perhaps his favorite thing to do when family was together was tell stories about his life. And Lord knows, he had a ton of stories. Even though I heard the same stories many times, I would find myself hanging on every word.

Beginning in the 1970s, Dad sat for a series of one-on-one interviews at the Country Music Hall of Fame and Museum for their oral history project. Over the course of his life, he spoke to many TV and radio interviewers and spoke to many writers for other projects. At my request, he also recorded a couple of self-interview cassettes, beginning in 2004.

When Dad was asked what he'd been doing lately, one of his favorite replies was, "Oh nothing, just slaving over a hot microphone all day." When people would tell him that he should write a book, he would almost always say, "Nobody would want to read that" or "I don't have the patience to sit down and do that." But I believe his story and, indeed, his life are worth taking the time to write about. That's one of the reasons I agreed to help Michael when he approached me with the idea for this book.

Dad always wanted to tell the world about the Jordanaires: who they were and what they accomplished. So what did they accomplish? Six decades performing as a solo act and supporting many of the greatest singers/performers in country, pop, rock and roll, and gospel/spiritual music. And his story in music goes back to his early childhood. He had quite a professional career before he even started singing with the Jordanaires, as you will find out from reading this book.

There's a lot to tell. He didn't really get to tell it during his lifetime, not like he wanted to. Instead, he gets to tell it now, nearly a decade after he left us. Much of what you read are his words and his memories and those of his fellow Jordanaires, his family, and his colleagues on Nashville's Music Row and around the world.

My dear friend Greg Hall told me once, "Your dad and the quartet saw the world of pop music change across the microphone from and over the shoulders of some of the biggest stars of the time." He's right. They were a big part of that change, and what they helped create stands immortal. Not bad for a country boy from a small West Tennessee town who grew up with a slight speech impediment that bothered him for much of his life.

He was a great father to me, my brother Brent, and my sister Venita; a great husband and grandfather; and a giving and loving brother, uncle, and friend.

I have to mention my mom, Jean. Dad would be the first to say that he wouldn't have been nearly as successful without her love, companionship, and attention to detail. Mom handled most of the quartet's bookings, did the bookkeeping, and made sure that everyone got paid. From their first meeting outside a church in Nashville at an all-night singing, they were destined to spend the rest of their lives together.

We are happy to have the opportunity to take these words and memories and present them so as to give you an idea of what the Jordanaires did to influence the music of those six decades.

PROLOGUE:
A PLANNED MEETING

H. Gordon Stoker

By the summer of 1955, I thought I'd seen it all. I'd been performing professionally as a musician or singer since I was eight and been doing recording sessions for more than 15 years. We were one of the most popular vocal quartets in the South, making gospel records for major labels, performing live concerts, and appearing on TV or radio shows. For several years, we were popular performers on WSM radio's all-powerful Grand Ole Opry. On this particular evening, we were in Memphis appearing on a bill with Eddy Arnold. Just another concert, we thought.

That hot August night in the Ellis Auditorium, we were approached backstage by a struggling singer who had had some success and was hoping to make it big.

I guess the first thing I remember about him was his shirt. Men just didn't wear pink shirts in those days. He also was a little dirty around the neck. But he was polite and had a warm smile. So when he approached me, I took the time to hear what he had to say.

What he said was, "I'm a big fan of y'all's. I . . . I . . . I'm a singer myself." He stammered a little. "I'm on the Sun label right now. That's a local Memphis label. I'm . . . I'm trying to get a deal with a major label. If I do, I'd, ah, I'd like you guys, the Jordanaires, to sing with me on my records." He'd been hearing us sing, see, on the Grand Ole Opry, and he'd come backstage to meet us. He didn't come backstage to meet Eddy Arnold; he came backstage to meet *us*. Somewhere in there, he told us his name. We didn't catch it. Not then. He said, "Hey fellas, I want to *sing* a little something with you." I don't even know what we sang, probably "Swing Down Chariot." What I remembered about him is that back in 1955, a guy didn't wear a pink shirt. He wore that pink shirt with black trousers and a white stripe down the side. This was just a little unusual. He looked a little unusual too in that he had sideburns (which nobody else had) and had his hair slicked back (his hair wasn't black, as you know, his hair was dirty blonde), but the main thing I remember about him was his beautiful smile. He had an exceptionally beautiful smile. It was something that you don't forget, know what I mean? And he was extremely kind, very cordial to us, and I guess we wasn't used to being treated that way by a young guy. Later, I'd find that he got a lot of his clothes from one of the many clothing stores on Beale Street.

When I think back to that day and that conversation, I remember that it would have been easy for me to brush him off or discourage him somehow: "A major label deal? Well, that's not going to be easy, you know. Singing's a lot of fun, but you need a real job. Do you have something to fall back on?"

I could've, but I didn't. What if I'd been in a bad mood that day, or in a hurry? What if I just didn't like pink shirts and told him so? What if one of the guys just told him to buzz off?

But we didn't. That's not who we were. Besides, I liked him. Maybe his stuttering reminded me of myself because I had my own speech problems, and maybe that made me feel close to him. So I told him that when he *did* get signed by a major label, the Jordanaires would be happy to work with him. We exchanged a little more small talk, but I think that was the extent of the conversation.

Less than a year later, my home phone rang. For much of our career, the Jordanaires' office has been located in my home, my wife Jean being the one who handled the quartet's booking and scheduling. It was Chet Atkins's office at RCA in Nashville calling, wanting to book me for a recording session at the Trafco studio in the United Methodist Television, Radio and Film Commission Building on 1525 McGavock Street in Nashville with a new artist they had just signed.

Eight days after the phone call, I entered that studio and at the same time walked into a world that for me—and that for many of the greatest pop, rock, and country singers of the 1950s, 1960s, and 1970s and music lovers the world over—would never be the same.

Chapter 1

GLEASON, TENNESSEE: JUST THE RIGHT TOWN FOR JUST THE RIGHT KID

In the 1950s and 1960s, rhythm-and-blues and country music elbowed their way into the American mainstream pop music world. These two musical genres had a lot in common. Both came out of the rural and small-town South, often the product of intuitive musicians with more talent than formal education. These people were largely influenced by an American culture that would be fading into the past by the time they were adults presenting their music to the rest of America.

We are taught to believe that nothing much goes on in small towns, but you'll see that enough went on in Gleason, Tennessee, and surrounding communities to prepare Gordon Stoker for a long, influential career in American country, pop, gospel, and rock-and-roll music.

Pop stars are often hailed by the American media as self-invented super-talents, but the best of them tend to be super-sponges, absorbing music from all around them and synthesizing them into fresh combinations that awaken us. The Jordanaires were a gospel group whose original members came together from Kentucky, Tennessee, Missouri, and Oklahoma. These young men journeyed from Springfield, Missouri, to Nashville and found success in Nashville's new but burgeoning radio and live performing industries. Circumstances gradually led them away from the Jordanaires, and they were replaced, in time, by a new combination of young southerners who would sing together for nearly a quarter of a century. All told, the Jordanaires would be a force in American music for 65 years.

One of those replacements, Hugh Gordon Stoker, became the leader, that is, the manager of the Jordanaires. That doesn't mean he sat around making musical decisions for all the members—"you

1

sing this note, you two guys do the do-wops" and so on. Neal Matthews was the arranger for the group, but there were no singing robots here; all were an active part of the creative process. Gordon was part manager, part booker, and part spokesman. He was the guy to fill the role called "somebody has to do it!"

Gordon Stoker

Twenty-four years have passed, 24 of the best years of our lives. Today is a big day for the kid we first met at Ellis Auditorium in Memphis, way back when. He kept the promise he made to us that night, and we got to know him well enough to learn that he always kept his promises. Tonight Nashville is remembering his birthday, and we're sharing it with the rest of America on a 90-minute TV special called "Nashville Remembers Elvis on His Birthday," hosted by celebrity TV host Jimmy Dean. Guests on this show include many of Nashville's greatest stars, including Merle Haggard, Roy Orbison, Tanya Tucker, Dottie West, Charlie Rich, Jerry Lee Lewis, and Larry Gatlin, plus a ton of Hollywood movie stars doing cameos. Also us, the Jordanaires. They couldn't not invite us to the party, because for nearly 15 years we'd sung on almost all of his big hits and all the 28 movies he'd made during our time with him.

Over those years we had worked with him on countless singles, and nearly all those records read "Elvis Presley with the Jordanaires" on the label, because Elvis insisted on it. Most of those records were Top 10 pop hits or albums, and I think 16 were huge number one national and international pop smashes. All told we recorded more than 260 sides with Elvis, and thousands more with many of the most famous singers of the era. Maybe someday the Rock and Roll Hall of Fame will discover us. I'm sure that if Elvis were alive today he would say we need to have a plaque right next to his, and he would promise to get us one, and somehow he would find a way to keep that promise the way he kept all the others.

Elvis and the Jordanaires. Without Elvis. Singing a medley of his hits, that day, was not the easiest thing we'd ever do, even though we had sung each of those songs hundreds of times over the years. The one person who really needed to be there and was notably absent was the birthday boy himself. He had died the year before, and as we stepped onto the stage to do our part in the celebration, I felt a terrible ache at the back of my throat. I had spent much of the past year *not* thinking about Elvis. I knew nothing good could come of thinking about all the sweetness and decency that made him so special. All that would just bring tears, so I kept my mind on my work and my family and everything that meant anything to me—except Elvis. But this night—this gala tribute show, brought it all out. We took our places on the stage; Hoyt, me, Neal and Ray, left to right, from the view of the audience, and as usually happened, I took strength and confidence from their presence as we sang our medley—"Blue Suede Shoes," "All Shook Up," "Loving You," "Don't Be Cruel," and "Hound Dog." It wasn't one of our flawless performances, but it was tough for us to smile and sing at the same time. Backup singers have feelings too.

Before they started calling rock and roll "rock," it was mostly black. The nation's teenagers hadn't made up their mind, at least, not until Elvis, what the next big thing was gonna be. "Don't Be Cruel" was pure do-wop rock and roll, and that song was so big that I believe it helped establish the sound as early standard mainstream rock and roll. Elvis and Neal surely realized it. Just listen to "Stuck on You," "All Shook Up," "Too Much," and "Teddy Bear." Strange things were happening during those early years. Journalists were beginning to make value judgments about rock and roll. "These records weren't black enough." "Those covers were white kids stealing black songs." Never mind that covering songs has been a part of the recording industry since it began. Never mind that it made a few black songwriters a lot of money (if their publishers ever got round to paying them).

In his early days with RCA, Elvis did few covers. And it's really satisfying to listen to those old, brand new hits. To me the best of them sound as fresh today as the day Elvis, and the Jordanaires, sang them.

We've traveled the world, and sung for millions. Some say we've sold more than eight *billion* records. I've never done the math. We've recorded with more than 2,000 acts and made thousands of friends over six decades. I think what we did was terribly interesting, us starting out so darn small and somehow getting so big and you know what? It happened all right, but I'm danged if I understand how.

My name is Hugh Gordon Stoker and I was born August 3, 1924, in a small town halfway between Memphis and Nashville, about 120 miles from Nashville, 120 miles from Memphis, and 50 miles from Jackson, Tennessee. A town named Gleason. Gleason, Tennessee, has a population of about 1,400 people. The old joke used to be that every time a baby was born in Gleason, somebody would leave town. It's really strange, after all these years, the population has stayed about the same as it was when I was born. And that's a long time ago.

Everybody comes from somewhere. It's where they go that just might separate them from everybody else on the planet. Look up Gleason, Tennessee, and you won't find much, but it had enough to raise kids in.

Gleason was known as the tater town of the world. They raise more potato slips in Gleason than any place. They were shipped all over the world, certainly all over the U.S. Gleason isn't nowhere. It's linked to the rest of the world by the products they bring forth from the land in West Tennessee. Gleason is also known for having clay mines, and they produce some of the best clay of any place in the U.S.

I was born in the kitchen area of our home, in a building right downtown, next to the railroad tracks. My mother sent my sister Imogene (pronounced EYE-ma-gene) and my two brothers, Arnice and Wayne down to my Aunt Lilly's house while Dr.

Goldsby delivered me in the afternoon of August 3. My brothers and sister were way older than me. My dad always thought I was an accident. Looking back at what they all did for me I'm sure I was their pet.

We shared the building with the little telephone company that my mother and dad worked for. We lived in the switchboard area of that building. It was a two-story building—all those buildings were two-story buildings and it was the second story that I was born on. The lower floor was a bank for a while, and then later it became the Gleason Post Office. The second floor was the switchboard area, where my mother and dad ran the telephone company. My daddy was a crackerjack repairman, for telephones or anything of that nature. He kept the telephones and the lines for about 300 subscribers in working condition. I don't ever remember anybody ever complaining, but I'm sure they must have. My mother would run the switchboard at night. Miss Jenny Taylor was the daytime operator. She answered the calls from 6 a.m. till 5 or 6 p.m., bless her heart. That's a lot of hours. And then my mother came on at six in the evening and she was on till nine in the evening. Then they closed the switchboard down, so from 9 p.m. to 6 a.m. you could not call unless it was an emergency or a fire or something like that.

That building where we lived—by the railroad tracks—we would have four passenger trains a day, run on those railroad tracks, and of course several freight trains that passed through every day. The building was there until last year [around 2003]. They tried to restore it, but, uh, during the process of restoring it, it kind of fell down so they tore down the rest of it and I'm sorry that they tore it down, 'cause it was part of a long line of other businesses there, which I'll always remember, places where I went when I was a child, to Trevathan's Grocery Store and Gleason Hardware Store and Brumitts Department Store where my mother bought socks and shoes for me—and the city drug store where I always loved to get milkshakes and things of that nature.

The passenger trains would run at 10 a.m. going in one direction, 12 noon going in the other, then 2 p.m. going back in the same . . . and then 6. In other words two trains going in one direction and two trains going in the other direction. And you could catch those trains and they'd take you pretty much anywhere you want to go. Later on in my life, I would catch one of those trains to go to Nashville.

I guess that's the reason I like to hear trains blow their whistles now, because I was a baby when I first heard those trains blow their whistles. We lived in that building by the railroad tracks until I must have been about two years old. Then my daddy built a house. The house is still standing. And we all moved out from the switchboard building, and they got another operator that lived there. In other words, you lived on the premises if you were the nighttime operator. So we all moved into the house that Dad built himself—I'm sure he did most of the work himself. He was very handy. Anything he set his head on doing, he could do.

His name was Hugh Ambus Stoker, but they always called him H. A. Stoker. And the Hugh of my name probably came from him. My dad's tombstone, it has Ambus Hugh Stoker, but A.H. just wasn't very good sounding, I guess, and so he used for his initials H.A.

Just across the railroad tracks, about a block's distance, was the Gleason High School, they called it, which actually went from grade 1 to grade 12. And that's where I went from grammar school through high school, and graduated in 1942. By the way, Gleason had *two* telephone companies. They had the rural telephone company, which my dad and mother operated. And then they had another, called Cumberland Telephone Company. And that's the only telephone company that you could call out of Gleason on. It was connected to the long-distance facilities.

My brother Arnice bought me my first tricycle and I still reminisce about those days when I used to pedal down the hill, past the front of our house. He also bought me my first little red wagon.

And he also bought—bless his heart—he and my other brother Wayne were working at Nance's Mill, which made what we called potato hampers, because they grew a lot of sweet potatoes around Gleason. I think they made a dollar working 10 or 12 hours a day at Nance's Mill. And my brother Arnice bought the family our first record player, a portable-type Victrola record player—which I still have—and it still plays.

My dad started buying records, 78 rpm records, breakable records, from Sears and Roebuck, and all these different companies that you could get recordings from. He especially liked to order the Carter Family recordings. And my sister loved Gene Austin, who was one of the biggest record sellers in those days. My dad would order records from Sears Roebuck in Chicago, or Montgomery Ward out of Memphis, which as I mentioned was only 120 miles away. You could get three recordings for a dollar. And do you know I don't remember a time that we got three 78s from Memphis that one of them was broken. They had a way of packing them that—they just didn't get broken very easily, but of course, at home *we* broke them many times: set down on them, or dropped 'em or just something, and you'd break um and boy there'd be plenty of tears when you'd break 78 records, I can assure you.

He bought a lot of quartet recordings. Ah, the ones I remember most was the Vaughan Quartet from over in the Lawrenceburg area. He would buy any quartet record he could get his hands on. I think that might have had an influence on my wanting to be in a male quartet, him buying all these male quartet recordings. But I was mainly interested in the way the Carter Family sang, 'cause they had unusual—it wasn't particularly perfect harmony by any means. But . . . the way that Maybelle Carter picked the melody on her guitar; I had never heard anyone pick the melody on a guitar like Maybelle Carter, and this really influenced my ear—a lot.

See, both of my brothers, and my dad and even my mother, played guitar. And a lot of my relatives around us played guitars.

So I heard a lot of people play guitars, even as a child. And the reason Maybelle's picking interested me so much was because hers was entirely different from anyone just beating on a guitar. At the time I could only dream about hearing her play live. Someday I would get that chance. I guess I am one very lucky person.

Chapter 2

I COULD HAVE ACTUALLY BEEN A GREAT MUSICIAN

Gordon Stoker

After we moved to the house up on the hill that my daddy built, I shared a bedroom with my sister, Imogene, who was 13 years older than me, and I had a speaking problem when I was 3 or 4 years old. Since I slept with her it was easy for her to try to correct me. But I had a problem talking plain and I even have a problem talking plain today. When I do these radio interviews I try to pronounce words right and do a good job of talking but I still have problems. So my sister Imogene would constantly drill me on saying words correctly. I said "twee" for tree, I'd say "penny" for twenty, just many things I couldn't say plain, and Imogene, bless her heart, would drill me by playing piano for me to sing solos. That got me to banging on the piano and my mother would put the lid down 'cause she didn't have a key to lock it, and she didn't want me to beat on the piano because they had some kind of thing in their mind that beatin' on the keys would get the thing out of tune, and I'm sure that at that age I wouldn't have beat hard enough to have knocked it out of tune.

So they kept the lid down on the piano but every chance I got, when I could slip around, I'd put the lid up on that piano and just play on notes. Imogene would try to teach me piano too, and she did teach me the very beginning of learning to play.

Gordon's family wasn't just humoring him. Even during his toddling years, they had to know that something musically special was going on inside his head. His niece, Jenna Stoker Wright, who also grew up in Gleason, recalls this family moment.

Jenna Stoker Wright

My grandmother once told me that when Uncle Gordon was only three years old, he came home from a gospel singing, pulled himself up on the piano bench, and started playing some of the music they had heard at the singing.

Gordon

Right from the beginning, I could sing. I had a very high voice before my voice changed. You couldn't hit a note that I couldn't reach. Imogene would play for me, and I mainly sang gospel songs, songs out of the songbook, "'Neath the Old Olive *Twee*" was one of them. We would sing at church functions, functions all over the county actually, and many places in Tennessee where we had transportation, I would go and sing and my sister would play. One time they had an amateur contest at the Gleason Auditorium, and my sister entered me into this contest. She played for me to sing, "Have you ever been lonely, have you ever been *boo.*"

There was a lot of people entered into the contest. Various musicians, singers, people from all over the county came to that contest. I won first prize, actually a bunch of prizes, a set of glassware and some other things I can't remember at the moment. But the main thing was, it got me noticed by so many people, and I was only six or seven years old and I don't know if the fact that I couldn't pronounce "blue," would have anything to do with me winning the contest, but they said I had such a beautiful voice and all that kind of carrying on, and I like to think *that's* the reason I won it.

Before I knew it, I was taking piano lessons from Ms. Tom Cates. Ms. Lucille Cates was her name, her husband was named Tom, he led the singing in our church, and she played the piano in our church, and she also taught piano at the Gleason High School. They had a piano in the basement of that grammar/high school and that's where I took lessons from her. I think the lessons were fifty cents a week. We could afford it 'cause my dad had a salary. Very few people in Gleason had a salary, and I've been told it was $50 a month, and in the twenties, in a small town like Gleason, $50 a month was good money. We had a cow and we had chickens and we had this and we had that, and he would pick up $10, $15 here and there; he always made the best out of anything. Soon we bought our first car—it was a 1928 Chevrolet. It had a curtain in the back window, and I can remember as a child, standing in the back seat and pulling that curtain down.

Then in 1934 he bought a Ford. It was only a two-door car, and the two doors opened out, from the windshield toward the back. He heard that doors like that were dangerous, so he got rid of the '34 Ford, and bought a brand new 1937 Ford. I can remember so well, that was a beautiful car. We've still got pictures of it, scattered around.

We had one cow, and I can remember so well, the cow saw her reflection on the car, ran into it, butted her head up against it and skint the door up real bad and, ooo I remember my dad was so upset, 'cause my dad didn't get too upset about many things, but, boy if he could have killed that cow he would of.

I think they drove that 1937 Ford until they got a '51 Pontiac, which I have today in my garage.

I took music from Ms. Cates starting at about seven years of age, and the next teacher I had was Ms. Reba Oliver. She was my main teacher. She played a lot of classical music, and that's what she wanted me to be, a classical musician. I played a few classical pieces, but nothing to speak of, I can assure you. I took from her more than from any other teacher. Of all the students she had, and I'm sure she had as many students as she could, I won a gold medal for my music in 1933, which I still have. And then I won another medal in 1934, a little gold piano, which I think I still have. We'd have these recitals, and I always had to play in these recitals, which I hated, but I did it anyway.

A lot of people laughed at me for playing and singing. That was always my main problem. Made me different, you know. Had not so many people laughed at me and called me sissy and called me this and called me that for playing and singing, and of course I had a high voice and that made for even more laughs—if only—I might have had a happier childhood. Of course, Imogene and my mom and dad and my brothers and a lot of people encouraged me, but I had a lot more people making fun of me than the ones that were encouraging me. I could have actually been a great musician, but there was something in my mind that kept telling me, if I don't practice, if I don't learn to play this music that I'm given to play, that I'm assigned in lessons each week, then they won't laugh at me.

Of course, that's not the way it worked, but that was in my mind. You know, they laugh at you every way you turn, for playin' piano, and for singing, but I can remember the very ones that didn't laugh at me—I'm talking about my classmates—that didn't laugh at me. I even had teachers laugh at me. I had one teacher that really put me down one day and this just nearly killed me. You know, these things are things that are very hard for you to overcome. And I've always thought that I would have been a much better musician—I *know* I would have been a much better musician, if people had just not laughed at me. So anyone who reads this, if people laugh at you, just smile at them and go ahead and say, "Someday I'm gonna be laughin' at *you*." You know what's funny about this? While I'm writing this I'm thinking of so many people that fell by the wayside long, long ago, and here I am, still going, and here I've done well financially and, I've been so blessed in so many ways, and if I had my time to go over it, maybe I could just look at those people and laugh right back.

But of course, at the time this is going on, you certainly don't think of looking at the ones that laugh at you and making a face at them or something like that; you're hurt, you're put down, and you go the sad way of so many people that *could* be great musicians or great singers.

A lot of the records that my father bought when I was a child were Jimmie Rodgers records. I guess he bought just about every recording that Jimmie Rodgers made. And I used to stand by the record player, as a five or six year old kid, and make out like I was playing the guitar, and singing. Of *course* I was singing, and every recording my dad bought, I knew every word and you know it's really strange, even today I remember the words of those recordings. And it mattered that my parents were singers; my mother'd sing alto and my daddy'd sing tenor, and I would sing the lead. And my brother Wayne if he was available, he would sing bass with us. We had a Stoker family quartet, and we sang at a lot of places. And when we were singing together at night it didn't matter so much that the kids had made fun of me in the daytime.

I got me an accordion at a very early age, and I started playing that accordion, and I would sing with my mother and dad, and if Wayne wasn't available, we'd just sing as a trio. And soon we were singin' in front of people, and they thought we were *fine*. There was a singin' every Sunday afternoon in different towns around Gleason, in Dresden every fourth Sunday, McKenzie every third Sunday, Huntingdon, I think, every second Sunday, and somewhere there'd be one every first Sunday, and we would go to these singin's. And at these singin's, different musicians would play the piano, but then all of a sudden, one girl appeared from Fulton, Kentucky, by the name of Ruth Byers, and she could play so good, she was the first person I ever heard that added something to her music, I mean, Imogene, and Ms. Reba Oliver and the various persons that played around Gleason, they played the music pretty much like it was written, pretty much by the book.

Now that's not saying that the others weren't good, they were, but here was this Ruth Byers, all of a sudden, that came on the scene, and she added stuff to her music, and, man, I thought it was something heavenly, I just couldn't believe it, and little by little, when I was either 9 or 10 years old, I started listening to her every chance I could get. If we knew she was gonna be anywhere near us, or even in Paducah, my mother and dad would drive me to wherever she was gonna be, just for me to get to listen to her play the piano, and then all of a sudden she took an eye to me, took an interest in me.

When I started taking piano lessons, I discovered that I had a God-given gift. But I tried to hide it, because I didn't want to be laughed at by the guys. The girls and the older folks loved it, of course, and that was okay. But when Ruth took an eye to me, that made a difference. Even to this day I still hear from her occasionally, and she still calls me Hugh Gordon, her dear friend of long ago. There was really no one that encouraged me as much as Ruth Byers did when I needed it.

Before I knew it, I was going to singing conventions, and they'd say, "Let that Hugh Gordon Stoker play the piano," and even Ruth Byers, when she would be at these places, she'd say, "Let that little ol' Stoker boy play." People started noticing *me*, and soon they would be applauding, and when I'd walk into these various places, in McKenzie, Dresden, Martin, wherever these singing conventions took place, they would give *me* a hand, and this attention really set me out to want to be a professional entertainer.

When I was about 10 years old, we went to McKenzie, and there was a trio, with a woman playing a piano for her three children, a little boy, Fred Junior, and his two sisters, Gloria and Rachel. This was the Clement Trio. Their father had been admiring my playing for some time. He wanted me to play for them. He asked me if he could come to Gleason and bring 'em, and we could rehearse, and I said, "Sure!" One of those things. My mother and dad loved it and I did too. This was the start of something. Tennessee, Kentucky, Illinois, we did a lot of work around, we even went to Detroit, and appeared before, I guess, 3,000 or 4,000 people, and in those days that was a lot of people.

Gloria Clement sang the low part, she was about six or seven years old, and she just absolutely took an audience by singing the alto, or the lead or whatever you would call it in the trio, but she was a hit everywhere she went. Fred Junior taught me quite a few things on the accordion, and he was a heck of an entertainer himself, but the trio really did well, appeared at a lot of places, and did a lot of music, and then, all of a sudden there was a girl's quartet, from Paris, Tennessee, and the father of two of the girls, Mr. Hastings, had been hearing me play, so he asked me if I would play for them, and here I was, all of a sudden, playing for the Clement Trio, for something they might have gotten booked, and then playing for the Girls Harmony Four from Paris, Tennessee. There was two sisters, Jo Nell and Sue Jean Ford. And then two other sisters, Betty and Nodgle Hastings and what was so funny about all these things was that Rachel, of the Clement trio, was wild about me, and then, here come Jo Nell Ford from the Girls Harmony Four, *she* was wild about me. She even corresponded with me when I went into the service.

All of a sudden you wake up and you've got two pretty little girls in two different groups that are crazy about you and I guess you'd call it puppy love, but anyway, whatever it was it sure didn't hurt my confidence.

Meanwhile I was singing solos in school programs, and at religious conventions all over West Tennessee and some parts of Kentucky, to the point where they would call and see if "Hugh Gordon Stoker," as they said, "could appear at our convention and sing for us." I went to a Baptist church, and the Baptists are always having various kinds of conventions, you know, association meetings, that type of thing. They'd want some sort of entertainment before they started, and they would call my sister and me to come and sing. West Tennessee, southern Kentucky, I really didn't know what I was doing, I was singing for people before I could even talk plain.

A lot of music people from Nashville would come through town. My dad and mother would take me to various programs in the area, so I could hear them. Some of them were from the Grand Ole Opry, and that got me wishing I could go to Nashville and see them there, along with all the other people from the Opry. They were like friends to me, you know, 'cause every Saturday night I got to hear them live on the radio. By the time I was in high school, it seemed like everyone from the Grand Ole Opry, from Roy Acuff to Pee Wee King (who fascinated me because he'd play the accordion, which I really dug) they'd come and play the schoolhouse in our area.

And of course, my mother and dad really loved quartets—religious quartets, like the Rangers Quartet, the Vaughan Quartet, the Stamps-Baxter Quartet—all these various music companies had their quartets that they had on salaries in those days. The Vaughan Company, they had people hired under them, on their staff, on their payroll is what I'm trying to say. So in addition to their jobs, they'd go out and play dates. And they would sell their songbooks, and give a certain portion of the songbook sales back to the company. The company guaranteed them the gas and the car to travel in, that type of thing.

I was always fascinated by the piano players who would play on those shows. I remember so well when James D. Walbert, and the Vaughan Quartet came to Gleason and played in a country church out from Gleason. It was one of those old wooden frame buildings that had a high roof, you know how those old churches used to have. It had a few wooden planks that used to make up the ceiling. One or two of those planks had fallen down kind of, and when James D. Walbert began pounding the keyboard—I don't mean so loud but he played great because he played so *much* piano—well, a snake was evidently vibrated in the roof of that church building, and that snake fell down into the audience while he was playing a solo.

Of course, all the women screamed. I can remember. I was still just a kid but believe me, I can remember that snake falling down from that ceiling when he played that piano. He played so much piano, and I'm sure that that church had never heard such piano as James D. Walbert played that day.

Chapter 3
TURNING PRO

One day, the future came charging into Gordon's life, though naturally he had no way of knowing it was about to happen.

Gordon Stoker

These singing conventions would usually be held in the auditorium or gymnasium of a school building, because the churches we had generally weren't big enough. They had what they called class singing, from songbooks. The songs in all those books were written in shape notes, which looked a lot like regular musical notes, except the bodies of the notes instead of them all being oval or round, had a variety of "shapes," such as triangles, diamonds, squares, and half-rounds. And the shapes of those notes were key to reading the music. I'd say 90 percent of the people who attended these conventions could read shape notes, and they could sing the darn things.

They'd have class singing in the morning, then they'd go break for lunch, then they'd go back and sing two or three hours in the afternoon. They used to do those things all over Tennessee. They had many of them even in Nashville. They'd sell songbooks for 50 cents a book at these conventions, and they'd sell every one they'd bring in. Everyone would buy one of them dang books, and they'd sing, and they'd learn 'em real good, because they'd attend singings on Fridays, Saturdays, and Sundays. Even every Sunday, there'd be a singing convention somewhere in our part of West Tennessee.

The Rangers appeared at these singings I'm telling you about, and the Vaughan Quartet, the Walbert Quartet—would you believe even the Speer Family appeared at these various things when Ben and Brock were little kids, and Rosa Nell and Mary Tom Speer. That's how I heard them. That's how I knew them, through these gospel singings.

As a matter of fact, when the Speer Family appeared—now this was, I'd say, in the '30s—'38, '39, somewhere along in there—they appeared at a place somewhere around Milan, Tennessee, and my dad and my mother took me there to hear them. First time I'd ever heard them.

Mrs. Speer played the accordion, Brock played the guitar, and Rosa Nell played the piano, and, man, when they started singing, the place went—just really, really got off to—it's hard to explain, but at that particular singin', they started singing and they moved the audience so much with their singing, that the whole place got to shouting. I was a very small boy, but I realized then how potent, how strong that was. I knew that a group could get up in front of an audience and move an audience to this state—and they didn't even have a loudspeaker. It had just been that class singing. That's where everybody sings. You place the baritones over here and the basses over there, the altos over here and the sopranos over here. Then you'd throw out these books to the crowd if they didn't have a book. Most people would buy their book for 50 cents, but if they didn't have a book, they'd be provided with one.

Most of them could read the parts. But those that *couldn't* read them knew what they were supposed to sing anyway—you know, they went to every singing, and they'd heard the songs so many times—you see, there were certain numbers in every book that were very, very popular. I can remember the song "I'm Going to Take a Ride," that G. T. Speer wrote, that moved the audience so much that the whole place got to shouting. If a quartet could get in front of an audience, and excite them so, well, I knew that was something that I wanted to do.

Actually, the Speer Family was the only group I ever heard that could move an audience to where they would form a shout. I mean, people got up and shouted all over the building! And it really impressed me, as a very young person, that that was something very strong, that the words of a song really meant something. I've talked with several people who, when I would say something like that, they'd say, "Well, really, I became converted through hearing some great song that moved me to the extent where I became a Christian."

I would go to those conventions, and I first really learned to play the piano after going to those things. And once I got to play really well, it got to a point where when I'd walk in, man, they'd say, "Gordon Stoker's here. You're gonna play the piano for us." A lot of times they'd give me a big hand when I'd come through the door. So indirectly, I became a star at the singing conventions, even though I didn't really want it. Had I wanted it, I would have been much greater than what I was, but, within my heart, I really didn't want to be a piano player. Isn't that funny?

When I was in my teens I went to the Vaughan Music School in Lawrenceburg, Tennessee, for a little while. They had a three-week course, and they would even give you one credit for your high school if you made a good grade. I did, and I got my one credit. We would meet like nine in the morning and they had teachers who would teach you. Then you'd take a piano lesson, or whatever instrument you wanted to take. They taught the rudiments of music, that included shape notes, and conventional notes too. Then in the afternoon, we'd start singing at two o'clock, and we'd sing till four. They had voice teachers, taught us a lot. I know they did. Gave me more confidence. And I kept singing at conventions and things. My sister would play for me and I'd sing, but at first I'd have to sing without a microphone. Then, when I started singing more in gymnasiums, we absolutely had to have a mic or the people couldn't hear us. So they'd rent just a mic, an amp, and two little speakers, which weren't capable of covering the auditorium with sound at all, but it was better than standing up there and singing so they couldn't hear nothing coming out of your mouth, you know.

And every now and then we'd get paid a little something, maybe a couple or $3. Then, sometimes, someone would ask you to play or sing on a radio station, and *they* might give you a couple or $3 for *that*. So I always managed to make a little something playing or singing, even when I was thirteen, 14 years old. I think that's how I bought my mother a living room suite and chairs and a dining room suite and various things. Things that she wanted I was able to buy for her. I didn't make much money, but I made enough. I would play all during the summer, and I would play on weekends, even when I was going to grammar school and high school.

And right about then, I found steady work in the world of gospel music. There was this radio station in Paducah, Kentucky, WPAD, and every Sunday morning a man named W. W. Hawkins had a show. He heard me play in an auditorium in Paris, Tennessee, and he told me, "Son, you've got something I want to hear. I want you every weekend to catch a bus or a train and come over to Paducah," and I said I would.

I'd leave Gleason on Friday afternoon and come back most of the time on Monday morning. The people in school knew why I'd come in late on Monday mornings but they'd go along with my schedule because I guess they knew I had a talent for playing the piano. They'd let me come in like noon on Monday and leave at noon on Friday so I could play the piano at the radio station. I played on that station for a long time with the Hawkins Brothers Quartet; the Hawkins Quartet they were called in those days. They were Hoyt Hawkins, Boyce, Charles, and Mr. Hawkins, and Hoyt will be turning up later in this story.

I was learning about radio. Our show had several sponsors. In those days, how you got your sponsors, you'd go out and get your sponsors for a program. So if you had three sponsors and that program cost $50 to get on the air, those sponsors would split the fee. You had to go out and contact those sponsors yourself, and collect the fee yourself, and you had to take that fee to the radio station. That's the way all those early shows were done. You built some profit for yourself into the fee, plus you would sell songbooks on the air, plus you would promote the dates that you was going to play: "Tonight, we're going to be in Paducah. Next Friday night you can catch us in McKenzie." All the people back there in the thirties really listened to the radio, and if they liked us, they'd go where we were playing and buy a ticket and maybe buy another book.

We would buy these songbooks from Stamps Company, you see. We'd pay 25 cents for the songbook, then sell it for 50, so we'd make a quarter a book. That sounded pretty good. Mr. Hawkins would let the three boys and myself go out and sell these songbooks and for boys like us that was real money to stick in our pockets.

And you'd write your own commercial and you would read that commercial on the radio station during the time that you bought from that station. The station had a flat fee that you paid, and you would go out and get your sponsors. Then on Sunday morning or whenever you had your program, you'd reserve a certain length of time to talk about what a great grocery store so-and-so's got, or what a great tire this was to buy for your car and all that type of thing. And the grocery store and the tire store would pay their fee and they'd sell more groceries and tires and you'd get more fees and that's how you made your money.

In 1936, while I was attending the Vaughan School of Music during the summer, I first met the Johnson Family Singers, a great gospel group. There was the twin boys, Bob and Jim, their older brother, who was called "Booger Red," their sister Betty, and Jesse and Lydia, who were Pa and Ma Johnson. Boy, listen, let me tell you, this group got up to sing one afternoon—the first day I was there, and man, I like to flipped, and everybody else did too, because they had a special arrangement on "Amazing Grace" that just absolutely thrilled everybody to death. I don't know if I can describe what they did. They didn't have a country accent, even though they were from North Carolina. They had a different brogue from what we had, as we called it in those days. It was just real neat and real clever, the way they sang their notes together. They were just different from anyone else.

They heard me play the piano for the class singing, and Pa Johnson asked me if I'd go with them on weekends to some churches. Believe me, I was poor, but they were even poorer than what I was. They didn't have the price of a newspaper. The little amount of money that they made on the weekends was really all the money that they had to eat on. Later, after the Vaughan School of Music, they came through Nashville. John Daniel—he was very popular in those days, and he had the Daniel Quartet—he told me that the Johnsons didn't have the money to get out of town, and John had to give them the money. Of course, that was not unusual with gospel singers. They would get out and sing and make a little money and buy them a little gas and a little food and a few clothes and move on down the road to another town. That's the way the Johnson family did at the time, but they had great talent.

I played for them the entire three weeks that I was in Lawrenceburg. We later became friends, and I played for them at various times. As a matter of fact, I was instrumental in getting Betty Johnson on the Grand Ole Opry here in Nashville, and on "Sunday Down South" and some other programs here in Nashville.

During that time I got by primarily on my piano style. In those days you just hauled off and sang, period. My voice was high like a girl's voice before it changed when I was 14. I sang what you would call, I guess, in falsetto, and I could really hit the high notes, believe me, before my voice changed.

But in those days, piano is what I really worked at, playing by ear, even though I could read the music; all the extra stuff you add to your playing is done strictly by ear. It's a talent, just like these singers who improvise on the hymns. Of course, some people play it just as they read it, but 90 percent of what you hear that gets on those various religious programs and sounds so great, they're doing it mainly by making it up as they go along, just strictly by ear.

Now, you might ask, when I was 15, 16, going to the music schools, did I think at the time that I would grow up and do this for a living. The answer is no. I thought I'd like to, but I didn't think

I had enough talent to. It's a funny thing. I've always been put in positions where I've been required to do more than I've been able to do. So, for example, I'd be required to play better piano than I knew how. Even when I was a kid, I was given more difficult stuff than what I could play, and I was required to play in various places for various people on various things that I didn't feel I was capable of doing. And somehow I was able to do it, sort of. I was able to bluff my way through it, but I didn't feel, after it was over, that I did nearly as good a job as what I should have done.

So, getting back to my high school days, what I really wanted to do was be a musical director in a church. I would have liked to do that, but here again, that takes a lot of training, and it takes a lot of knowledge. Now, my parents, they wanted me to make my living in music. Looking back a little, they pushed me to be in music. Any band program that they could take me to, they took me. Lots of times they probably would not have gone if it had not been for me.

There's moments when something happens that will someday change your life forever, and you don't know at the time that it's happening. I was playing the piano with the Girls Harmony Four, at the Sneed Grove Picnic in McKenzie. There were several others on this picnic show that Mr. Sneed invited, several groups from Nashville and what have you, huge crowd, an outdoor affair, and John Daniel, who had the Daniel Quartet from Nashville, who appeared on the Grand Ole Opry and were on WSM every morning, he asked me, "Son, how old are you?" and I said, I guess, I was 14. He said, "When you gonna be out of high school?" I told him and he said, "Son, I'm gonna call you, and I'm gonna bring you to Nashville and make a star out of you."

The Daniel Quartet was the first gospel quartet to sing on the Opry network, *The Prince Albert Show*. So what he said should have meant something to me. And he said, "Son, I want you to play for my group one day." Well you know, I figured, so what? I'd been told that I was a good piano player, a good singer, since I was a very small kid, and really, I didn't pay much attention to it, but I *was* thrilled that he said that to me.

Like I said you don't always know a big moment in your life when it hits you. I want you to know that almost the very day I finished high school, one of those moments came back to hit me between the eyes. I finished high school on a Friday night and on Saturday morning I got a call from the Esso filling station in downtown Gleason. You might recall there were two phone systems in town, the rural system my dad and mother worked for, and the Cumberland system, from which you could call out of town. The filling station had both systems. So the guy at the filling station called us on the rural phone and said, "John Daniel called for you and if you get on down here, he'll be calling back for you in a few minutes."

I hurried on down to the Esso and the phone rang and there was John Daniel, on the other end, keeping a promise. "Hey," he said. "Didn't you finish high school yesterday?"

I said, "Yes, sir."

He said, "How soon can you get to Nashville? I want you to come to Nashville as soon as you can, let me know when you'll be here, and I'll meet you at the train station." I was 17. You know, I knew he believed in me, but I'm not sure that *I* believed in me. Not completely. I was thrilled to death and scared to death, and I didn't have any more sense than to come. I got my things ready, and here I came to Nashville.

On that train that ran by the switchboard building in Gleason. As soon as I got to Nashville John took me to the studio to rehearse. They really had great dreams for me to play the piano for them. And they were right. Before I knew it, I was playing piano on their early morning radio programs, on a 50,000-watt station. We were on every morning, and boy in those days, that was in 1942, a 50,000-watt station reached a lot of territory.

I'd never lived in the city before in my life. It was a scary thing for me, but John was very kind to me. I lived in John's house out here at 2607 Belcourt Avenue. The house is still there.

Mrs. Daniel took me under her wing and made me feel at home. I lived with them and started appearing with the Daniel Quartet on the Grand Ole Opry. I was the youngest person on the Opry in those days. This was in 1942 and '43. John paid me a weekly salary and then he gave me a commission on songbooks that I'd sell. We appeared at a lot of conventions. We appeared at a lot of auditoriums. We played high schools, and we appeared on a lot of shows with the Grand Ole Opry people. Bill Monroe was one. A lot of people I'd listened to on Saturday nights were on those programs.

The Carter Family was on some program that we were on. I met them and of course I was so excited, I will never forget it. Here I am, playing piano with the Daniel Quartet, and we played some personal appearance in some auditorium somewhere and the Carter Family's on the bill. I said, to nobody really, "I can't believe I'm going to get right up close to Maybelle Carter and hear her play the guitar." Well, the time came and I asked her to play something, and she did. I will never forget her kindness. After all, who was I? I was no one, and she was a star, but Maybelle wasn't that way. Maybelle never considered herself a star, and I always appreciated that.

Then there was us, the Daniel Quartet. Actually there was five of us including me on the piano, but you still called us a quartet, because there were four male singers. One of them was Wally Fowler—he was Wallace Fowler in those days, before he became famous in gospel music. Jesse McCurdy sang bass. John sang first tenor and his brother, Troy, sang second tenor. We stole almost every show we went on with "I Found a Hiding Place." We broke up the Grand Ole Opry every Saturday night with "I Found a Hiding Place." I guess we were one of the few acts on the Grand Ole Opry that got an encore. We always did, with just one song, really.

We'd sing one chorus through, and then John would take the chorus and sing real loud. And Wallace Fowler would jump up— he was a fat boy, first of all—and as John would hit the high note, Wallace would jump up off the floor, and everybody would laugh.

As a result, why, they would applaud, and bring us back to the chorus to see Wallace jump up again when John would hit the high note.

We did the same types of songs as all the other quartets. Most gospel quartets had their own special hits, certain songs that they could sing better than other groups. Occasionally there'd be a little group that would get out and sing your hits before you got on the program, but you'd still go out there and you'd also sing those songs, because you were known for singing those certain songs. A few quartets, like the Rangers and the Vaughan Quartet, had a recording contract, and those groups would take their records and sell them. Or you might appear on a radio show singing your songs and the people who heard them and liked them might follow you around as you sang on the different conventions, because they wanted to hear you sing them live.

Part of my job was transposing the material that we did on the *John Daniel Early Morning Radio Show*. After each show was over John would come to me and say, "You know, tomorrow, we're gonna do this number." And the sheet music he'd hand me might be in the key of C, and he'd say, "That's too high, we're gonna have to do it in B-flat." We had little time to rehearse it the day before, and I didn't have enough time to write it out, so the next morning, with just a little bit of practice, I'm trying to read the sheet music in front of me in the key of C, but I'm trying to play it in B-flat. It forced me to learn quickly how to transpose in my head. So I would look at some of it, quickly, and start playing, hoping that I'd get close enough to get it right.

I got to where I *could* get it right, most of the time. But there was this one time on the show, where I started out playing in the key that was on the sheet music in front of me, not the key we were gonna sing it in, a couple of steps too high, and the singer, I think it was John Daniel's brother Troy, started off, and his voice squeaked and squealed something awful, and we were alive on the air, and the other guys *died* laughing!

But before long I learned how to do it right, and that really helped me years later with the Jordanaires.

I was living in a completely different world than during my high school years playing for little or no money. We'd go out on weekends, play anywhere from 100 to 300 miles from Nashville. We appeared on WSM Radio every morning, Monday through Friday, around 6, 6:15, and you had a lot of listeners at that time. And let me tell you, I drew more mail just being the piano player for the Daniel Quartet than what I imagine every act put together on the Grand Ole Opry pulls now.

Alan Stoker

Dad told me that he played on the radio in the morning before he left to go by train to basic training. John Daniel mentioned on the air that this would be the last time listeners would get to hear "Hugh Gordon" on the radio with them for a while as he was going in the service, and told where he was heading. Dad said that when he got off the train in Tullahoma and all the boys were lined up, the Sergeant asked if there was a Hugh Gordon Stoker in line. Dad raised his hand while thinking, what have I done now? The Sergeant asked if he was the Hugh Gordon that played on WSM radio. Dad said he was. The Sergeant told him to go on down to the officer's club right now as they needed a piano player. Fortune smiled on him again.

Gordon Stoker

I'm just talking about being the *piano player* for the Daniel Quartet. WSM was a clear channel station; it didn't have all those little interference stations, and we reached out 500, 600 miles. Early in the morning we reached out even farther. And there was no TV. You had a lot of listeners. In 1943 I went into the Air Corps. John had to hire another piano player and he hired Boyce Hawkins, Hoyt's brother. I was stationed in Tullahoma, Tennessee, and John would announce on WSM my address in the service.

"You be sure to write to Hugh Gordon Stoker because Gordon would like to hear from you," he'd say. And the people flooded me with mail.

I got so much mail that the man in charge of the post office on the base said, "Stoker, if you don't quit getting so much mail, we're gonna have to put another mailman in the mail room." So I wrote a letter to John and told him to stop announcing my address. I'm talking about I'd get 100 to 200 letters a day. Of course I appreciated it, but what could I do? A lot of people sent me packages, which I really appreciated, cookies and cakes and just about anything else they could think of, candies, and stuff like that, which I appreciated. I've never forgotten.

When I was still with the quartet, most of the people would say things like, "Would you dedicate a certain song to my mother, or father, who is going to be 77 years old?" Or they'd ask me to dedicate to anniversaries. I got a lady that said, "I have named my son Hugh Gordon after you because I hope he grows up to play the piano as great as you do." I've never forgotten that. I'd love to meet him. I remembered he was from Alabama, but I don't remember what town in Alabama. Somewhere in Alabama there is a kid—I say a kid, an old man of course, this was in 1943—that was named Hugh Gordon after me.

Most of the time they just wanted to know where we would be playing next, and "Would you dedicate me a song?" or "Would you play a certain song?" "Would you send me a picture?" "Would you send me an autographed picture?" We mailed out pictures free, or charged a quarter for them. I can't remember which. These people thought of us as their friends. And I came to respect their feelings.

I learned a whole lot about the business watching John. He was more than just the boss of the quartet; he had a thousand details to take care of. He mailed out the songbooks, booked the dates, dealt with the Artist Service Bureau at WSM. The station didn't charge you for time, like the little stations did. You'd sell a certain item and give the station a percentage of what you sold, as well as a percentage of the dates you played. John took care of all that and made all the decisions.

We traveled in style. We always kept a brand new Packard, a big, large Packard. Wouldn't it be great if we'd had buses in those days? But we always had a big car, and five of us went in the car. A lot of times we'd take Zeke Clements, or Paul Howard or Eddy Arnold along with us as an extra-added attraction. We had the Hatch Show Print print up these posters, and we would send 200 or 300 to whatever town we were playing, and we would hire someone there that would put them up on trees and lampposts, telling them when and where we'd be appearing.

John had a good business head on him, which most people didn't have in the entertainment world. I think I have been wonderfully blessed myself, financially and otherwise, and I think one reason for it is that I admired John Daniel's ability to bluff his way through—to push his way and get onto various things. You have to be able to go in and talk. You have to be at the right time at the right place and say the right thing in order to get things done. Baby, after you get there, you have to know how to toot that horn, how to carry that ball after you get there. Once you get that job you fought for, you're gonna have to produce, because if you can't, they're going to kick you right out of the way. You've got to deliver.

I learned how to bluff my way in, watching John Daniel, how he did it. I learned a lot from him. He was uncouth about a lot of things. I never admired how he used the Lord's name in vain, which I couldn't stand. I was brought up to go to church and to believe in not using the Lord's name in vain and certainly not when you're singing gospel songs. He'd curse like a sailor, but then he would walk out having got what he wanted. That's always been amazing to me, how the Lord would actually bless somebody that took His name in vain like John Daniel did. Yet he was able to promote himself and promote the quartet and get what he wanted.

It's a funny thing. An awful lot of people that have made their living singing religious songs and singing in quartets live right the opposite from what they—I've often wondered, will you have to pay more when you stand before the judgment of Jesus, having professed to do His work and living the exact opposite? I've wondered if the payment's going to be much greater.

When I got out of the Air Corps in 1946, I went to college for two years at Oklahoma Baptist University, in Shawnee, Oklahoma. I didn't get a degree. Nashville was always in my heart. This is a funny darn town. Once you live here, you never quite get away from this place. Nashville will never be anything but a country town, no matter how big it gets, but if you live here, there's something about this place that, once you move away, you just *have* to come back.

After I got out of college, I went to Oklahoma City and started working there, playing with a group and also working at a civil service job I had gotten as the result of being in service. I didn't like it. By that time Boyce and Hoyt Hawkins were asking me to come back to Nashville. Boyce, who had taken my place with the Daniel Quartet, which was now called the John Daniel Quartet, had started playing piano for the Oak Ridge Quartet, so they called me and asked me would I come back and consider taking a job playing piano again for John Daniel. I said yeah, 'cause I wanted to come back to Nashville. That was the latter part of 1948. The John Daniel Quartet had left WSM for WLAC. We were on early morning on WLAC, which at this time was very hot, and offered a much more inviting deal for us to sell our merchandise on the radio.

Chapter 4

THE FIRST JORDANAIRES

Back in the 1940s in Springfield, Missouri, four brothers who were all ordained ministers named Matthews formed a really good gospel group called the Matthews Brothers Quartet. For a time, they were regulars on radio station KWTO in Springfield, then Matt and Jack Matthews decided to leave the group and become full-time ministers. But the other two brothers, Bill and Monty, decided to stay in music, and Monty thought that another local singer, Bob Hubbard, might be interested in joining the group. Hubbard had a friend named Culley Holt, who sang with him in a local quartet called the 4 H's, and Hubbard agreed to join the group if they would also take in his buddy Holt, who was the 4 H's bass singer.

They felt they needed a new name for the group since they were now only half Matthews Brothers. There was a creek that wound through Springfield called Jordan Creek, and the name pricked Monty's brain perhaps because it was almost—but not quite—the Jordan River. "Jordanaires" had a sound to it. And Jordanaires they became. Soon, they were doing two shows a day on local radio station KWTO. In those days, it was not uncommon for a local group to build a local reputation and stay local forever, but the Jordanaires were ambitious. After six months as Springfield gospel radio stars, they thought they might take a shot at the big time, so they headed for Nashville with dreams of WSM's Grand Ole Opry. Instead, they found a spot on WSM rival WLAC, which was no small potatoes itself. Their slot was 5:30 a.m. weekday mornings, right after the great black quartet, the Fairfield Four.

There was nothing wrong with WLAC, but the Jordanaires still had one eye out for WSM, and they were really good, so WSM invited them to audition. Country star Red Foley was their one-man audition audience, and he must have liked them because soon they were appearing regularly on the Grand Ole Opry along with Minnie Pearl, Rod Brasfield, and Foley. They sang a lot of spirituals, powerful up-tempo songs that rocked evangelical audiences all over the southern United States, and the Opry crowds loved them immediately. Before long, they were being booked around the country by the prestigious William Morris Agency, and thanks to their place on the Opry, they were beginning to cross over into the world of country music. They recorded for Columbia, Decca, Capitol, and RCA Records, and while they were on Decca, they had a chance to dip their toe into the world of pop recording. Decca records had an A&R (artist and repertoire) man named Paul Cohen, who would someday become a major force in country music, and Cohen was interested in a catchy song called "Rag Mop" that a young group from New England called the Ames Brothers would soon be recording on the Coral label. Cohen wanted one of his acts to record it, and the song seemed to require a group, so Cohen went to the Jordanaires and suggested that they do the song.

The group protested that the song was not appropriate for the image of a quartet that sang gospel and spiritual songs, so Cohen suggested that they record the song under the name "Foggy River Boys"—all for naught because the Ames Brothers had a huge hit with the song, while the Foggy River Boys version swiftly sank.

Gordon Stoker

While I was in service, Wally Fowler had started a series of gospel programs called All-Night Singings at the Ryman Auditorium, which was about to become the longtime home of the Grand Ole Opry, and it had developed into a big event. He'd heard the Jordanaires in Springfield, Missouri, and he invited them to appear on one of his all-night singing programs. They came and while they were in Nashville, working at WLAC, they auditioned for WSM and WSM hired them.

Hoyt Hawkins and myself were still working with John Daniel, and we happened to tell him how great we thought the Jordanaires were, and he said, "Well, you be nice to them as long as you want to, because they ain't gonna be around long no way!" Hoyt and I really liked to hear them. We heard that they were going to be appearing at some show down at the Ryman Auditorium on Friday night and Hoyt and I went down there to catch their show. And we went backstage and met them. Bill and Monty Matthews ran the group. Bob Money was the piano player, Bob Hubbard was the second tenor singer, and Culley Holt sang bass.

Well, the Korean War was going on and Bob Money, who was a very good piano player, was drafted. So they started auditioning piano players, and several people said to me "Aren't you gonna audition?" and I said, "Me?" But I was one of the guys they decided to audition, even though I was still with John Daniel. I remember Hoyt's brother Boyce auditioned. He was with Wally Fowler and the Oak Ridge Quartet, but he auditioned for the Jordanaires. Marvin Hughes auditioned. He was a very good piano player. And there were others who auditioned to play for the Jordanaires. And the group asked me to come and audition, so I did. I couldn't believe it, all these great people that auditioned with them. But Bill and Monty and Culley Holt called me in and said, we've been thinking about all the people we brought in to audition, and we decided to hire you to play piano.

I said, "You mean that you chose me over Boyce Hawkins and Marvin Hughes and all these people that were so much better than me?"—at least I thought they were much better than me. They said, no, we like your style, the main thing, you don't add so much stuff when you play. We're the singers, we're the stars. The piano player's not supposed to be anything but just, do your thing, play the chords and what have you, in other words, don't try to be a star on the piano.

Well, now I was thrilled beyond words. I've always felt that the Lord had a big hand in me getting a job playing the piano for the Jordanaires. We had early morning radio programs, we appeared on the Grand Ole Opry on Saturday nights, we had several dates that we did out of town; it was a great job to have. Before I knew it, I was singing a fifth-part harmony on some of the songs. Soon we were doing a lot of dates in town and out of town, and still appeared on WSM radio.

I don't know if John ever knew that I was going to audition for the Jordanaires, but soon enough he found out that I did. He called me a little greasy-headed SOB. "Go on over and play piano for them if you want to!" he said. But that's the way things go in this business. He would have fired me anyway, I'm sure, once he'd heard that I had gone over and auditioned for them. The Jordanaires had a lot on the ball. I knew they had a lot more to offer. They were on WSM. They were on the Grand Ole Opry. They weren't yet on the *Red Foley Jewel Shortening Show* but soon enough they would be.

Anyway, they hired me, and that was a big deal.

Off we went to Hollywood, where we did some movie shorts. In those days the TV stations needed "fillers" in case a show they had on didn't take up the complete time. They'd run musical shorts that actually looked like small movies. There was one company in particular that produced these little films and they were called Snader Telescriptions, in Hollywood, and that's where we went to do this.

After Hollywood we went to Yeaman's supper club in Detroit to do a 10-day gig, a very classy supper club. When we went in I didn't notice anything different about Bill Matthews, but they all said later that he did act different when we got there. We had a huge crowd that first night; why I don't know. Maybe it was the great food and drinks. I thought it was a little unusual for a spiritual quartet to appear in a club that had drinks. Bill Matthews booked it because they offered us pretty good money for the week. Well, the opening night, Bill Matthews had a complete nervous breakdown.

Right in the middle, when Monty was doing the emceeing— Monty Matthews always did the talking—Bill walked down off the stage and went to the back and started to shake hands with all the men sitting around the bar, and Monty tried to call him back on stage, but Bill was too busy shaking hands, so we did another song, without him. We finally got him back on the stage and when he got back on stage he started fightin' with the spotlights. *Fightin' with the spotlights*, if you can imagine. We didn't know what in the world had happened to him. From there things went down hill the rest of the night, though I don't quite remember how. It was a long time ago and it was something you wanted to forget. But I do remember. It was bad.

To make a long story short, the manager of the club, Mr. Yeaman, called in a doctor, and the doctor said, "This man is undergoing a major breakdown, and we need to get him to a hospital as soon as we can." So they did, and the next time I saw him after that night was the next morning, and he didn't know who I was, so I knew that he was really sick. They took him away, I think in a strait jacket, and I didn't see Bill again for some 40 years. Bill and his wife, Juanita came to Nashville in 2002. I'm so glad I got to see him, one more time.

We couldn't believe it. We had 8 or 10 nights to go. We had a contract. We had to live up to it. We needed all our singers.

Monty Matthews says to me, "You'll absolutely have to sing. You'll have to sing Bill's part on every song."

I said, "I can't do it."

This goes back to what I said earlier. I've always been thrown in positions that I didn't feel I could do. Me sing Bill Matthews high tenor part?

I said, "I can sing second tenor." Monty said, "Well *I* sure can't sing first tenor. You've got a higher voice than I've got, and nobody else can sing it at all. Don't even give me another word, Stoker. You've got to sing the part." Bob Hubbard and Culley said the same. "You've got to!" We were desperate.

And I was forced to sing, way higher than I could so what I did, I took the arrangements, and we rehearsed a lot. Monty was very, *very* kind to me. But he was also very demanding. He actually *made* me sing Bill's high tenor parts.

We walked out onstage the next night, and I sang Bill's parts. Scared me absolutely to death, but I sang every one of his parts, and evidently I did a good enough job because Monty and them complimented me on the job I did. I'm sure I didn't do as good a job as they led me to believe that I did, but at least it got us through. We called Hoyt and had him get up to Detroit the quickest way he could get there, and this is how Hoyt joined the Jordanaires, because when I started doing Bill's parts, we brought him in to take my place as the piano player.

After Detroit we had a recording date with George Beverly Shea for RCA in New York. We did "Roll, Jordan, Roll" and "Goodbye Pharaoh," and, again, I had to do Bill's high part. Again, scared me to death, but the record came off very good and I've often thought, so many times, that you call upon the Lord to help you in various ways. This time was a very crucial point in my life. He grabbed hold of my falsetto and pulled me through, and I'll always remember that Monty *made* me sing Bill's part, that I knew I could not do, and yet I did it.

This is a place that I hold today, still singing the first tenor with the Jordanaires, 55 years later.

Gordon and his older sister, Imogene. Thirteen years old when he was born, she treated him as her baby doll. His number 1 fan and encourager all her life. Unknown date. COURTESY OF THE ESTATE OF GORDON STOKER

THE CLEMENT TRIO

•

(Left to Right)

HUGH GORDON STOKER, Pianist;

RACHEL CLEMENT, Soprano;

FRED CLEMENT, Jr., Bass;

GLORIA CLEMENT, Alto.

•

FRED CLEMENT, Sr., Manager
McKenzie, Tennessee

The Clement Family Trio out of McKenzie, Tennessee. Gordon started playing piano with them onstage and local radio at age 10. Circa 1936. COURTESY OF THE ESTATE OF GORDON STOKER

Gordon with his siblings on the front steps of the Gleason, Tennessee, home that their dad, H. A. Stoker, built. Circa 1938. Left to right: Imogene (age 26), Arnice (age 19), Wayne (age 20), and Gordon (age 13). Music ran in the family. COURTESY OF THE ESTATE OF GORDON STOKER

The Girls Harmony Four Quartet out of Paris, Tennessee. It was during a picnic appearance playing with this group that John Daniel of WSM's John Daniel Quartet first heard Gordon play. Left to right: Betty Hastings, Jo Nell Ford, Gordon Stoker, Sue Jean Ford, and Nodgle Hastings. This picture was made in the early 1940s. COURTESY OF THE ESTATE OF GORDON STOKER

Gordon on piano with the John Daniel Quartet at WSM Radio. Circa 1942. Left to right standing: John Daniel, Troy Daniel, Percy White (WSM engineer), Wally Fowler, and Jess McCurdy. COURTESY OF THE ESTATE OF GORDON STOKER

527 NW 15th
Oklahoma City 3, Oklahoma

Dear Friends:

When my brother, Hugh Gordon Stoker, was called
into service, he was with the Daniel Quartet, WSM,
Nashville, Tennessee. You helped to make his going
easier by your encouraging letters. He dearly loves
to get mail and kept your letters, from which I have
taken your names and addresses. Of course it was
impossible for him to write to all of you after en-
tering the service, and I hope you will take this as
a personal letter from him and will join me in shower-
ing him with letters.

Gordon is with the Army Airways Communication
and is in the South Pacific. He is satisfied with
his work as he serves our country but is looking forward to the day when he can return to America and
his piano playing.

His address is:

Cpl. Hugh Gordon Stoker
34710767
5th AACS
APO 923, C/o Postmaster
San Francisco, California

I have read many of your nice letters and note
that many kindly say you will remember Gordon in
your prayers. I do hope you have not forgotten and
assure you he appreciates your interests and says he
knows now that prayers for him have been answered.

I shall look forward to hearing from Gordon
that he has received hundreds of letters from radio
friends.

Sincerely,

Imogene Stoker
Imogene Stoker

*A letter written by Gordon's sister Imogene, which was copied and sent to the
many fans who wrote to him after he was drafted. Keeping his name out there
like a good sister would do.* COURTESY OF THE ESTATE OF GORDON STOKER

Hoyt Hawkins (left) and Gordon Stoker, attending the Stamps Quartet School of Music, 1948 in Dallas, Texas. Gordon was teaching gospel piano at the school that year. Gordon and Hoyt had been good friends for 10 years by this time, since meeting as teenagers. COURTESY OF THE ESTATE OF GORDON STOKER

The Hawkins Brothers Quartet. Circa 1949. Gordon couldn't stay away from music and Nashville for long. Left to right: Gordon, Hoyt Hawkins, Charles Hawkins, Neal Matthews Jr., with Boyce Hawkins on piano. Three future Jordanaires, along with Boyce Hawkins, who was to become a Nashville television personality for many years.

Chapter 5
THE ROAD TO ELVIS

In November 1974, Gordon Stoker stopped by the Country Music Hall of Fame to give an interview. By this time, the Jordanaires had been in business for two and a half decades and had made a huge impact in gospel, spiritual, country, and pop music. The interviewer was Douglas B. Green, then an employee of the Country Music Hall of Fame. He later came to be known as "Ranger Doug" as a member of the popular cowboy musical group Riders in the Sky. The time line of this interview begins shortly after Gordon joined the Jordanaires.

Gordon Stoker

After Detroit the next thing I knew, we were back in Nashville, still singing on the Grand Ole Opry, me still singing Bill's part, and Hoyt playing the piano. Monty, who sang baritone with the Jordanaires, was doing arrangements for the group, really good arrangements that hold up even today. Then Monty got in financial trouble with somebody in Nashville. I don't know exactly what the details were, but the next thing I knew, Monty was forced to leave town, and he went back to Springfield. This again left us in a hard spot. We moved Hoyt off the piano and had him take the baritone slot, Monty's part, while Monty and his wife, Betty, got out of town in a hurry.

Meanwhile, Bill was in an institution. Bill went from Detroit into this institution and was there I think for some 10 years. So you see how very serious his nervous breakdown was.

This left Culley Holt, Bob Hubbard, Hoyt, and myself as the quartet. We'd use Marvin Hughes and occasionally Boyce Hawkins as the piano player. WSM didn't require us to have a piano player because we used the musicians that played on WSM.

In 1952, Don Bruce was brought in to be first tenor, but the next year, he was drafted, so Gordon went back to being the Jordanaires' first tenor.

Then Bob Hubbard was drafted, just right out of a clear blue sky. I think this was in 1953. We had worked with Neal Matthews on WLAC radio and knew Neal, so we called him and had him audition for Bob's position.

Neal's son, Greg, tells us that Neal Matthews (no relation to Monty and Bill Matthews) was born in Nashville on October 29, 1929. Like most of the other Jordanaires, he came from a musical family and began his music education at a very early age. In a book he wrote about his now-famous "Nashville Numbering System," Neal recalled that his dad played guitar and "taught us western and gospel songs from the time we were cutting our first teeth." At the age of 10, Neal, his brother Roger, and his cousin Rachel were singing at banquets and in theaters. By the time he turned 13, he was playing guitar with his dad on the Grand Ole Opry. After high school graduation, he played guitar and sang with Wally Fowler and the Oak Ridge Quartet, which would later become the hit-making country group the Oak Ridge Boys.

In 1951, he began a hitch in the army and went off to Korea, where he won a bronze star with a combat "V."

Greg Matthews

He was on a tank retrieval team. That was a tank with a big crane on it instead of a big gun. If a tank went out and threw a track, this retrieval tank would go out and drag the wounded tank back to where they would fix it. One day they went out to grab a tank and they started coming under enemy fire from a nearby hill and he just got tired of being shot at, so he jumped up on the tank they were towing and grabbed a .50 caliber machine gun and of course it jammed, so then he grabbed his M-1 carbine and just started laying down fire, enough to where everybody could get out of the tank and somebody put him up for an award.

After 21 months in uniform, Neal returned to civilian life, where opportunity awaited him. Gordon and the other Jordanaires were familiar with Neal, his experience, and his talent. Not long after he arrived home from overseas, he passed his audition and joined up with the quartet. For a while, he was able to pursue his singing career and an education at Belmont College in Nashville, but later, when their career really heated up, Neal would decide to concentrate on his career with the Jordanaires.

This brings us back to Gordon.

Gordon Stoker

The year is 1954. We did several albums with Capitol Records, several singles for them. They called us country gospel, I think it was, but we were not really that. We could sing barbershop, sing country songs, just about anything the producer wanted us to sing. I think that if we'd been given the right exposure we could have been Capitol Records recording stars.

Eddy Arnold had been hearing us on the Grand Ole Opry and around town and what have you, so he called us out to his home on Granny White Pike and said, "I'm thinking about doing a TV show in Chicago, and I wondered if you guys would be interested in doing this show with me. I'm gonna use Betty Johnson of the Johnson family, and we'll syndicate it out to various TV stations all over the country." This may have been the first syndicated country TV show. It was shot at Kling Studios in Chicago and was called *Eddy Arnold Time*. At that time we didn't have video tape. It was all done on film. We went to Chicago for six months, four days a week. It was a rough show to do, but it paid pretty good, even then. Eddy paid us $250 a week per man, plus expenses, and he paid our hotel bill and travel expenses. We got through doing the film series on Friday, and came back to do the Opry on Saturday night.

Now, Culley Holt's wife did not want him going out of town four days a week, so he had to resign. Culley was a handsome man. A lot of girls found him interesting, and his wife Betty was insanely jealous of him, so she did not want him to go to Chicago at all and do this film show with us. We had worked around town and had sung a little bit with Hugh Jarrett—he'd auditioned with us for bass and done some dates with us when Culley was either sick or was taking off. Culley told us, "Boys, I guess I'll just have to quit, I can't go out of town, it's either Chicago or my marriage." So he would continue to do the Opry on Saturday night and we called Hugh Jarrett and hired him to do "Eddy Arnold Time" with us in Chicago. Well this didn't work out. I just said, "Look, Culley, in Chicago we're learning songs that we should be singing when we come back to the Opry," and he said, "Fellas, I'll just bow out, quit completely." So he did quit, and took a job with the Metropolitan Life Insurance Company. But I'll always regret that it happened the way it did, because I liked Culley. I liked his bass singing, and it was just an unfair situation that it happened the way it did, but I could understand—this thing happened to a lot of entertainers. That's the reason I'm thankful that our wives never gave us a hard time about anything; they always went along with us, and did the best they could do under the circumstances, and so did we.

At the time he quit, Culley Holt was the manager of the group. Bill Matthews had been the manager of the group but when he had to cut out because of illness, Culley started managing the group full time. So when Culley resigned from the group, that meant that we needed a manager, and Neal and Hoyt said, "Well, Stoker, here, take over." Now here I was, with no managerial experience, knew a lot of people, and I guess they thought that I had a good relationship with so many people that just automatically Neal and Hoyt could appoint me the manager of the group, and then everything would take care of itself. There were so many reasons why I didn't feel I was capable of being the manager, but they wanted me to do it, and so I did the best I could do, and the Lord blessed me in so many ways I can't believe it.

We did those Eddy Arnold shows in Chicago for six months, driving all the way to Chicago to do it because Nashville didn't have the facilities necessary to do a syndicated TV show like this one. I'll always give credit to Eddy Arnold because Eddy believed in us when others did not, and he knew that we could sing all kinds of songs. I have recordings of a lot of those things and when I listen to them to this day, I can hear that we did a good job. We did some personal appearances around to publicize those shows, and the shows were running on a station in Memphis, and so we were booked to play in Memphis at the Ellis Auditorium, and during the intermission of one of the shows was when we met a young man named Elvis.

As you might imagine, that meeting is the most important event in the history of the Jordanaires, and I described it in detail earlier in this book. If you're the kind of reader who skips around, you would have skipped that meeting. You need to go back to the front of this book and take a look.

I remember that Hoyt Hawkins was really friendly to him, he just really took a liking to Hoyt and Hoyt took a liking to him, and Hoyt was the only one who later remembered him coming back stage. Except now of course I *do* remember this unusual looking guy, handsome kid, with the long sideburns, who stuttered that he loved the Jordanaires and said he wanted to sing with us.

Except for Hoyt, *we* may have been slow to remember that meeting, but the kid did not forget. Those backstage moments in Memphis, and Elvis's memory of those moments, kicked off a relationship we would have with him for almost 15 years, and a deep friendship that would endure until his death.

They were on the road, the Jordanaires, the first time they heard an Elvis record, the four of them in one car traveling along the back roads of America in the mid-1950s. There's not much you can do to ease the boredom of four weary grown men tucked into one car, doing 60 on the straights, 30 on the curves, and 20 on an uphill slope following a local delivery truck. Just about all they had to help them pass the time on the road was an AM car radio, which they listened to as much out of habit as for entertainment.

One late afternoon, driving straight into the afternoon sun, they heard a record that caught their attention. It was a secular record, but they all agreed that it had a gospel feel to it, and they agreed that the singer sounded like a gospel singer, and the song contained a little here, a little there, that almost added up to a gospel sound without being a gospel song. The song was "Mystery Train."

Over the next few days, they heard the record several more times on the radio, and finally they heard a deejay clearly announce the name of the singer.

"Hey, wasn't that the name of that kid wearing a pink shirt that came to meet us backstage at the Ellis Auditorium in Memphis?" Hoyt might have asked. "Didn't he talk us into singing a song with him?"

They might have agreed that you don't forget meeting someone with a name like that who was wearing a pink shirt. Anyway, at that point, they remembered him. But meanwhile:

We were doing a certain amount of backup with Red Foley and Hank Snow. I guess they were about the first ones in Nashville that used vocal backing on records before Elvis Presley came along. When Elvis arrived, he really boomed the vocal backing business for lots of people. Before Elvis there were actually no vocal groups making fat livings doing vocal backing. He opened a lot of doors for a lot of people, not only in Nashville, but in New York and Hollywood too.

So now the Jordanaires consisted of me, Neal Matthews, Hoyt Hawkins, and Hugh Jarrett singing bass. Neal, Hoyt and I would be three fourths of the Jordanaires for years to come. Hugh worked with us until, oh, we had done about three movies with Elvis.

Gordon's son, Alan, has been working for the Country Music Hall of Fame for many years, and he has an encyclopedic memory for events that occurred during the long history of the Jordanaires. He recalled that his dad, as manager of the group, took great care to preserve the image of the Jordanaires as thoroughly reliable studio performers.

Brent Stoker

Dad was always concerned about how the group was perceived, especially on the sets of movies. 'Cause he wanted to make sure that they would continue to be invited to work on the soundtracks of Elvis movies. I think it was during the taping of the film, "Loving You," that Hugh, who had suffered from polio as a child, tripped over some of the instruments that were set up onstage and broke some of them, and Dad got really upset, I can see him now turning all red, trying to keep calm. The prop guy had to get new instruments and bring them back up. They had an insurance adjuster come up on the set, and someone else come in to make sure that Hugh wasn't hurt. This was not the image that Dad wanted to give to the production company "officials" as Dad always called 'em, just a bit snidely, you know.

Hugh stayed with the Jordanaires for about four years. The Jordanaires were not Hugh Jarrett's primary professional interest, and Gordon was not pleased.

Gordon Stoker

Hugh had outside interests, and we fired him. He was still our friend. He was on WLAC here for years, and he had a big successful TV show in Atlanta. He was interested in promoting himself with either radio stations or with a hit record as a solo act. Hugh wanted to be a biggie on his own, you know. So he kept promoting himself on the side, even though he was making, at that time, at least a minimum of $500 a week with us. That was a lot of money in those days. He wanted to be a famous disc jockey. Big Hugh Baby, he called himself. He was very popular. He wanted to be a disc jockey more than a background singer. And we said, "Either you make up your mind to be a member of the Jordanaires, or you make up your mind to be a disc jockey." And he couldn't make up his mind. So anyway, to make a long story short, I called him up one day and said, we've replaced you. Kind of blunt! And he cried, and cried, and all that, you know.

So that's how we came to hire Ray Walker as our bass singer. Now the classic Jordanaires quartet was complete. To be in a group, you must live and breathe for that group. This is the reason so many of your groups break up today. If you'll notice, there aren't many gospel groups that have kept the same personnel. I mean, a lot of times, well, now, there'll be gospel groups that come to Nashville to record, and only one member will be of the original. Same thing with rock groups. Your rock groups constantly change personnel, the reason being, they can't get along, and they have so many things going, that they just have to agree to disagree. We've been very fortunate to keep the same personnel for many many years, because we can get along. You must work for the group you're in, or it just isn't going to go. I've always lived and breathed the Jordanaires. We're all I've pushed for years. Now we were the Jordanaires that you all heard for so many years on so many records. There was me, still enjoying my first experience of singing first tenor. Hoyt Hawkins sang baritone, Neal Matthews didn't have a falsetto at all, so he couldn't sing first tenor, he sang second tenor, and played very good guitar, and Hoyt's brother Boyce played excellent piano. And Ray was our bass.

We signed with Capitol Records back in 1953, and during the time we recorded for Capitol Records we almost made it, with a song called "Sugaree," a song written by Marty Robbins that almost broke into the big time. It sold pretty good, and got high up on the charts of some radio stations. One time when we were in Hollywood, Lee Gillette, who was with Capitol Records, sat me down and talked to me. We were pushing them to promote "Sugaree." We couldn't help it. We wanted our own hit. He said, "Let me tell you fellas, you guys don't want a hit record." He shook his head and said, "You guys pushin' us, wanting a hit record, believe me. You guys are masters. If you will stay in the background field, it'll be good to you for years. If you have a hit record you might have one or two, three or four, like this group and that group," and he said, "They're all gone by the wayside by now. If you have a hit record, you must go on the road and promote it. You must do free shows to promote it. You've got to do this, that and the other all over the country to promote it. Take it from me. Stay in the background and treat the background right, and it'll be good to you." Little did we feel, at that time, that he was telling us the truth. All we could see was a hit record. But believe me, he was really right. I never dreamed it. I said, "Yeah, but I'd still like to have a biggie."

We've been very fortunate to have lots of biggies with other people. Of course, over the years, our names have been on their album or their record but we just had to console ourselves with that. And you know what, once we got used to seeing the records we sang on hit the top of the charts, it didn't bother us that the disc jockeys didn't mention us. *We* knew we were there.

Just this morning we worked in the studio with a guy who had two great numbers. I'd never heard him sing—I'd never even met the guy. It's just really a joy to meet new artists all the time, and we get to do that quite often. Did we cut a hit with that guy this morning? I don't know. You never know, till the stations start playing the song, and the public makes up its mind. I think it's funny though—it's gotten so, in the last ten years, when we go do a session with somebody, the first thing they wanna do is have a picture made with us, before we ever start recording. They say, "Hey, can I have a picture made with the Jordanaires?" and you feel like saying, "Hey, did we come here to cut a recording or did we come here to make pictures?" But we're always happy that they wanna have a picture made with us. That's all right.

At the Opry, when we were not onstage I'd stay in the wings and just watch people, and watch the show, because I really enjoyed it. I loved country music, and I like the operation of the whole thing [the Opry], and I was always hoping that it would get better, and that we'd get an air-conditioned building. I knew someday that we'd have something much nicer than what we had in those days.

And many years later, they built a brand-new Grand Ole Opry house, a big place with cushiony seats, air conditioning, lots of dressing rooms and space to hang out, and good sound.

Great place to make music.

Sentimental country fans love the Ryman, the old home of the Opry. Gordon remembered it differently.

Hot, terrible. We had a huge floor fan over on the right side of the stage—an enormous fan, I'd say, four foot high, and that's the only comfort we got. And of course, it was only blowing dust and odors from the right side to the left side, is about all that boiled down to. Terrible! It was a terrible place. Always was—terribly hot, I mean. It wasn't cold in the wintertime, but it was really hot in the summer.

But all those great singers!

We're the most fortunate group in the world, in that we've been able to, first of all, mostly keep the same personnel, to get along, and secondly, to be able to work with the biggest names and be able to please them. A guy called me yesterday, well-known artist, wanted us to do a session for him that another group had done, and he didn't like the way they sounded. He wanted the sound *we* have. Of course, I'm sure that along the way we did something for somebody and they didn't like what we did, because every group has their in and out days, of course, so they called another group to try and do better. We'd do from one to four sessions a day, five, six days a week, and on each session, we'll do from three to four—in some cases five—numbers. That's an awful lot of songs. We're not always perfect, but we work hard at it, and give it our best. It's not always easy, but it's interesting, all those different songs, different singers, different musicians.

Neal Matthews, the quartet's second tenor and arranger, was of prime importance in the Jordanaires' journey to the top of the heap among backup vocal groups of the 1950s–1970s. His son Greg explains:

Greg Matthews

Most of the time when I was there, dad had some sort of work tape, and he would go to the piano sometimes, and start to play around. From listening to the song, to writing up the charts, to creating those background sounds was a matter of a few minutes. As far as drawing stuff up on the spot, the other members of the quartet definitely looked to him to do that, and he was just gifted, creatively, to do the four voice arrangements. They might be catchy vocal licks, syllables as simple and choppy as "bop-bop," or they might be beautiful harmonic oohs and aahs. But he'd been doin' it for so long, 'cause he'd started out with the Stone Mountain Quartet, Wally Fowler and the Oak Ridge quartet, gosh, he was traveling around at 17, 18 years old, doing the gospel quartet thing, the all-night singin' thing, years and years and years. He was around music all his life.

Gordon Stoker

We've been asked how we work on developing a sound that's uniquely our own. I don't know the answer. It's the kind of thing that just happened. We try to make a real true country sound with pretty harmony. Like the stuff we'd do with Kitty Wells, I'd sing her part in a male's range, you see. We do a lot of things with Tammy Wynette the same way, and Loretta Lynn. We sing the same part the artist does—the tenor takes the same part the artist will take, and then the other three voices fit their part under it, and the sound just more or less comes. You know, it's one of those things. We just get into the song. A lot of times they want us to sound black, or they want us to sound spiritual, or they'll tell you, say, "Hey, can you guys rough this up a little bit? I don't want it smooth," and they'll demonstrate. And of course, there's two or three records we did with Elvis that you'd have thought it was a trio of black girls. We were all singing falsetto. People would say, "Hey, I don't like those girls," or, "I *do* like those girls on this record." And I'd say, "Well, that was us." Because we have to do whatever it takes to give the artists what they want.

And we can do it, because we've been doing it for so long. People will say, "Hey, don't you need a copy of the song I'm going to do on the session next week?" If they haven't recorded here before— "Don't you need to have a pre-rehearsal? Don't you need to get together in advance for the session?" We don't do that at all. We don't have to. It comes from knowing harmonies, having a background in music. We're able to hear the song once and go right in and work the harmonies immediately. You have to have a photographic mind of the tone at the time, photograph in your mind the exact song you're singing, the part you're singing, where, when, and how. But, like, if you ask me right now what songs I did in yesterday morning's session, I couldn't tell you, see, I couldn't tell you a one of them. [Longtime Nashville arranger] Bill Justis referred to Nashville as "fakesville." Background singers, studio musicians, we come in for the session, listen to the song once, and we make up "head" arrangements on the spot instead of having to follow prewritten arrangements. That's why Capitol wanted us to move out to Hollywood. We'd make up the arrangements in our head and then they don't have to pay an arranger $500 to write a vocal arrangement.

We didn't go, because the pay scale's the same there as it is here, you see. Scale's the same in Nashville, New York, Hollywood. We work for scale here just the same as we work for scale out there, and we work all we want to here, so there wouldn't have been any advantage in going to Hollywood and being in the rat race out there, and this is home with our families, so why would we move?

We might also add that when Gordon was recording this, Nashville was a much cheaper place to live than it is now.

To get back to Elvis, RCA had bought from Sam Philips of Sun Records in Memphis, Elvis's contract for 30,000, some say 25,000 some say 30,000, then they gave him an extra 5,000 to buy his mother a Cadillac. They came to Nashville to do their first sessions for RCA in January of 1956. They brought in D. J. Fontana, Scotty Moore, and Bill Black, who backed Elvis on all his shows, and then they added musicians here in Nashville to the session. We had been hearing stories for a while. Hank Snow was the first guy who told us about Elvis. He'd been doing shows with Elvis, and the Carter Family, and other people were on the show, and he told us that "There's a kid that you just can't follow on stage, ain't nobody can follow him, he just completely walks away with the audience." There's many funny stories about this that you can read in other books about Hank Snow but anyways, to give Hank Snow credit, Hank Snow was the first person that told us about this kid who had appeared with him, that was just absolutely tearing the audience up.

Steve Sholes from New York worked through Chet Atkins in Nashville to set up Elvis's first session on RCA, and Chet, who was the head of RCA in Nashville at that time, called me and said, "We just signed this long side-burned kid from Memphis, would you mind using Ben and Brock Speer [on the session]?" Well, of course, I knew Ben and Brock Speer, known them since I was a kid, but I said, "I've never worked with them, I've never sung with them," and

Chet said, "Well, that doesn't make any difference. He's not gonna be around long, he's just a passing fad, come on in and do some oo's and aahs. I've just signed the Speer Family to the RCA label, and I would like to give them a little work, and if you could use Ben and Brock Speer, it would be really great." I guess I could have said, "No, I'm not about to use them" and then he would have said, "Okay, I'll get somebody else in your place." But you didn't give that kind of static to the head of a record company so I said, "Okay."

The session was set for January 10, 1956, at Trafco, on McGavock Street, just off Music Row. When we got to the studio, Elvis was of course a little late, as [I would learn] he always was, on sessions, but he always had the kindest air about him in that when he walked in, he walked around and shook hands with each person in the studio. When he got to me, he remembered meeting me. He did not know Ben and Brock Speer, but he remembered meeting me in Memphis, and being one of the Jordanaires, so, I introduced myself, I'm sure, as Gordon Stoker of the Jordanaires, and he said, "oh-oh-oh-ah-ah, where's the other guys?" And I said, "Well, Chet didn't want me to use them. He wanted me to use Ben and Brock Speer." And because of that, Elvis did not like Chet Atkins till the day he died; he always called him "The sneaky sonofabitch." Chet was as sweet and nice to me as he could be. He used the Jordanaires on many many sessions, so I'm not putting Chet Atkins down, except I am saying that Chet Atkins pulled something over on Elvis by not using the other three Jordanaires. But Elvis told me at the end of the session, he said if anything from this session is a hit, "That I want the Jordanaires on my upcoming sessions."

I was there that day, at Trafco, when "Heartbreak Hotel" was recorded, even though that song did not call for backup vocals. Just sittin' there. Ben and Brock left but I stayed because I was fascinated by Elvis. He was just a very interesting person. He was entirely different from anybody that I had recorded with. He had a beautiful smile and just was extremely friendly. He actually kind of seemed to want me to stay. And I respected that.

He had been hearing us sing on the Grand Ole Opry on a Saturday night, on the NBC portion of the Grand Ole Opry, which was a 30-minute portion sponsored by Prince Albert Tobacco. We'd sing a lot of country songs but often we'd sing a finger-snappin' hand-clappin' spiritual, and this is what he loved.

We did one more session with Ben and Brock, and by that time, "Heartbreak Hotel" and "I Was the One" had just absolutely swept the country [and Elvis could get what he wanted] and so soon enough, the Jordanaires were on the road with Elvis. And the first show date we did with him was in Atlanta, Georgia, at the Fox Theater, and he said if these dates are hits, if we have big crowds, and we did, we had sold-out crowds at the Fox Theater, I never will forget he said that "if these dates I'm doing are a success, I want the Jordanaires to work with me from now on." And that was a beautiful arrangement to have with one of the nicest people that you could ever imagine, for almost 15 years."

According to Gordon's son Alan, when Elvis found out that RCA had booked Ben and Brock Speer for the April 14, 1956, Nashville session ("I Want You, I Need You, I Love You"), he was furious.

Alan Stoker

Pop told me that RCA had only hired *him*, not the quartet. After that date, though, Elvis got who he wanted on his sessions. The mixture of the Jordanaires' pop and gospel styles was the sound Elvis was looking for.

And you could hear traces of that mixture in Elvis's records for many years to come.

Gordon Stoker

After the Elvis sessions in Nashville that Chet Atkins produced, we went to New York to do the *Ed Sullivan Show*, and while we were up there, we had a session set in RCA, New York. On that session the first thing we did was "Don't Be Cruel." And then we did "Any Way You Want Me." Now this was the fourth Elvis recording that I had sung on: "I Want You, I Need You, I Love You," "I Was the One," "Don't Be Cruel," and "Any Way You Want Me." But I had been in the studio when he did "Money Honey," and many other things. And so I'd heard him sing *many* songs. But do you know, he did not really reach me until he started singing "Any Way You Want Me." It had a spiritual feel about it. And I said to the guys, I said, "Hey! (chill bumps on my arm) This guy can sing!" He'd heard us sing "Dig a Little Deeper" on the Grand Ole Opry and he liked that ending and he wanted us to put the same ending on "Any Way You Want Me" as we did on "Dig a Little Deeper." And so that's what we did on the recording.

"Right after that the next number was one that remained on the charts for 35 years. It's been about the biggest recording of all times which is "You Ain't Nothing but a Hound Dog," and Shorty Long who had played piano on "Any Way You Want Me" and "Don't Be Cruel," said, "Now I've got another session, and I've got to leave." It was then 5:30, the session had started at two o'clock in the afternoon, so Steve Sholes said to me, "Gordon, get over to that piano and play the piano on this recording," and that's what I did. However, they could not mic me (vocally) at the piano, see, nowadays that's no problem at all, but in those days we didn't have enough tracks to mic my vocal at the piano, and so I couldn't play and sing too, I'm sorry to say. This meant that Hugh Jarrett, who had been singing bass and couldn't fake a baritone part, *tried* to fake a baritone part, and Neal and Hoyt both were singing the two top parts. Turned out to be one of the worst sounds we ever got on any recording, but, *hoo*, Lord has it really sold. But vocal-wise, vocal group-wise, I'm talking about, it was terrible. Awful. We always tried to do the very best—we demanded for each member to do the very best, and of course, Hugh sang as good as he could, but he just couldn't fake that part very well.

But I guess he got by. Because the world liked "Hound Dog" then, and it has ever since, and never mind what I think.

Chapter 6

WHEN IT ALL CAME TOGETHER

While the Jordanaires were enjoying their early success with Elvis, they were becoming an important cog in the Nashville recording machine. And Nashville, against all odds, was becoming a powerful force in America's recording industry, pop as well as country. By 1957, the Bradleys' Studio B [the Quonset hut] on 16th Avenue South was humming along at a furious rate, and RCA's brand-new studio a block away was already attracting big business. The Jordanaires could be found in one or both of those studios nearly every weekday, oohing and aahing, syllableizing, and singing powerhouse choruses, often rewriting the book of background singing. Nashville was a big small town in those days. Living costs were reasonable, and scale for sessions was good, so the Jordanaires could live very well. And besides the incredibly successful Elvis sessions, it seemed like any session any day might turn up another new crossover classic that would blast the sound of the Jordanaires across the country.

On December 3, 1957, the Jordanaires stepped into RCA's brand-new studio, which would eventually be known as RCA's Studio B, with Don Gibson. Alan Stoker tells us that this was the first session that RCA executive Chet Atkins produced that resulted in a double-sided hit (and what a hit it was), "Oh, Lonesome Me" and "I Can't Stop Loving You." This session, along with an earlier recording by Jim Reeves [also with backing vocals by the Jordanaires] reportedly proved to RCA brass that Chet could produce hit records.

Gordon Stoker

Early in 1957, Don Gibson wrote "I Can't Stop Loving You" and "Oh Lonesome Me" in Knoxville while living in a trailer and without a regular job, after his vacuum cleaner and TV had been repossessed A year later, his first songwriting royalty check from Acuff-Rose publishing was $36,000. Don was quoted as saying, "I couldn't fathom that much money."

"Oh Lonesome Me," backed with "I Can't Stop Loving You," by Don Gibson and the Jordanaires, were smash hit country and pop records. Both were Top 10 hits with "Oh Lonesome Me" reaching number 1 on the country charts and number 7 on the Billboard Hot 100 *pop chart. It stayed on the charts for 34 weeks in 1958. Four years later, Ray Charles took "I Can't Stop Loving You" to number 1 on the* Billboard Hot 100, *the R&B chart, and the Adult Contemporary chart.*

The quartet was on many great records with Don Gibson. His versions of "Blue Blue Day," "I Can't Stop Loving You," "Don't Tell Me Your Troubles," "(I'd Be) A Legend in My Time," and "Sweet Dreams" are considered standards.

Alan Stoker
On "Oh Lonesome Me," I particularly like their oo badda wadda waddas during the bridge and the baddi op bop bops answering the guitar solo. Also the "Oh me" at the end fade out.

Alan's comment is a reminder that the Jordanaires' arranger Neal Matthews did more than music; you might say that he and the others, as they created the syllables that we all remember today, were sort of lyricists too.

Interviewer John Rumble asked Gordon to talk about those syllables. He, like Alan, was fascinated by the badda wadda waddas on "Oh Lonesome Me."

Gordon Stoker
Yeah, that's just something we come up with, you know. Don wanted us to do something different, come up with an idea, come

up with something here. Of course, you don't tell the Jordanaires to come up with something that they don't come up. We'll come up with something, I can assure you. That's always been a challenge for us to go into a studio and record. If you tell us to just—"You guys just use your own—," lots of times, we'll go into the studio without an idea and we'll say, "Lord, have mercy" [and he does]. Matter of fact, I finished a session just like that before I came here (for this interview), three songs. What are you going to do with a song like this? Many times, bless his heart, Elvis would walk over to us on the session, as many artists do, and say, "What can you do with a piece of crap like this?"

In September 1957, the Jordanaires flew out to Hollywood to back Elvis on a Christmas album. Out of that session came Elvis's most popular Christmas recording, but he sure picked an odd way of getting there. Sometimes, things work out no matter how hard you try to screw them up.

Elvis and the Jordanaires were preparing to do a Christmas album when RCA executive Steve Sholes told Elvis that RCA had "made a deal" on "Blue Christmas," so Elvis was going to have to record it. In the record business in those days, it was not uncommon for a label to ask a publisher to cut their royalty rate on a song if the publisher wanted the song to be cut by a major artist on that label.

Elvis didn't want to record the song because Ernest Tubb had had a big hit on it. Elvis said, "Mr. Sholes, I don't want to do this song at all." Elvis had great respect for country acts. He thought that song was a signature song for Ernest, so he objected, but Sholes insisted, and they went round and round until Elvis came up with his own way to resist.

Millie Kirkham, who had been hired to sing a high part on the session, continues the story.

Millie Kirkham

Elvis turned to the musicians and singers and said, "Okay, let's just get this over with, have fun, have a good time, do something silly, so when it came to my part, I started going "oo-hoo-hoo-hoo-hoo," and he motioned to me to keep doing it, so we just laughed, I did it throughout the whole song and when we got through we all laughed and said, "Well that's one record that the record company will never release. But they did, and if I was getting royalties on it I'd be a rich old woman."

If you listen to the record, you can hear Millie singing, "oo-hoo-hoo-hoo-hoo," and somehow it became the most popular moment on the record.

Gordon Stoker

Elvis would step up to the mic to sing, "I'll have a blue *Ka-ristmas*, without you," and Sholes would stop it every time. He'd say, "Elvis, we can't release it that way. People will think you're making fun of the way they talk." And again he'd sing, "I'll have a blue *Ka-ristmas*, without you," The only time he said, "I'll have a blue Christmas," is the recording that you hear on the record. Neal finally said something to him. We still don't know exactly what it was. Elvis listened to the Jordanaires. He really liked us, he loved us and we loved him. Neal said something like, "It looks like we're not gonna get out of recording this, so you're gonna have to sing it."

Millie said she's gonna have that lick, "oo-hoo-hoo-hoo-hoo," engraved on her tombstone because everybody knows her by that. And when we tour with Millie, we sing that song even in the middle of the summer . . . because they wanna hear Millie do that.

Alan Stoker

An entry on the internet about Blue Christmas says "Presley's version is notable musicologically as well as culturally in that the vocal group, the Jordanaires, replace many major and minor thirds with neutral and septimal minor thirds, respectively. In addition to contributing to the overall tone of the song, the resulting 'blue notes' constitute a musical play on words that provides an 'inside joke' or 'Easter egg' to trained ears."

Sounds like a blues harmonica lick to me.

Gordon Stoker

The thing was, Scotty Moore and the guys who were playing the introduction played it correctly and they kept on having to do it over and over [while Elvis played his game with Steve Sholes]. He didn't want them to release it, and he thought that if he stuck to that ridiculous background on it, that they wouldn't release it. He was having fun with it. Elvis had fun with almost everything. He had the best attitude. Like this morning we had to do the remake of a different version of "Stuck on You." Elvis called the song, "Stuck in You." He didn't like the song. He didn't want to do the song. The colonel had made a deal on that song too.

Readers, go to your computer. Go to YouTube or one of the music streaming services and find Elvis's "Stuck on You" performance on a 1960 Frank Sinatra TV show, the one with the good stereo sound synced in. Elvis gestures with his right arm to the Jordanaires, who are standing to his right, in formation. The four Jordanaires nod their heads, almost in unison, a graceful group bow, as two great acts pay tribute to each other. Elvis may not have liked the song, but Neal had come up with a snappy vocal arrangement. The quartet did their bah doo doos, Elvis did his part, the studio players did their part, and the result was another big hit they could all be proud of or at least live with.

Were there a lot of songs he recorded that he didn't like?

He didn't like Teddy bears and from everywhere all over the world they'd send him Teddy bears. That's only a song in the movie! He wasn't endorsing stuffed Teddy bears! When we do Elvis impersonator shows right now, the people in the audience still throw stuffed Teddy bears to the guy on the stage.

We'd always go down there [to Graceland] right after Christmas to take him a Christmas present and a birthday present—we tied that together because his birthday was January 8. The year that song came out we went down and they had stuffed Teddy bears from the floor to the ceiling all around the wall in the dining room. He said, "I guess I'll have to call Good Will, and the Children's Homes and everybody else to come out and get these damned Teddy bears outa here."

There were so many songs he had to do that he didn't like. "Won't You Wear My Ring around Your Neck." Freddy Bienstock, he worked for Hill and Range [publishing company], had his way of playing a demo for Elvis and Elvis would say, no, I don't like it, I don't like it, so, he'd play several more songs, and then let that first one surface back up again. And on that demo, they had a girls' trio, and Elvis said, "Well, we ain't got no damn girls' trio, Freddy," and Ray said to him, "well, if you want a girls' trio, we'll sing a girls' trio for you," and Freddy said, "Yeah, I'll bet." But, if you hear the record, that's Hoyt, Ray, and I—not Neal, because he didn't have a falsetto voice—and "Stuck on You," we did a girls' trio on that too. There was one or two others we did a girls' trio on. We'd always do what Elvis would want us to, you know, he was such a super nice guy, anything he wanted, we tried to come up with.

Gordon goes on to explain why, if he resisted Steve Sholes so much on "Blue Christmas," he gave in on so many songs.

Well you see, the colonel would come out there and, "Hey, we made a deal on this song, you know, we need you to do it"—he would have a way of saying to Elvis—and many times *we'd* say to Elvis, "If you don't want to do it, just tell 'em you don't want to do it," and he would finally get worn down to the point that he'd say,

"Aw, no, I'd just rather do it than to argue with him." And we'd say, "You don't have to argue with them! You're the hoss. You're the boss."

'Cause he was his own producer. Steve Sholes, Chet Atkins, Felton Jarvis, these guys had their name on it as being the producer, but *Elvis* was the real producer, not those guys. He knew exactly what he wanted, and he knew what sounded good, and you know, it's amazing, if you put on a Frank Sinatra record that's 40 years old right now, it would sound 40 years old. If you put on an Elvis Presley record that's 40 years old, it sounds like it was done yesterday, and I think that the reason is, he was there, he knew what sounded good, he knew what *was* good, and I think that's the reason those records have been around so long.

Today the song "Blue Suede Shoes" is often associated with Elvis, but the hit version was recorded by the writer of the song, Carl Perkins, who had his own brand of charisma and was expected by many to be the coming rock-and-roll star back in 1955.

Well, you know Carl had that serious accident on the way to New York to tape the *Perry Como Show*. The accident occurred in March of 1956, during the time that "Heartbreak Hotel" was making Elvis America's new big thing of rock and roll. As a matter of fact, Steve Sholes wanted Elvis to record "Blue Suede Shoes," and Elvis said, "No, Carl's my friend and I'm not gonna do it, because it'll interfere with his sales." And then, when Carl had that serious accident, Elvis said, let's go in and do it right now because it'll help him royalty-wise. Carl said, "The first royalty check I got from Elvis's first album: seven thousand dollars! Man it was like finding a gold mine somewhere for me."

One of Elvis's biggest hits was "Are You Lonesome Tonight," a record with an outstanding recitation. Gordon liked to talk about it because interesting things just happened around that song. Keep in mind that this interview took place in 2001, long after that record was a hit.

Well, you know, the little part where he's doing the talking in there, some lady called me about 10 years ago, and she said, "I *wrote* what Elvis said on that song. You know, the talking part down in there."

I said, "You did? With who? I'm sure that you have gone through the proper authorities and you're getting paid."

"Oh, no," she said. "They cheated me out of every bit of it. You remember I was in the studio when you recorded that song with Elvis."

I said, "No, I don't remember you being in the studio, because Elvis wouldn't allow anybody to be in the studio except the people who was on the session. He was very funny about that. So I certainly couldn't stand up for you that you wrote it or that you was in the studio, because if I remember correctly, you wouldn't have been in the studio."

What she was trying to do, of course, was to get in on the money part of it. But I thought it was so strange that somebody would call me years and years and years after that song had been recorded.

"Are You Lonesome Tonight" was very special to Elvis, because he liked anything that told a story. Elvis was a good one, to tell stories. You know, he once said, "I can't sing, I can't dance, I can't play the guitar. What the hell do they want with me?"

We always told him, "You've got what it takes. Give it to them. Let them have it." That was one song that just told a story that he liked, and he could do it good. Any song that told a good story, Elvis could sing it, and that one did.

In an interview with John Rumble, Gordon explains that events in the studio that night were a bit unusual.

Gordon Stoker

Bill Porter [the engineer] told me that he was about to wind the tape off from the previous song. He looks up, the lights are off in the studio. Steve Sholes, the producer, says, "Bill, roll the tape."

Bill says, "But I haven't set any levels yet."

Steve said, "Roll the tape, Bill."

"Yes, sir." So Elvis starts to sing. There's just a guitar, I think, and a bass, and the Jordanaires. All these mics are open. So Bill starts trying to turn the volume of those mics down. But then he thinks, oh, no, I'm ruining this song. So he left the levels alone, and it actually kind of gave it a bigger sound.

Elvis liked the lights off in the studio, because in the dark he could think. He had a super memory, but he didn't want anything to distract him. If the lights were low or down or completely out—he always said that's the reason Ray Charles could do so well, is because Ray Charles couldn't see, so he could concentrate. So Elvis liked the lights out on a lot of recordings.

Many of the songs that we did with him, the lights were out. We'd write our chords down. That's the only way we could remember where to come in or what to do or so forth, what to say. Elvis had it all right up here in his head. He could remember. He could listen to a demo one time and be able to cut that darn thing. Something like "Joshua Fought the Battle of Jericho," now listen to the words on that. Lots of words. Every artist that we record with uses a word sheet, and they keep their eyes glued to that word sheet. I don't blame them. We do, too. But Elvis didn't. He'd listen to a demo a few times and get up and sing every bit of it without a word sheet.

So he liked the lights down low. But the lights being down low, *we* couldn't see our lyrics. A lot of times, well, we was—like a song—you take a song like "Crying in the Chapel," I can hear mistakes that we made. Of course, it didn't have anything to do with the sale of the records, because the sales of the records were huge and still are, I'm thankful to say, all over the world. But I could hear the little mistakes that we made here and there, because we didn't have the lights on.

A lot of times, they'd fix us a light on the stand. But Elvis didn't even like this if we were standing close to him. We'd often have a baffle in front of us, and then the light didn't bother him.

We have already read more than once the strong feelings the Jordanaires had for Elvis. Stoker now explains why.

He had a lot of situations that, if you and I were confronted with them, we'd throw up our hands and walk out. His mother and dad, I think it was his mother mainly, embedded in him to be nice and kind and sweet to people, and that was just something he carried through to his grave.

Did the pressures of his career change his ability to enjoy his life?

Yeah, the pressures—the colonel—he wanted to get rid of the colonel . . . because the colonel had no love for him. You do your job and I'll do my job. You stay on your side of the fence and I'll stay on my side of the fence. That's the way the colonel felt. If the colonel had just shown a little love and respect for him—he showed no respect for him! No love for him! Elvis wanted people to love him. We loved him and we showed it. And D.J., Scotty and Bill Black, they loved him and they showed it.

As I've said many many times, the reason we had to quit working with him, is that he went into Vegas doing two shows a night, and we could not do two shows a night, at least we didn't want to do two shows a night in those days—and we don't even do two shows a night now—I've always felt that doing two shows a night is what took Elvis Presley's life. He was not *able* to do two shows a night, because he wanted that second show to be as good as that first show, and that was very hard on him; he just couldn't do it. Elvis took his shows very seriously. The fans meant everything to him, and actually there was nothing that really mattered to him except doing a good show. He was a perfectionist. He wanted everything to be right. He wanted the musicians, the music to be right, he wanted to sing everything right, and he wanted that second show to be just as good as that first show, and he intended for it to be. And this meant taking uppers and downers. He'd take uppers to get him going because he'd sleep most of the day and was always tired. Between the first show and the second show he would take a shower and do all the things that you'd try to do to refresh yourself, and rest, but there wasn't much rest he could do with all those guys he had around him, 'cause they'd always bring in stars that wanted to meet him, and girls that wanted to meet him and things like that, and he would be so kicked up by the end of that second show, that he had to take a downer to get him to sleep—he still didn't go to sleep till, they said, way up in the morning a lot of times. And he'd sleep most of the day, or stay in bed most of the day, and then it was the same thing over again, first to get him going, and then the downers to put him to sleep. We were asked many times in interviews about the drugs that Elvis was on. He would take various things to give him a kick, to get him going, and then something to put him to sleep, and it did lead to Percodan and stuff like that, so he could go out and do a good show. I never liked to think of him as being a drug addict, as a lot of people try to make him out to be. He was not that. He had a great attitude. There are so many good things I could say about him, I wouldn't know where to start.

But, here again, I say, if Elvis had set his foot down, things would have been different. What killed Elvis is he should not have had to do two shows a night in Vegas. He wasn't doing anything like that before Vegas. You know, you could see him for $40 a show, this was in the late '60s and '70s. You'd have paid $80 just as quick as you'd have paid $40. He wasn't on the hard stuff. He was on Dilaudid and stuff like that which was strong medicine, but Elvis always thought that as long as the doctor prescribed it, it was okay. And of course, Dr. Nick prescribed everything.

Like Scotty used to say about Elvis, "You can ask him what you want to, but you can't tell him what you want to." Of course, Elvis, not having any brothers and any sisters, that was the way he was brought up. He was an only child thinker, and he carried that through to his death. He was the only one, in his mind. And that goes for Priscilla and Lisa too. They existed, and he knew they existed, and he loved them, but it was still "me."

Over the years, there have been a number of books written about Elvis, often by people who were close to him or who thought they were close to him. Some thought he was this way, and some thought he was that way, and the readers would often choose the Elvis that best fit their fantasies. Gordon saw a lot of Elvis and different sides of Elvis. It doesn't make sense to judge Gordon or anybody else. He saw what he saw, and for those of us who never knew Elvis, does it really matter whether or not we know what the King was like? We loved him for his music, not for what he was like.

"All I want to do is sing and make people happy with my music," he'd say. "I ain't much of a singer, I can't dance"—and you know a lot of people laughed when he would say he can't dance, but all that stuff he did, that wasn't dancing, that was just moving, he said he got that movement from the church. He was brought up in the Assemblies of God, and they *move* when they sing. And that's where he got that. And you know, because of the *Ed Sullivan Shows* they'd call him vulgar? He said, "Man, you know, that's the farthest thing from my mind, to be vulgar. My mama'd whup me if I was vulgar." But that's what they called him, they called him vulgar, which really brought him down.

He wanted to be a member of a gospel quartet, really. And before he made it, he auditioned for two male quartets in Memphis. I ran into one of the guys from one of the quartets, his name was Cecil Blackwood, and I said, "You mean Elvis auditioned with you guys and didn't pass the audition?" He said, "Yeah, we sure did. To tell you the truth, Gordon, he could sing any part and sing it good, but when you're singing in a quartet you've got to stay on the part you're given, and before you knew it, Elvis was singing the tenor, the next thing you knew he wanted to sing the bass." Elvis told Ray, our bass singer, that the Lord messed up on him in two ways, He didn't make him a bass singer and He didn't make him black.

It's difficult to explain today just what Elvis meant to the pop music world. Before Elvis, it was obvious that rock and roll was coming, and adult America had better be ready for it, but following the success of "Heartbreak Hotel" and the unparalleled phenomenon of one huge hit after another, Elvis would be the focus of millions of Americans every day. Teenage girls swooned over him. Clergymen who didn't like the way he moved when he sang said terrible things about him. He appeared on myriad TV shows, and the celebrity hosts of those shows always seemed astounded at his respectful attitude toward them, his frequent use of the word "sir," and his bright smile. This "nice young man" was not America's values-wrecking rebel, he was the boy next door, they were pleased to say.

While Americans were getting used to constant tidbits about their new "next big thing," Elvis and the traveling show built around him had to get used to their new life. His band, his business staff, and of course his backup vocal group had a brand-new existence, and they had to learn to live it on the fly. Hylton Hawkins, son of Jordanaire baritone Hoyt Hawkins, talked about life in the early Elvis circus.

Hylton Hawkins

Back in, I guess it was the late '50s, when Elvis was scared to death to fly, they would all take a train out of Union Station here in Nashville. The wives would help the Jordanaires board the train, help them get their luggage in their suites, whatever, so my mom was walking through one of the cars, saw Elvis in his suite, and said, "Hey Elvis, what's happening?"

He was not at the moment, his usual happy self. He said, "Aw, Miz Dot, I need your help." She looked at him in the daylight that streamed through the window of the car and saw that he had black hair dye all over his forehead.

And he said, "Miz Dot, what am I gonna do? We got a show in Chicago tomorrow night. I gotta get this off. It won't come off." She said, "Elvis, what in the world have you done? You just stay right here. I'll be right back." And she walked out of the railroad car, up the hill to a little store right near Music Row, on the corner of, I guess it was 18th and Demonbreun, I think it was called Brenda's Market, or something like that, so she went up there and got some Comet Cleanser, and a sponge, and came back to the train, put Comet Cleanser all over the sponge and scrubbed his forehead down to the skin, and she said, "Now, Elvis, don't you be dyeing your hair anymore. If you need to dye your hair you let me know and I'll come dye your hair." She scrubbed the hair dye off his forehead, probably gave him a bit more advice about hair dye, and got off the train, leaving Elvis and his traveling crew to ride their train to Chicago.

The memories flow. Presley memories.

When we used to go to Graceland, Elvis's mom, Gladys, would always bring us in the kitchen and make us banana and peanut butter sandwiches, and I never had a peanut butter and banana sandwich until I went to Graceland. Peanut butter and banana sandwich was southern poor-boy food. Miz Gladys, she was the sweetest thing, she'd always give my mother a plant for Christmas, and one of those plants, I remember, mama probably had it for 20, 30 years, and she'd say, often enough, "Miz Gladys Presley gave me that plant, Hylton," and she had it in her home all those years, kept it carefully watered, and treasured it.

Mama and daddy had a houseboat out on Old Hickory Lake, and Elvis, you know, he was just a regular old guy. The stardom, he wanted to get away from it, so daddy would take Elvis and Colonel Parker out to the houseboat, just take 'em for a boat ride, you know, and Elvis would lean back and say, "Man, Hoyt, this is great!" and Dad understood that Elvis could just be Elvis on a friend's houseboat, in an unofficial world, and so Elvis and the colonel both really loved doing that. A great escape for them, you know.

And then, when the Jordanaires were scheduled to record with Elvis, I remember mama saying to Dad, "Aw, mercy, the Jordanaires have a 10, 2, 6 and 10 with Elvis in RCA Studio B, and then you've got 10, 2, 6 and 10 tomorrow with Patsy Cline [or Marty Robbins or Johnny Cash, whoever], and the money for all that round the clock recording is good, but this is your life we're talking about," and mama said, "Lord. Elvis will keep you up till 9:30 in the morning, y'all will have to leave Studio B and get over to Woodland Sound Studios [or Pete's Place or wherever they were going to record next], and, sure enough, it's early morning, after the 10 p.m. session, Elvis would say, "All right, guys, come on, come on, come on over here to the piano," and they would gather round him at the piano and harmonize, singing spirituals past dawn and then, they'd have to leave the studio at say 9:15 or 9:30 [a.m.] to get to Bradley's Barn or wherever they had to go, so it was a tough day for them, you know, 'cause they've been up for 48 hours including that last 7, 8 hours wearing out their voices singing nonstop spirituals.

As he got a little bit older, I would ask Daddy from time to time, "Well, Dad, who'd you all record with last night," and he'd say, "Aw, gosh, I don't remember, some guy named Marty, Marty something." Sort of another day at the office with them. Who'd you record with last night? I don't know, Jimmy something, I don't know, had this song called—did this thing called "Big Bad John" or Big Bad Jack or whatever, I don't know.

It wasn't that they didn't care. It was the workload, day after day, and the same was true for a lot of the musicians. You might ask why didn't they lighten their load. They'd still be doing plenty of business. But they knew that if they weren't available for a session, there was always someone else who could take their place, and there was no guarantee that all this profitable steady work would be there for them a year from now.

These skillful, hardworking artisans were not about to take their foot off the gas, and many of them had a long, happy ride until new, young musicians and singers came to town and gave the old ones some serious competition.

Like many gospel singers, Hoyt had a family pedigree. Hylton explains.

Daddy, he grew up performing. My grandfather had a gospel quartet. His name was Wavel Hawkins, and there was my uncle Boyce, who later become the weatherman on Nashville's Channel 4 and Dad's brother Charles, and then my dad. They had a gospel radio show on WPAD in Paducah, Kentucky, every Sunday morning. Daddy was performing at 7 years old, and Boyce was 5, and Charles was 9, and they and my grandfather did a bunch of tent revivals, stuff like that. Daddy and Gordon were old buddies from way back, and I remember going up to my grandparents' house, and after we'd have the Sunday dinner, you know, they'd call the old quartet guys in Paducah, 'cause my grandfather continued to sing after Daddy went into the army, and then went to Peabody College in Nashville, where he majored in music. And they would sing spirituals and gospel songs in the front room of my grandparents' house. Oh man, you talk about some great harmonies, golly, and my grandfather had a tape recorder, and he'd record what they did, it was really cool to hear them and they were, just, right on key.

Being in the music business in Nashville did come with occasional perks, and you didn't have to be a star to enjoy those perks. Hylton tells this one on Hoyt, who might have been the least disciplined of the Jordanaires during the long era of the classic quartet.

Daddy was always kind of notorious for running late to recording sessions. He had been fined a couple of times by AFTRA. So one day he was running late again, headin' out to Bradley's Barn, in Mount Juliet, determined not to be *too* tardy. He jumped on the interstate at I-24 and Harding Place, in his 1968 Pontiac Grand Prix with the biggest engine that they made at the time. He got on that interstate, and put the pedal to the floor. He's flying down I-40, almost to the Mount Juliet exit, and he sees a state trooper, slowly gaining on him.

"Aw heck" he says. So he pulls over, the state trooper gets out of the car, his *gun drawn*, yells at him, "Get out of the car! Put your hands on top of the roof!" He said, "Mister, I have no idea where you're goin', but I have been chasing you from I-24 and Harding Place, almost here to Mount Juliet. Where are you goin'?"

"Well, officer, I'm running late for a recording session."

"What is your name?"

"I'm Hoyt Hawkins."

"The trooper says, slowly, 'Hoyt Hawkins.'" "Mr. Hawkins, are you from Paducah, Kentucky?"

"Yes sir."

"Are you a member of the Jordanaires Quartet?"

"Yes sir."

"Was your grandfather W. W. Hawkins of the Hawkins Brothers Quartet that used to play on WPAD radio?"

"Yes sir."

"Is your brother Boyce Hawkins, the weatherman on WSM, Channel 4?"

"Yes sir."

"Mr. Hawkins, I've been wanting to meet you all my life." He said, "I grew up in Paducah and I used to go with my mom and dad to all these tent revivals and gospel sings, and you and your grandfather and your brothers, y'all were fantastic, I used to listen to y'all on the radio, and Mr. Hawkins, if you would, please slow down! Please. . . . And by the way, could I get your autograph?"

"Yes sir, sure can."

Hoyt might well have been the most colorful of the Jordanaires, with a sly, laid-back sense of humor that could get him out of tight spots. Alan recalled a Hoyt story told by Gordon, known to the group as the "ferry boat story."

Alan Stoker

In the early days the quartet was in a car going somewhere maybe to an engagement, and they came to a ferry crossing, and the ferry was not there, and there was a car parked pretty far back from the dock. Hoyt, he was driving, just pulled around the car and stopped his car in front of the other. Well a woman who was driving the car, she got out, she blew her top, she walked up to Hoyt's car and stuck her face up to the window on his side and cussed him out a blue streak. "You SOB, how dare you, blah blah blah, she went on and on and on and on. Hoyt sat there in total silence while she blathered on, until she finally got finished hollerin', and then he rolled down the window and he said, "Uh, Madam, uh, would you mind repeating that?"

Chapter 7

HOYT, NEAL, AND RAY

The last of the classic quartet to join the Jordanaires was Ray Walker, who arrived in 1958. Ray's father was a minister, a pioneer in working with youth groups, and Ray's education pointed him in the direction of a faith-based career.

Ray Walker

He was so far ahead of his time. He would take children, as soon as they could sit away from their parents [in church] and start them waving their little hands and singing, and learning memory verses, and so, the week I was six years old, I made my first talk, and led my first song [in church].

I made my talk on "The Broad and Narrow Way," and got confused. I couldn't figure out which was right, because, I thought, If it's narrow, looks like everybody who's gonna be saved is gonna have to line up in a long line, and that's not fair, and I don't see how it could be wide enough for everybody, and I cried. My daddy put his hand upon my shoulder and he said, "Son, one failure's good for any preacher."

Ray was born in Centreville, Mississippi. He started singing four-part harmony in the second and third grade, and from third grade through college, he was always in the "quartet" of whichever school he attended. "Every time we moved, every two to four years, the education got better," he says.

In 1958, he was teaching school when he got a message from a friend saying that Gordon Stoker of the Jordanaires quartet had told him that the group needed a bass singer and asked whether Ray would be interested.

Ray Walker

I was interested. I had no way of knowing that Gordon generally didn't get up until nine [because the group often worked late in the studio the night before]. Gordon called me back at four o'clock on a Wednesday afternoon, and I went down [to WSM] and tried out.

And they decided that he was just fine. Before he was an official member of the Jordanaires, he sang on several Jordanaire recordings. Soon, he was singing on the Opry, a genuine Jordanaire, and he remained with them for the next 55 years, when Gordon's death marked the end of the Jordanaires as a live performing group.

Ray has said that he never wanted to be a solo singer and that the only quartet he wanted to sing with was the Jordanaires.

I began working away from home when I was 13. And I've never filled out a job app in my life. It's always been there. I've never gone looking for work. A new job would come up first when the other job was just about over and I'd just make a change and go do it. And this [the gig with the Jordanaires] has been a most fortunate thing. It's opened a lot of doors for all of us in our lives.

Ray has opened some doors for people over the years. He's just that kind of a man. Artists such as Patsy Cline and Loretta Lynn found him easy to talk to on a session, and on those session occasions when life in the studio was getting tense, it was often Ray who knew what to say to ease the nerves of an agitated artist.

But Ray, like Gordon, was also there for the young nobodies. There was this new guy in town. The kid was given a full name at birth, but he went by the name of Cole. Just Cole. He was born in Michigan to a set of parents that split up while he was a little boy, but he grew up with a desire to get into music. Cole was never a Jordanaire; he was a musician whose life was changed for the better because he got to know the Jordanaires.

Cole

As soon as I graduated from high school I moved south to Hendersonville, Tennessee, which is just north of Nashville. There I started writing songs and doing what so many others do to try to break into the music business, including working in television at Country Music Television and the Tennessee Television Network. In 1992 I took a trip up to Canada and saw the Jordanaires in a show for the first time. I got to know Duane West, who took over for Hoyt Hawkins as baritone in the group after Hoyt died in 1982. We became pretty good buddies, and I let him know that I wanted to make a record and I wanted to have the Jordanaires sing on it.

Cole was not your usual dreamer or country fan.

Over the years I got to know Gordon a little bit but I didn't know Ray at all. So I tried to reach out to Gordon, but he was vacationing in Florida.

Cole had enough nerve to chase a dream full throttle once he thought he'd figured out a pathway.

So I picked up a phone book and said to myself, Let me see about Ray Walker. I didn't know if he was listed or what, but I found some Ray Walkers in the book and I took a gamble and I called one and lo and behold he answered the phone and I right away went into business mode and asked if he was the Jordanaires' Ray Walker. I almost choked when he said yes, but I got it together enough to say, "Hi, my name is Cole. I want to make a recording. I've tried to reach out to Gordon but I can't find him, would you be willing to talk to me?" And I asked him what rates they charged and started peppering him with all sorts of questions, but he quickly stopped me.

"Whoa there! What did you say is your name?"

I started to tell him, but he stopped me again. "Wait a minute," he said. "You're that kid who keeps popping up at all our shows, you always show up with a pretty girl under your arm." And I said, "Yeah, that's me."

And he said, "Yeah, we've all wondered about you," and he says, "Where are you at?"

"Hendersonville, Tennessee."

"What are you doing there?"

And I said, "I live here now." This was turning into a real conversation.

He said, "Well, we live in Goodlettsville, which is real close to you. What are you doing right now?"

"I'm just calling you."

"Tell you what," he replied. "Mama's fixin' dinner, you wanna come over for dinner?" Now, mind you, I'm 19 years old at the time, I'm nervous to have even made the phone call in the first place, I'm talking to a hero of mine, and it quickly went from that phone call to a 26 year-plus best friend relationship. I did join them for dinner that night. My best decision ever.

Cole has never become a star. He's done better than that: he's carved out a career playing and singing in good bands, often in Las Vegas, where the fans are excited and the pay is good enough to live on. As for Ray, the last of the classic lineup Jordanaires, who gave a huge leg up to a very young, very gutsy musician a quarter century back—what was he like?

Of all the Jordanaires I got to know, Ray had the biggest personality. It's hard to explain because it's bigger than life. But they were all such a cool, self-controlled bunch. On a session they'd make you go from nervousness to almost like them. Just having them on your session would make you feel that way. They might mention, you know, that, "we just worked in the studio with George Jones or Dwight Yoakam or Billy Ray Cyrus," and here it is the next day they're working with you and they're treating you just like they treated those big famous guys on their sessions.

And Cole tells a story about the Jordanaires that has nothing to do with him, but it's about the Jordanaires, and it's about Jerry Lee Lewis, and everybody in the business has a Jerry Lee Lewis story that'll shake your foundation, so:

They were doing a session with Jerry Lee Lewis. I think it was around 1982, '83, 'cause it was just when Duane West had started working regularly with the group. So they're all standing around the piano in the studio, learning their parts and kind of warming up, running through the next song. They're really focused on Jerry Lee, watching him closely as he sings, because as backup singers, you gotta watch his lips to phrase along with him, you know—and all of a sudden, Jerry Lee stops singing and throws a hard look at Duane, super great guy, awesome, but very quiet, very sincere. Anyway, Jerry Lee stops, looks Duane—of all people—in the eye, and says, "I see you looking into my soul, boy! You tryin' to steal my soul?" And the Jordanaires are all going like, "What?!" And Duane's like, "No sir, I'm just rehearsing!"

Jerry Lee repeats, "You're trying to *steal* my soul!" And he reaches for his briefcase, and they all suspect what's in the briefcase. He flips it open, and now he's got a small gun in his hand. Duane is scared to death, and the other Jordanaires are trying to calm Jerry Lee down, 'cause he is convinced that Duane West and the Jordanaires are trying to steal his soul—or is he?

The story ends there, without a climax.

You know, he's really mellowed out over the years but at the same time he's still the same Jerry Lee.

Back in 1956, when the Jordanaires were first connecting with Elvis, Ray was a young college student at David Lipscomb College in Nashville.

Ray Walker

I was working at a radio station in Centerville—WHLP, the voice and choice of Middle Tennessee—and as a disc jockey I played Elvis's first record. I'd say, "Folks, you may not like the sound of his voice, I don't know what it is, but you gotta listen to this record." And people would request it, and it was just raw, it wasn't country, and it wasn't named rock yet. Then when I came to school I saw the Jordanaires on television, and I was dorm supervisor, so when I graduated that year, I was kind of ready to be a Jordanaire.

Once he was a part of the Jordanaires, Ray found that the quartet had a special relationship with Elvis.

He trusted us. He knew we wouldn't tell him something that wasn't true.

And life was good.

When Elvis did the movies we would sing on the tracks, but he wanted us in the movies with him. But we were doing lots of sessions in Nashville and a lot of the songs we cut on those sessions were hits. We were averaging five records a week in the Top 10. One week I think we were on nine. We couldn't afford to stay out there [in Hollywood] and wait to see if they would use us this day or that day."

These were the days when country records were crossing over into pop again and again, and a whole lot of them featured the Jordanaires: Johnny Horton's recordings of "The Battle of New Orleans" and "North to Alaska," Jim Reeves and "Four Walls," Ricky

Nelson's "Poor Little Fool" and "Lonesome Town," Sonny James and "Young Love," and, of course, the Patsy Cline trilogy "I Fall to Pieces," "Crazy," and "She's Got You." And many more.

Ray remembered Patsy.

She was feisty. She had her opinions and she and Owen Bradley, her producer, fought before every session.

She was doing "I Fall to Pieces" and, aw, it was just great and we were mesmerized with her low tones. And then toward the end she broke into this western [brassy vocal] sound, and we looked horrified. She came over to me, said, "What's the matter, Hoss? Don't you like that?"

I was still new. And I said, "Well, do you want me to say?"

She said, "Spit it out!"

I said, "Patsy, you had us in the palm of your hand and all of a sudden you come up with this ending. It ruins the song."

She said, "Well that's what Owen said!" I said, "Aw, Patsy, stick with Owen. He knows more about you than you do. He'll take you places you never dreamed you could go. Don't worry."

"Well, western swing's always been good to me and I'm just afraid to leave it."

This little exchange is a great example of the many values the Jordanaires brought to their sessions. Ray had a gentle way of explaining his point of view. Gordon could be direct. But both were able to let the artists know they cared and were on their side. I've mentioned that most Nashville sessions tended to be low key. Most—not all—of the session musicians were easygoing and were both creative and capable of taking direction, even when they thought the person giving that direction was out of his mind. But the musicians mostly sat with their instruments, focused on their playing and what the other musicians were doing. The Jordanaires were on their feet, working as a team, often interacting with the artist, very much aware of the total vocal approach to the song, and many of the artists they worked with respected what these four men were bringing to the session.

To the artists who recorded with the Jordanaires, these sessions were terribly important insofar as their careers were concerned. For many of them, having a legendary group like the Jordanaires by their side supplying hooks, licks, and encouragement added confidence and gravitas to the experience. Over the years, fans and media people would want to know the reasons for the Jordanaires' long success. Here was one of Ray's responses.

When Elvis hit so big with "Don't Be Cruel," that two-sided hit (with "Hound Dog") was considered by many to be the biggest selling hit of the era. When he hit so phenomenally, [other artists] wanted the same sound that Elvis had. Well, we couldn't do *all* the sessions—so they would get four other people to sound like us. At that period in the '60s and the '70s, the Jordanaires and the Anita Kerrs were the only two groups in the world making a living doing just vocal background. We didn't give up our paper routes, we let our children do 'em so in case we needed them again, they'd be there for us, you know.

We did so many sessions we all had subs, and Joe Babcock was one of the subs that we used and Dolores Edgin, who sang with Millie on many many recordings, we used her. We were always blessed to be able to adapt to the different styles of music on all the sessions. We *had* to do that. If you don't do that, they get rid of you. A lot of groups come into Nashville, they say, "We're gonna get in on the big money. Move over, we're gonna be a big background group in Nashville, and I'd always say, 'If you've got it, you'll stay around,' and then, before you knew it, they were gone."

As always, second tenor and arranger Neal Matthews was a critical part of the Jordanaires sound.

Gordon Stoker

Neal was with us right from the beginning, you might say. Neal did the vocal arrangements on so many things, everything, really. And he never really got credit for anything he did, all those great arrangements. For Elvis, Ricky Nelson, Patsy, Charley Pride, Conway and Loretta, Crystal Gayle, the Judds, K.D. Lang, the list goes on and on. Great records, great sounds. Neal never got credit.

Brent and Alan Stoker, Gordon's two sons, recall that Gordon often talked about how important Neal's arrangements were to the success of the Jordanaires.

Brent and Alan Stoker

Brent: The key to their work was the arrangements. Dad talked to me about that. Neal had to get it right. He had to pay attention to the song, to the singer, and to whatever the producer might say, and he had to make that arrangement perfect, and you know, they only had 20 minutes or so from the first time they heard the song until they were starting to stand around the mic and get some harmonies going, and that arrangement had to be right, 'cause every minute mattered.

Alan: And when you think, two, three, four songs every session, four sessions a day sometimes, you're looking at twelve arrangements in a day, or more, and that's a lot to have to create, on the spot.

Brent: You know, the other thing that comes to mind, if I may, I remember Dad talking about, "Not only did the arrangement have to be right, but we had to sing it right because we knew we were only gonna be remembered for the last mistake we just made." Brent explained. "On those old one- and two-track sessions, the artist could make a mistake, but we couldn't." Dad said, "If Elvis made a mistake, well, nobody thought anything about it, he'd just do it again, but if we made a mistake during what might have been Elvis's best take, we'd all have to do our parts over, including Elvis.

That'd make us look bad and we couldn't afford that. And that was four of us, *all* of us had to get it perfect, so yeah, we always felt some pressure."

Dad always said that Neal was a perfectionist. He said if you made a mistake, he'd cut you the evil eye, during the take. So you didn't want to make a mistake. Hoyt was a piece of work; I loved Hoyt Hawkins. They would tell a story about "Bossa Nova Baby," that they recorded with Elvis. It had some really fast phrasing, which Dad hated. And Hoyt couldn't do it, he couldn't make all those syllables, so Neal told him, "Just sing every other word."

Brent: Dad sometimes would complain, that *he* could not get a lyric straight. I remember they did a cover of "The Name Game," the Shirley Ellis song, you know, "Shirley Shirley boberley, banana fanna foferly,"—well, dad complained about that because he just couldn't get all those words. He just couldn't do it!

There's a photo of the quartet onstage with Elvis singing something and Neal is right in—Hoyt's ear maybe, and Dad says he's pointing out the mistake Hoyt just made. It's a live show, and Neal is right in Hoyt's ear!

Alan: Reading him the riot act!

Brent: Only to make it perfect. Because he wanted it perfect. You know that Dad makes a mistake on "She's Got You" with Patsy Cline. And it's on the record.

Now, that's a bit of a revelation because "She's Got You" is recognized by many as one of Patsy's best, and the Jordanaire harmonies could wring tears from an executioner. So where's Gordon's mistake?

Brent: The first time they come out of the bridge, when she sings, "I really don't know," Dad hits it wrong, and he slides down to the right note. The story I remember, that Dad told me, was that there had been a scene, before they got to recording the song—Owen had argued with Patsy, or she had argued with him, or they had almost come to blows, or somebody had threatened to—whatever it was—and Dad said, "The scene was so tense I thought, I can't say anything. I don't want to be the one to say I made a mistake, I don't want them to turn on *me*. I thought, if Owen didn't hear it and Patsy didn't hear it, I'm not gonna say a word. I was afraid Owen would get mad or Patsy would get mad, so I just didn't know what to do. So I kept my mouth shut."

So it's on the record.

Readers, music streaming will lead you to "She's Got You." If Brent says it's in there, it's in there, but you can bet it's not sticking out like a sore thumb, or Owen Bradley, Patsy Cline, or Neal Matthews would have heard it, and it would not have stood. And when you get tired of looking for the glitch, listen to the record to enjoy the precise, heart-catching Jordanaire moments; the inspired licks of the A-team; and, of course, Patsy, sharing another heartbreak with her devoted fans. Alan points out that in that song, many of those Jordanaire lines were delivered in unison.

Alan Stoker

They sound almost like one voice. Their unison lines were really *really* good, and they knew when to back off from their mic and not have one voice overwhelm. And their blend in the studio, especially after Ray joined. When Ray joined the Jordanaires, all of a sudden, they had that great bottom end. Really rounded out the sound and made 'em a full-sounding quartet.

As Dad mentioned earlier, Neal did not have a falsetto. Gordon and Ray and Hoyt had a falsetto, and I've even heard Dad say, when they would be singing, Neal had a cue, somehow with his fingers, and they would know to invert the chord, so Dad or Ray would move up and sing falsetto, change the positioning of who was singing what, and on the fly they would alter the chord inversion.

Elvis said, "I want you to do a 'Jake Hess and the Imperials' sound. I sure wish they [the Imperials] were here to do this." Dad said, "Well, we can get that sound!" Elvis said, "Yeah, right."

"My Wish Came True" is the song. And you listen to it, it doesn't sound like the Jordanaires; with the help of Millie on the high parts, it's that real big Jake Hess sound, and Elvis heard what he needed to hear. "Okay!" he said. They could do pretty much anything that he'd ask them to do.

But they didn't always have it their way. Brent pointed out that when they sang for the movies, they'd be nagged by movie people to do it the movie people's way.

Brent Stoker

A lot of that Elvis soundtrack stuff doesn't sound like them. "You need to sound like 'Men on the Dock' on this one (they'd say)." Don't make it a sweet sound. You need to sound like rough and tumble guys on the dock." Sometimes, to me, they sound a little less like the Jordanaires, on purpose. Dad always complained about what he called "The officials," you know, the movie studio people wanted us to do this or do that. In Hollywood, there were always people in their face.

Life didn't always go smoothly in Nashville, either, especially when Gordon brought a union to town.

Gordon Stoker

Oo, yes. Every time we went to New York or Hollywood, we'd have to get a temporary card from AFTRA, the union for singers. I got a lot of static from Chet Atkins.

So Gordon decided they should have an AFTRA chapter in Nashville.

Chet chewed me out *so* royally. So did Hubert Long and Buddy Killen. I said, "But Chet, *you've* got the musicians union." He said, "Yeah, but—huh, singers union. We don't need another union!"

I went to Bud Wolfe in New York and told him, "We need an AFTRA office in Nashville." For some reason he took a liking to me, and he said, "I'll tell you what I'll do. I'll come to Nashville and I'll hire you guys an attorney," and he got Cecil Branstetter [a well-respected Nashville lawyer] down on 3rd Avenue, and we got 11 members, Millie, Dolores, Winnie Breast, the four Jordanaires and the four Anita Kerr Singers. Eleven members was all we had, when we started. Now we've got right at a thousand.

Ray Walker

They go and come or there'd be more than that. I remember we were having a vote on the leaders of the union. And I had to go to the bathroom. So I went to the bathroom and when I came back I found that in my absence they'd voted me union president. That was not a happy place to be right then. And the first thing Gordon said to me after I got elected was "I know you're president, but don't you say anything!" And I said, "I don't have anything to say, I'm never going to the bathroom again."

Gordon Stoker

I'll always be grateful that Owen Bradley, Jim Vienneau, Don Law, Ken Nelson especially, so many of the A&R men were happy that we got a union. AFTRA offers so many things to singers: union insurance, retirement funds, so many things. I can't believe that Buddy Killen, of all people, and Hubert Long, and Chet Atkins fought us tooth and nail. This was in 1961 when we actually chartered our office in Nashville.

Throughout the 1960s and early 1970s, the voices of the Jordanaires continued to be heard on major hits like Conway Twitty's country classic "Hello Darlin'," Loretta Lynn's immortal "Coal Miner's Daughter," Tammy Wynette's "Stand by Your Man," and so many more.

Conway's "It's Only Make Believe," is one of the greatest records we ever did. Huge pop hit. That's what Conway was, back in the late '50s.

Ray Walker

We recorded with Dolly Parton down on 7th Avenue when she was still in high school. Curtis Young, our lead singer now, used to date her in high school.

It is difficult to explain what being a Jordanaire meant to the Jordanaires. They didn't work for anybody, but they worked for everybody. They were in constant demand, often to the point of overwork, and yet they knew that if music styles changed, it could all come tumbling down. Once, an interviewer asked Ray when in the course of his time with the quartet did he realize that they had carved out for themselves a lifelong career. Ray's response says an awful lot in very few words.

I never realized, I still don't, we just did every day what we did. That's probably not the answer you want but, I don't have favorites [records that we did] and we never considered it a career, we were doing a job. We were church people and family people, and we went to work.

Although Ray was not with the Jordanaires when they and Elvis first got together, he saw how the relationship developed, and he understood the role of the music in that development.

Elvis loved the Spiritual sound, and Gordon, defiantly, would say that we're not gospel, mainly because he said we couldn't compete in the gospel field, and we were so surprised [many years later] when they put us in the Gospel Hall of Fame. What they said was, "As far as we're concerned, these guys began everything, and that's why we're working today."

Elvis used to listen to the Opry, and he would hear the Jordanaires sing, and he always wanted them to sing with him, 'cause he thought he was country, and he really was. When Chet Atkins brought in Ben and Brock Speer to sing with Gordon on two of Elvis's early sessions, contrary to Elvis's wishes, the colonel went to Chet and said, "When Elvis asks for something, he gets what he asks for!"

If Chet responded to Colonel Parker, that response was not recorded, but by the end of 1956, it was pretty obvious that the Jordanaires were going to be an important part of the Elvis sound, both on record and in his live performances.

Through the '60s, '70s, and '80s, one of Nashville's top studio arrangers was Bergen White, another son of a preacher man, who came from Oklahoma to carve out an outstanding and diversified music career in Nashville. Like many other musicians, Bergen credits Gordon with helping him get a solid start in a successful music career. Bergen's freelance arranger career frequently found him working on sessions with the Jordanaires, and when the Jordanaires needed a fill-in voice for one of their sessions, they often turned to Bergen, who could deliver vocals from baritone through top tenor.

When I first got into the business, Gordon started calling me to fill in for either Neal or Hoyt, and I found out right away that when I filled in for Neal, I was supposed to do the quartet's vocal arrangements. I'd be scribblin' the chords, writin' in badda-waddas—gotta tell you, it's not hard to do a little bit, but if you can do it as good as Neal did, you can make a big difference in the quality of the records. I mean it!

One of the first times I was filling in with the Jordanaires—I was taking Hoyt's place, I think—I was watching Neal as he filled in the parts, and he's writing shape notes! I told Gordon I remembered as a kid seeing those things in the hymnbooks, but . . . I can't read shape notes!

With the Jordanaires, mostly I filled in on baritone and second tenor. Sometimes I actually filled in for Gordon on first tenor. I had a great falsetto. You know, I worked in a group called Ronnie and the Daytonas, who had a big hit called "Little GTO," and with them I got used to singing tenor. Over the years I wrote arrangements for dozens of country hits.

He also was well known for some of his soft pop arrangements and all in all had a long, lucrative, and satisfactory career creating music. Bergen had this to say about the Jordanaires' role in the country and pop music explosion that spawned the creation of the modern Nashville music industry:

Bergen White

When the Jordanaires were doing that stuff with Elvis, that was pop, and the Jordanaires were all over those records. For years people setting up sessions would call me if they couldn't get the Jordanaires and they'd say, "We need the Jordanaires' kind of sound." So I would call my friend Don Gant and different people, and we would try to be the Jordanaires on that session. I'm sure there were pop producers in L.A. and New York asking their backup groups to give *them* a Jordanaires kind of sound.

A lot of people I know have asked me, what was the magic of the Jordanaires that made them so successful. I've thought about that some, and I think this: Neal was so good with the arrangements he did, he was the brains. Now Gordon, with his high tenor, he was the sound. The other guys were really good with what they did, but you could replace them with another really good singer, and they'd still sound like the Jordanaires. But if you were to replace Gordon with a different high tenor, the Jordanaires would not sound like the Jordanaires.

Chapter 8
PATSY

*If you go to your computer and listen to some of the Jordanaires'
great gospel recordings, you might find a commenter complaining
that the Jordanaires' background arrangements on many of Elvis's
records were "old school background vocals." What he and some
other music lovers seem to forget is that those records were done
more than 60 years ago, when those sounds were every teenager's
earworm. Far from being old school, they were the* beginning *of a
time when doo-wop conquered the mainstream pop world. "Don't
Be Cruel" came out in 1956, the same year as "Why Do Fools Fall in
Love." The Dion and the Belmonts classic "I Wonder Why" arrived
in 1958, and the Marcels' wild version of Rodgers and Hart's "Blue
Moon" was a huge record in 1961. These records are representa-
tive of the flood of period rock and roll that hit the airwaves in the
late 1950s and early 1960s. So it seems that, far from being passé,
out of date, old-fashioned, obsolete, or whatever, Neal Matthews's
Jordanaire background arrangements for Elvis were exactly what
much of pop music was in those days.*

*How fortunate for the Jordanaires that they had an Elvis in their
career. One Elvis was more than any backup vocal group could
hope for. And how fortunate for them to have all these other great
artists who wanted them. But it wasn't an accident. It was talent
meets opportunity.*

*Among those artists, one stands out in a special way. Her star
shined so briefly compared to Elvis and some of the other Jordanaire singing partners. But so what? She was Patsy Cline. She
made her own space. And her later records would open up a brand-
new chapter in the career of the Jordanaires. This is Patsy's chapter,
but first, a little more Elvis.*

Gordon Stoker

I'd like to go back to give you an idea of where we are—and were, musically, and how it changed our career. We started out as a gospel group, and we loved to sing spirituals. We were one of the first white groups to take the black spirituals and bring them to diverse audiences. We introduced "Something Within," "Working on a Building," and I guess we were the first [white group] that sang "Peace in the Valley," and "Dig a Little Deeper." I could go on. Elvis loved the spirituals we did, because Elvis could sing spirituals all day long. As a matter of fact, sometimes we'd almost get thrown off the sets when we'd go to Hollywood to do a picture with him. All he wanted to do was sit down at the piano and start singing spirituals, and we'd sing along. He liked to do spirituals, and he would sing them until he was blue in the face, no matter that they had a movie to shoot. He loved to hear us sing, and he loved to sing with us, which is why, when he first wanted to do a session with background singers, he said he would like to have the Jordanaires.

Working with Elvis was always memorable because he was our friend, and such a fun person to be around. Sometimes, we were torn as to what our friend wanted us to do, and what we were to do as "hired hands" on recording sessions. I've never forgotten a time at Radio Recorders studio out in Hollywood, while we were there recording songs for the Jailhouse Rock soundtrack in 1957. In those days, Elvis always wanted to warm up singing his favorite gospel songs. When the session started, all Elvis wanted to do was play piano and sing the gospel songs that he loved, with us backing him up, singing with him. This went on for a couple of hours until finally, they called for a lunch break.

Elvis and his boys left to grab lunch, but we stayed at the studio and ate there with the musicians. One of the movie officials came up to me and told me "Look, we're wasting time and money here. When Elvis comes back from lunch, if he goes back to the piano and starts that again, don't you guys go and join him." I said okay, but I knew that Elvis wasn't going to like it.

When Elvis came back from lunch, he went straight to the piano and took up where he'd left off. When we stayed seated and didn't go up to sing with him, he turned to us and said "uh, uh, uh . . . what's the matter with you guys?" When I told him that the officials told us not to join him, fire flew in his eyes. He said "Look, if I want to come here and sing gospel songs all day, that's what I'll do." With that, he got up and walked out the studio door, with all those Memphis boys following him. The officials were stunned. Needless to say, that was it for the day. Nothing got recorded.

The next morning, Elvis walked in, and got to work recording the soundtrack, as if nothing had happened. I'm not sure if the colonel said something to him, but if I had to guess, I'd say that he did.

We did 28 movies with him—some of them we appeared in, a lot of them we didn't. We'd go out to California and do the soundtrack, but we couldn't appear in the movie because we had sessions going on here in Nashville all the time, and to go to Hollywood to be in a movie, you had to be out there from five weeks to two months, sitting around, waiting for our scenes to come up. *King Creole*, we all had parts in that. We were out there seven weeks. Well, our work in Nashville, you know, these people that we'd been working with for years, they want you to continue doing their sessions. So if we'd gone out there for all the movies, and stayed the length of time— all those movies were a big disorganized mess, every one of them. They may come off when you're viewing them, but when they're being made, they're a disorganized mess. A lot of times they didn't even know what the name of the movie was going to be when they started shooting. I remember one time, back in the 1960s, in a movie we did with Twentieth Century Fox, we went out and sang the title song for the movie (it was called "Black Star" then), and we did several other songs while we were there, and then we went home. About a week later, they called me and said, "You guys are going to have to fly back out here." They had to pay us the entire original guarantee again just to change the title song for the movie from Black Star to "Flaming Star." Isn't that wild?'

But for that reason, we usually could not leave Nashville and go out there to work onscreen with Elvis. We recorded with him all those years, which was a beautiful relationship with him. We loved it and he loved it. When the movie deal was over, he said, "Now I'm going to play Vegas." We couldn't do that, and we told him, so he got a little hurt. He got a little put out with us. But he never did put us down even though he may have thought we belonged to him.

Alan remembered that his father was upset when they couldn't do Vegas with Elvis. He said that he looked in his session book for the time period, and they had a lot of sessions booked.

Alan Stoker

Colonel Parker's assistant, Tom Diskin, is the one that called Pop to book them for the Vegas shows. Pop called Owen Bradley to see if there was anything they could do about it. Owen told him that, if they go to Vegas, he'd have to hire another male quartet to take their place. That pretty much settled it for Pop.

Pop called Diskin back, and told him they couldn't work it out. Tom replied with something like "Well, that's okay. We want to go in a different direction anyway." I don't think there was any press about it. Pop certainly didn't pursue press.

I don't know for certain, but I would almost bet that the quartet collectively made that decision to stay back in Nashville, not Pop on his own.

I've heard a lot of interviews, and the various things Elvis said. At one interview, when asked, "Whatever happened to the Jordanaires," he said, "I can't get 'em out of Nashville, man, they got stuck in Nashville and, they make so much money in Nashville that you can't get 'em out of there". Pop said he could sense a feeling of resentment, or abandonment.

Gordon Stoker

Elvis told us that if it hadn't been for us, with the attitude we had toward him, always being willing to help him with his songs, willing to help him with this, that, and the other, there just wouldn't have been an Elvis. I don't really agree with that. But this is what he told us on the last movie set that we did, when he knew the movies were over. He said, "Let's just face it. If there hadn't been a Jordanaires, I don't know if there'd have been a me. You guys have always tried to help me. You've always pushed me. A lot of times I'd come in and wouldn't want to do the crap [songs] that they'd give me." He had a few other words for it. They'd make him record these various songs. He didn't like a lot of them. Naturally we'd always go in and try to do the best job we could do with what they gave us. It didn't make any difference to us. We'd just as soon do one song as the other, but he didn't like a lot of them.

You know, it was one of those things. He said, "I have never made a movie." He did make, as I said, 28 of them, and yet he said, "I have never made a movie yet." Actually, Elvis is capable of making a good movie. He could be a good actor. He is capable. Elvis had to have like a million dollars up front before he stepped onstage the first time, and this was a lot of money for a movie scene. Hal Wallis and a few other people were the only ones that could come up with it. So because they had to pay Elvis so much up front they could not pay any real money for good scripts or pay any money for a song. A lot of the [movie] songs, as you know, *were* a bunch of crap. He knew they were too.

Readers may be surprised to learn that the group didn't necessarily care about the song, but it's not so hard to understand when you realize that to the Jordanaires, much of the material was not so much songs as it was melodies, harmonies, rhythms, and phrasing—a challenge in sound for Neal to sketch out and the rest of the group to fill in, in a short time, the best they could, then on to the next song.

* * *

Early in the history of the Jordanaires, producers like Owen Brad-
ley and Chet Atkins found that the Jordanaires made their records
sound better than they did without backup harmonies. The Jor-
danaires were special. Their harmonies were precise. Their timing
was precise, and, with Neal Matthews as their arranger, their vocal
parts were creative and entertaining. They were an accomplished
gospel/spiritual quartet, and their musical vocabulary was vast.
They knew their business. Their job was the same as that of the
Nashville studio musicians: to support the producers and artists by
giving them the sounds they wanted and using their creative talents
to help make the best sounding record they could.

Nashville sessions almost never involved formal arrangements
except when the producers wanted to "sweeten" the records by add-
ing "strings"—violins, violas, and cellos—when they felt the songs
called for these additions or "horns," like the trumpets in the Bob
Moore hit "Mexico," or Johnny Cash's "Ring of Fire." To this day,
self-proclaimed experts insist that adding strings or horns ruins
country music. They have a point—to a point. If you are making a
record that's supposed to sound like a Roy Acuff record from 1940,
then you shouldn't add strings or, for that matter, virtuoso four-part
background vocals because that's not what Roy would have done.
But after the Hank Williams–Lefty Frizzell era, Nashville found its
music in demand for the new Top 40 formats that were beginning to
dominate radio. The result was a new, energetic, hybrid Nashville
music that had a great influence on both pop and country music—
and sold a whole lot of records because lots of listeners really liked
that music. This music came to be called the "Nashville Sound."
Producers still tailored their records to the artists they produced.
Jim Reeves records did not sound like Hank Snow records. Jeanie
Pruett records did not sound like Osborne Brothers records, and
Johnny Paycheck records did not sound like Charlie Rich records.

But as country music became more popular in the 1960s
and 1970s and music journalists started to pay attention, these

journalists began to complain that traditional steel guitar sounds and fiddles were being replaced by string sections and smooth-sounding vocal groups. Ray Price and Eddy Arnold were crooning instead of yodeling, and these new country journalists didn't like it. They were not wrong about these changes. Where they erred was when they seemed to insist that country music, unlike other commercial music forms, had no right to evolve. They didn't complain that soul music had moved on from the raw rhythm and blues of the 1950s, and they didn't seem to notice that there was still a place in country music for stone country artists like Loretta Lynn, Porter Wagoner and Dolly Parton, Merle Haggard, Charley Pride, Mel Street, Gene Watson, and many more. They seemed to want country music to sound forever like Hank Williams, Ernest Tubb, and Kitty Wells, and that wasn't going to happen. Some country fans complained too, but over the years, as country continued to grow, many old country fans could find new country artists that moved them.

The Nashville Sound was a powerful force in country music for years, and one of the early beneficiaries of this new musical development was Patsy Cline, a bluesy, gutsy lady from Winchester, Virginia, who revolutionized the role of female singers in the world of country music. The Jordanaires played a critical part in the sound of Patsy's records. It took some doing to make her want to work with them, but it's hard to imagine how her greatest hits might have sounded without their sensitive harmonies. Gordon had a lot to say about Patsy, one of the most memorable vocalists in the history of country or pop or any other music, this from a 1991 Gordon Stoker interview with the Country Music Hall of Fame's John Rumble and Paul Kingsbury.

Gordon Stoker

We saw Patsy Cline at the Grand Ole Opry, of course, and we met her and sang with her on the Opry, I think, before our first recordings with her. We did many, many recordings with Owen Bradley, and when Patsy got her foot in the door, so to speak, with recordings, why, Owen told Patsy, "Hey, I want to bring the Jordanaires in to work with you on these songs." And she really didn't want us. She said [something like], "Four male voices covering me up? What am I gonna do with that?" Owen said, "Just leave it to me, Patsy. Don't worry about a thing. Let me bring them in for certain effects, and you're gonna like it." And then, a real funny thing, from the very first session we did with her, why she really got to liking us—just seemed like we had a family gathering, the first session we did with her at the Quonset Hut. So many recordings and so many years ago, I certainly don't remember the first songs, but I remember the session.

The reason I remember the session is because you could tell she was reluctant to record with us. She really didn't want a male quartet in the studio with her. She had already recorded many songs with the Anita Kerrs, which were a mixed group.

I kind of resented her feeling that she didn't want us there. It was a feeling like, if you don't want me, I don't want you. If you don't want us on the session, we certainly don't need you. We've got all the sessions we can handle. At that time, of course, we were doing, often, four sessions in a day. We were averaging anywhere from 15 to 20 sessions a week, so we didn't need Patsy Cline. You know, I don't mean it in the wrong way, but we didn't need her sessions to make our list of session work complete.

But Owen wanted us on those sessions because he thought we could add some beautiful oohs and aahs and what have you, *with* her. Owen sat down at the piano and started running over the first number, and Neal was close by. We all gathered around the piano, with Owen playing. And Patsy pretty well already knew the song. And then, little by little, we started filling in our parts.

Pretty quickly, Gordon explains, Patsy, and the Jordanaires got into the rhythm of the routine.

She wasn't overly friendly at first; for those first two or three sessions, Patsy *really* did not want a male vocal group. It was strictly Owen who insisted. And of course, he knew what was good for the recording, and naturally he won out. You can't imagine how much we all respected Owen, even Patsy. Later—I say later, maybe after the first two or three recording sessions, she became very friendly. I mean, she began to actually lean on us, in that she would say, "Hey, does this sound right?" And many times she didn't know how to pronounce a word. I remember so well. You know, she wasn't the most educated person in the world, by any means. And if she didn't know how to pronounce a word, she'd walk over to Ray Walker. The bass singer was usually closer to the [featured vocalist] the way we were standing in the Quonset Hut. She would walk over to Ray and say, "Hey, Buster," or something like that. Usually she had something cute that she'd call you. Half the time she wouldn't call you by your name. "Hey Buster," or "Hey Flippo," or, "Hey Handsome."

"Hey Hoss, how do you pronounce this word?" She used the word "hoss" a lot. And sometimes her language—she was liable to use a cuss word here and there, a dirty word here or there. She couldn't have cared less. But if she didn't know how to say a word, or something like that, she'd walk over to us and say, "How do you pronounce this word?" Or "Am I singing this tune right?" or, "Do you think I oughta do this?" or "Do you think I oughta do that?" The reason I'm telling you this is, I thought it was so strange, you see, the way it all turned around. After about three sessions, she began to realize that we could work with her. And then she didn't want to do a session without us. She began to want us on everything. She asked for us on everything she did. And I thought that was a wonderful compliment, the fact that she did that, because she really felt that we were important to all her recordings. If we missed something occasionally, if we had another session and we missed a session with her, why, she would tell us at the Grand Ole

Opry on a Saturday night, "Hey, I missed you on my session this week."

Some of the many artists the Jordanaires recorded with found the quartet to be good confidantes, sympathetic ears who were experienced enough in the business to understand their problems. Patsy Cline was one of them.

What she said I don't remember, but I know she didn't like the association she had with Four Star Records. She always felt like they were screwing her, except a lot of times she said it in a bit plainer words than that. I can distinctly remember the bitterness she had against her recording relationship before she got her contract with Decca. I think that may have prevented her doing her best work in her early days. Like she said many times—I heard her say, "What the hell!" That's how frank she was. "Who in hell cares, anyway?" I've heard her say that. And I think those kinds of remarks were a product of her background, what she'd gone through to get where she was.

She talked about the hard times she had before she came to Nashville. They didn't have the price of a pot. They didn't have any money for anything. When she came to town the first time, Wally Fowler encouraged her. She could sing. And he knew that. Anybody could recognize the fact that she had a voice, a great voice—loud and clear. And she had a certain gleam in her eye.

She came in a borrowed car and did not have any money to spend the night. She and her mother came so she could audition for someone, I've forgotten who. If she could've stayed and pursued a record deal then, she might have gained [success] much sooner. But she didn't have the money to even spend the night in a hotel. Later on, she must have been making guest appearances at the Opry, 'cause that's where we met her. She was cute. She had a certain look about her. I mean, she wasn't just an average girl, you know what I mean, that sang country music in those days. They weren't cute in those days like they are now. And she was a good-looking girl.

On the Opry she always had those little outfits with the little fringe all around. She always wore quite a bit of makeup, which is what she should have worn for the lights of the Opry. A lot of stars didn't. I always remember that she seemed to have good taste in her makeup, where a lot of girls didn't have, in those days and a lot of girls don't have these days. But *she* did. I never really saw her looking crummy at all. Now, a lot of sessions we did with her, she'd come in with her hair done up and her handkerchief tied around her head. Even then, she'd have on some makeup. And there was a couple of sessions that she came in where she made a remark that she and Charlie [Charlie Dick, her husband] had had a few rounds. And I think that Charlie has denied it, but she led us to believe that she and Charlie had had a little fight here and there, a few words, and a little fight. And it seems that I distinctly remember—and I may be wrong, but I've thought about this many times, and the other guys remember it too—there was one time on one of the sessions, she came in and had a semi-black eye. Now, you know, she could have hit herself on a doorknob, or she could have hit herself on the door of a car, or anything. The only thing I can remember is she said something about her and Charlie having words. But she said, "So what? I love the sonofabitch anyway." I can distinctly remember her saying that because not every girl used that word. I mean no disrespect. She was sweet. But she let the words fly by.

Oh, there's a couple of times when she and Owen got into it in the studio, man, that I thought she was going to hit him. He wanted the song a certain way. He wanted the tempo of the song a certain way. Owen, of course, was very knowledgeable. Owen knew what was best, and Patsy wanted to do it another way. She wanted to do the song faster. I don't know if it was particularly tempos that we're talking about here, where the argument started. But I do know that they got into it a couple of times when I really thought that either the session was gonna be called off because he'd take just so much, and then *he'd* fire back. She really got her dander up, I remember—I think one of those times was "Faded Love." I remember so well when she did that song, man, right at the end when she took a sad breath then sang "love." Man, chill bumps all over my arm, I never will forget it, even in the studio, when we were recording it.

YouTube or music streaming, you'll find Patsy in there singing "Faded Love" like nobody else could or ever will, right down to the last brokenhearted sigh at the end of that record. You'll hear the Nashville A-team musicians at their best and softly, softly, just right in the distant background, the Jordanaires. You'll hear strings too, a gorgeous, heart-grabbing just-right arrangement written by Bill McElhiney. Before Patsy, "Faded Love" was associated mostly with the song's cowriter, Bob Wills, and his band the Texas Playboys. It was one of their signature songs. The Patsy Cline cover of "Faded Love" discovered a beauty of its own. This is the Nashville Sound as it played in the early 1960s.

When we walked out of the studio after doing a session with Patsy, the songs that we recorded rang in my ear the rest of the night. She just had that magnitude, that magnetic sound, and a certain look she had on her face too. It was kind of like Elvis in that respect. Man, when she did a song, you might as well just hang it up, 'cause can't nobody else do it. She was just that way. She'd worked hard to get where she was. And let me tell you, when she set her head for any particular thing, she had to have her way or there was a fight. And I'm sure that same thing carried at home with her and Charlie. Charlie seemed like a pretty easygoing guy, but I bet they had some battles—fights, fusses, and what have you!

And she would mention them to us. Charlie would deny this, but I distinctly remember her saying it in the studio, and Ray does too. And Ray was closer to her. She liked Ray Walker more than the rest of the Jordanaires. I guess maybe him being closer to her

*Elvis and Gordon working on "All Shook Up" at Radio
Recorders on January 12, 1957. One of three duets they sang
together, "All Shook Up" also features Elvis slapping the back
of his guitar as a drum. Elvis's cousin, Gene Smith is on the
left.* COURTESY OF THE ESTATE OF GORDON STOKER

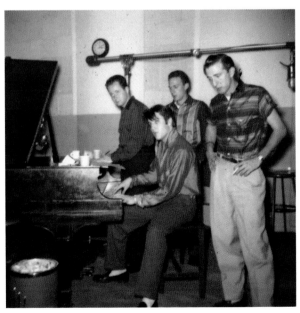

*Radio Recorders, Hollywood, California, on January 12,
1957. Standing left to right: Gordon, Hoyt , D. J. Fontana.
Elvis at the piano.* COURTESY OF THE ESTATE OF GORDON
STOKER

RCA Studio, Nashville, Tennessee, early morning of October 31, 1960. Long night of recording songs for the "His Hand in Mine" album, and just after recording "Crying in the Chapel." Left to right: Neal, Gordon, soprano and dear friend Millie Kirkham, Elvis, Hoyt, and Ray. COURTESY OF MILLIE KIRKHAM

With Connie Francis, August 1961, at Bradley Studio, Nashville, Tennessee. Connie, considered at the time to be one of the most popular female vocalists in the world, and the quartet worked together on numerous albums and singles. Left to right: Gordon, Hoyt, Connie Francis, soprano Millie Kirkham, and Ray. COURTESY OF THE ESTATE OF GORDON STOKER

The Jordanaires were cast members of the Grand Ole Opry for many years, backing featured artists and performing solo. Here they are on May 2, 1964, performing a solo spot. Left to right: Gordon, Neal, Ray, and Hoyt. COURTESY OF THE ESTATE OF GORDON STOKER

With Les Paul and Mary Ford, 1962, at Bradley Studio, Nashville, Tennessee. The quartet recorded a couple of albums with them. Left to right: Hoyt, Les Paul, Mary Ford, Gordon, soprano Millie Kirkham, Neal, and Ray. COURTESY OF THE ESTATE OF GORDON STOKER

June 27, 1970, in studio with Ringo Starr. The last day of three days recording Ringo's solo album "Beaucoups of Blues" at Music City Recorders, Nashville, Tennessee. Ringo seen here running down his song "Coochie, Coochie" with Jerry Shook on six-string electric bass. Left to right (standing): Gordon, Hoyt, Neal, and Ray. COURTESY OF THE ESTATE OF GORDON STOKER

In studio with Jerry Lee Lewis. Circa 1975. Left to right: Gordon, Neal, Ray, and Hoyt. Jerry Lee (seated) COURTESY OF THE ESTATE OF GORDON STOKER

With Dolly Parton during the recording of her "The Great Pretender" album. Circa 1983. Left to right: Neal, Ray, Dolly Parton, Duane West, and Gordon. COURTESY OF THE ESTATE OF GORDON STOKER

In 1985, the quartet appeared many times with Rick Nelson on a double bill with Fats Domino, or with Rick and his band solo. This photo was taken the last time the Jordanaires worked with Rick in September of 1985, backstage at the Sands Hotel in Las Vegas. Four months later, they sang at his memorial service at the request of the family. Left to right: Duane West, Louis Nunley, Rick Nelson, Fats Domino, Neal Matthews Jr., Gordon Stoker. COURTESY OF THE ESTATE OF GORDON STOKER

The quartet first got to know Naomi and Wynonna Judd on January 26, 1987, in Los Angeles, when they appeared together on the 14th Annual American Music Awards TV show, produced by Dick Clark. In December of 1991, the quartet was asked by the Judds to be part of their farewell concert, filmed at Murphy Center on the campus of Middle Tennessee State University. Left to right: Neal Matthews Jr., Naomi Judd, Gordon Stoker, Wynonna Judd, Ray Walker, Duane West. COURTESY OF THE ESTATE OF GORDON STOKER

The Jordanaires recorded many songs with the great Roy Orbison, including one where Roy was unsure of his entry note. He asked Gordon to stand behind him and sing the note in his ear while it was being recorded. This photo was taken on January 8, 1988, at the taping of "Elvis: A National Tribute," celebrating what would have been Elvis's 53rd birthday at the Showboat Hotel in Atlantic City. COURTESY OF THE ESTATE OF GORDON STOKER

A 2000 promotional picture of the last iteration of the Jordanaires. Left to right: Gordon, Curtis Young, Louis Nunley, and Ray. COURTESY OF THE ESTATE OF GORDON STOKER

Gordon Stoker with Hank Williams Jr. at an event at the Country Music Hall of Fame and Museum. Circa 2008. They'd been friends since Hank's mother, Audrey, asked Gordon to come to their house and teach a teenage Hank Jr. some of his Dad's songs on piano. COURTESY OF THE ESTATE OF GORDON STOKER

This was the last time the original Jordanaires were photographed together, June of 2000, when Bob and Reba Hubbard celebrated their 50th wedding anniversary. Left to right: Bill Matthews, Gordon, Monty Matthews, Bob Hubbard. Culley Holt had passed away 20 years earlier, at the age of 54. COURTESY BOB HUBBARD ESTATE in the studio and he always kindly made over her more than we did. We'd say, "Hey, Patsy, good to be working with you. Blah blah." And we'd go about our business. But Ray would take some time with her. He was very kind.

Now as for Owen, she wouldn't argue with him on every song, not on every song. But she argued with him almost any time— when he would start playing the piano and we'd start running something down, she would find something about the song that she didn't like that Owen was doing. You know, the initial rundown in the studio before we recorded it. Maybe she was listening, in her mind, to the demo at home, and she had in her mind, maybe, how she wanted to record it. And of course, when you go in the studio and you sit down with the A&R man at the piano, most of the time it comes off different from what you thought in your mind it was gonna come off. My point: she was very headstrong, extremely headstrong. I remember there were times when I thought it was all gonna blow up, and she was gonna walk out. I mean, voices were raised! And when Owen raised his voice, you'd better sit up and take notice, because if you ain't ever been told off by Owen Bradley, you ain't ever been told off. Owen was a fair man, but musically speaking, he was a perfectionist. That's why we had to be on our toes every moment. We had to have every chord perfect. We had to do everything perfect on everything we did with Owen, as a matter of fact. Because he'd catch you the very moment you did anything wrong. If you were singing the wrong inversion of the chord, he knew it, and he let you know it. Of course, that's good. I deeply respect an A&R man who has that knowledge. I know that in other parts of this book I talk about us occasionally missing a note, but remember, over the weeks, months, years, we sang an awful lot of notes!

I think what's wrong in our business these days is that we have A&R men that don't know one thing about music. Mash the button and let it roll. But back then we had Owen and Chet and a few others. Not very many others. Of course, Columbia producers

Don Law and Frank Jones didn't know a whole lot about music, and yet they produced a lot of hit records. But I think it's great to have a man who does know about music. And Owen did.

What I remember most of all is the songs, and what we were able to do for Patsy on those songs. Listen to "She's Got You." It still hits me right *here* when I hear it. "Sweet Dreams" was super. And "Crazy." Man, the buildup that Owen had us do on that was just great.

Alan Stoker

Written by Hugh "Willie" Nelson, "Crazy" was released first by Paul Buskirk and his Little Men with vocals by Hugh Nelson in 1959. It was that version that was played in August of 1961 at the session as a demo. To say the least, it was unlike most country songs at the time. It had seven or eight chords, for crying out loud.

Pop was quoted as saying, "I remember when the quartet and Patsy heard the demo, she said, 'Look, Hoss, there ain't no way I could sing it like that guy's a-singin' it.' By that she meant Willie's phrasing of it. She didn't wanna do it like that. She wasn't gonna do it that way."

The recording of this song was different from most sessions at the time. Patsy had been in a major auto accident not quite two months earlier, and had some trouble breathing—hitting the high notes. Because of that, she was in the studio when the track was recorded, but she didn't add her vocal part until weeks later. According to published reports her vocal on "Crazy" was a "one take," meaning that she sang it one time and that's the vocal track we hear today on the record.

Pop didn't hear the final version with her vocal on it until he heard it on the radio in October. "I remember how much I loved it," he said. "I know I remember that. I remember I was pleasantly surprised at how great she did it, with how much feeling she did it."

Reportedly, Patsy didn't like singing "vulnerable" songs, as she herself was nothing of the sort. But she had a way of singing hurting songs that made you feel like, at that very moment, she was torn up inside. You could make the argument that this was producer Owen Bradley's signature Nashville Sound production. "Crazy," by Patsy Cline with the Jordanaires is the number 1 most played song on jukeboxes in the United States, according to the Amusement and Music Operators Association. Unbelievably, it only reached number 2 on the *Billboard* C&W charts, kept out of the number 1 spot by Leroy van Dyke's "Walk on By." It reached number 9 on the *Billboard* pop chart.

The first woman inducted into the Country Music Hall of Fame and the first country female artist to perform at New York's Carnegie Hall, Patsy's recording career was relatively short, but many of her recordings are timeless. I hear people say that they don't like country music. But if you ask them about Patsy Cline and "Crazy," all of them will say, "Well, that's different."

There's no telling how many interviewers asked Gordon Stoker what made Patsy Cline special. John Rumble put the question this way: "I wonder if we could somehow describe what that magnetism was and how she achieved it."

Gordon Stoker

The hard way [said Gordon]. Singing at work and what have you. But it's just a gift. Just a gift. She had heart and soul with everything she sang. Let me tell you one reason, I think, that she did. Those songs were her life! "I've got those little things, but she's got you." That's the way she thought about her love life. These songs were the story of her life, and I think when she was singing, she was saying, that's the way I feel about you, about him, about whatever.

A lot of people have asked me, "How do you think Patsy's career would have survived if she'd been alive today?" This may not be fair to say, but Patsy was rude to a lot of people. She was rude to disc jockeys. If she didn't like you, it made no difference if you were a disc jockey. I don't care if you played her record on every program, if you said something she didn't like, she'd tell you off. Or if she just didn't like *you*, she's liable to have told you off, and you, in turn, might have quit playing her records, and then she might not have been quite as big in the days to come. Because how long can you be rude to people? And she was rude to a lot of people. I saw her be rude at the Grand Ole Opry to various people. She had a chip on her shoulder for some reason. And I don't know if it was because of her marriages, or because of her home life, or just what it was. There's got to be reasons that she was bitter, at times, to Owen Bradley, because Owen is always in a jolly mood. I never remember Owen Bradley coming into a session when he was mad. Never heard Owen Bradley coming into a session cussing out everybody or telling people off. But Patsy would walk into the studio and have Owen with fire in his eyes before you know it. Like I said, I guess she had a certain chip on her shoulder. I've never really known. Let me put it this way. Had I thought I would have been questioned about her 30 years later, I'd have paid more attention. But you know, she was like many of the artists we were working with, so I didn't think too much about it.

Gordon recalled that he never heard Patsy mention other singers or musicians who influenced her, but he put that in perspective.

Like most people that are very headstrong and think that they are a winner, she knew she was good. You can't have this great voice and not know it. The girl could sing anything that she wanted to sing; anything Owen Bradley or anybody else asked her to sing. And when they've got that on their mind and they know it, they're not gonna say, "Hey man, I know I can sing, but I can't sing near as good as Molly Bee." They're just not gon' do it.

I think we can compare the two [Patsy and Elvis]. Elvis seldom talked about liking the music of other artists. He just didn't compliment other singers, or other piano players, or other quartets. He told somebody one time that we were his favorite quartet, but he only told *us* that one time, and that was about a year or so before we quit working with him. He didn't [go round sayin'] we were his favorite quartet. Just that one time when he said, "Hadn't have been a Jordanaires, there just wouldn't have been a me." We [felt that way about him] because we loved him and respected him, and we did the same thing for Patsy. We loved and respected her. We loved her as a person, and respected her talent. Of course we encouraged her. Of course we complimented her. I can remember so well, 'cause there was a woman that was dying for a compliment. And the musicians, you know, they don't compliment people. When [the studio engineer and producer are] listening to the playbacks, the musicians are usually getting coffee or smoking or telling jokes among themselves. But we've always tried to stand around the artist when they were listening to the playback, not just with Patsy but all the singers, if we felt that they wanted us to hear them and to be constructive, give them constructive criticism, which Patsy did. Patsy would say to us, "Do you think this is good? Is that note too high?" Or, "Is this the right key?" I remember her asking that, about the keys. I can't think of any specific songs just now, but I can remember her saying. "You think this is too high for me? Or too low?" And if we thought it was, we'd say so.

Owen was very cooperative with all that give and take that went on between us. And he appreciated the fact that she was interested enough in us that she would ask us. There's not any artist I've ever worked with that was as headstrong as Patsy or Elvis. They were very set in their ways, very set about what they wanted to do, and very headstrong in what they wanted to hear. I can't remember any girl singer that we've ever recorded with, that's been as strong-willed. We did many sessions with Loretta Lynn. But Loretta was never as headstrong as Patsy, by any means. There was no comparison between the two. Patsy was a tough ol' gal. That's the perfect thing you can think about Patsy. Both she and Elvis come up the hard way and they both thought someone was out to rip them off. They thought they were gonna get the wrong end of the deal. Both of them pretty much had the same deal [thought the same way] and they didn't even know each other. It's very strange. They were a lot alike on many many things. Elvis was not rude to people, like Patsy was. She wasn't rude to you if she liked you, or if you were able to get in and maybe say a nice thing to her before she reacted. But there was a part of her that didn't trust people.

I'm sure she lost some disc jockeys that way. They couldn't deny her great records. But there wasn't a lot of love exposed between many people and Patsy Cline, the reason being she was very bold. She was very frank. I don't care what you'd say to her, if she didn't like you, if she didn't like your looks, she'd tell you, Get out of my way, boy. I ain't got time for you. That was just the way she could be if you rubbed her wrong. And many things she said, we thought she was kidding. And she might have been. On her behalf, let's say she might have been. Like I said about her and Charlie's fights. She might have been kidding about her and Charlie's fights. Who knows?

Now, Owen, see, was in charge. And she knew the steep bridge she had to cross was Owen Bradley. In other words, she might as well have been fighting a brick wall. If Owen didn't want it that way, it wasn't gonna be that way. Because Owen was the one who drew the final line. Owen Bradley was the one that made the final decision. Owen Bradley was the one that would get blamed for it if it wasn't a hit. So Owen was in charge, and Owen ruled. And she knew it and she resented it; it was very obvious that she resented it, a lot of times. Mostly the sessions went smooth [laughing], but then there were times it didn't. And when they got to jawin' back and forth we'd all stand there wondering, with our hands behind our backs, wondering what's gonna happen. What are we gon' do? Are we gon' go home, or what? You'd just watch 'em fight it out to see what would happen. But no session was ever torn up. Every-thing was always smoothed out. I don't ever remember—well maybe only one time that I can remember us sitting back there on those seats in the Quonset Hut when I really think Patsy left mad, because she didn't get her way. No, oh no. You do too many, and then you don't remember *which* session, you just remember that there *was* a session. And the only reason I do, it being so many years ago, is 'cause we respected her as a singer so much. And she had a certain gleam in her eye. Kind of like the same gleam that Elvis always had in his eye. She was just cute about the way she expressed herself. Wasn't always the best English, or it wasn't always in the best manner, but it was cute, and she was different. And that's the reason we liked her. That's the reason we all became very good friends with her. And we always looked forward to working with her, because she was a lot of fun. You never knew what she was gonna say, whether it was a smutty joke, or what.

But most of all she just had a great warm voice. Just a God-given voice, that's all. Some people are blessed with it, and some people aren't. She was blessed with the way of being able to get that feeling across in a song that a lot of singers can't. She was not formally trained. Her training was just learning by singing. She sang in nightclubs and joints and things like that to get a start. And that just gave her the lungs to sing. I don't remember her having any trouble with her voice, but as I've said, she'd ask us, "Is that the right note here?"

When she was singing a song, she lived and breathed it. Each song that she sang, she was singing it from her heart.

Patsy never spoke much about her family life.

She'd say little things all along, but she didn't really say much about her personal life, other than—a lot of times—jokingly. You don't know if it was really the truth or if it was a joke. But everything was just the hard way. She just had a hard way to go. She couldn't always make ends meet, financially. But she was very determined. She showed an extreme determination to move forward right from when we first met her. She knew she was gonna be a singing star. She had a lot of drive, which many girl singers do not have. What solidified Patsy's professional relationship with the Jordanaires, was that she appreciated what the group added to the sound of the record. She liked the oohs and aahs, the places that we built up, and the places where we would come in when she was holding a note. She felt comfortable in suggesting vocal ideas for us. "Can you come in here?" "Can you aah there?" "What about . . . ?" If Owen liked it, he'd say, "Yeah, fine. You all try that." And we'd try. Sometimes it didn't work. Sometimes it did.

I think what we did on Patsy's recordings was often a little more tasteful than a lot of our other sessions. I think that was because she inspired us. We loved to hear her sing. We didn't feel that way about every artist we worked with, I can assure you. Because we respected her talent, we gave her a lot of room to sing. I think all the time we had in our mind that she thought we were gonna cover her up. And if you listen to the recordings, we *don't* cover her up. We just come in kinda like strings, at various places. She liked what we did. And she liked the recordings. And she liked us because we encouraged her, and we smiled at her, and we stood around listening to the playbacks of her singing, because we actually loved to hear her sing.

Like many major country artists, Patsy recorded some gospel material, and one of Gordon's interviewers, John Rumble, wanted to know how she felt about her gospel sessions, asking Gordon, "In your estimation, was she capable and successful and believable in her handling of gospel material, sacred material, however you want to phrase it?"

She liked "Just a Closer Walk with Thee" because she thought it was a good piece of material. If you're asking me did she sing it because it was a religious song, not particularly. Owen evidently wanted her to do it. She never struck me as being in any form, shape, or fashion a religious person. "Elvis [on the other hand] was brought up in the church. I think she had heard the recordings, of course, and she knew how to sing the songs. Red Foley could do the same thing. He certainly didn't live a Christian life, but nobody could sing a hymn any better than Red Foley. Man, Red Foley could make everybody in the whole audience have tears in their eyes and then he'd turn right around and live different from the song he was singing."

The other interviewer on this session, Paul Kingsbury, wanted to know how Opry audiences responded to Patsy. The Jordanaires backed her many times on the Opry, and Gordon knew the answer.

She knew how to enthrall an audience. Everybody loved Patsy because she could belt out a song. And there was something about the—the word wouldn't be cocky—way that Patsy had about her. Confidence is a better word, though that word doesn't tell the whole story either. When she walked out on that stage, she didn't walk out with a mousy air. She walked out on that stage as if to say, "Look, you so-and-sos. I'm gonna sing you a song; you sit there and listen to me." And people liked that. She didn't walk out there trying to be Miss Cutey-Pie. As I told you before, she'd use any word she wanted to. "Listen to me sing. I'm fixin' to sing, and you gon' listen to me!" That's the attitude she had. And it was a change from the other people [who sang on the Opry]. It's hard to describe, but it's just the way she came out on the stage. It was a very demanding air. A very secure air. Which, maybe she wasn't a secure person at all. She might've been, some people would say, a very insecure person inside. She never *ever* impressed me, though, as being an insecure person, the way Elvis did. Elvis was extremely insecure. I would certainly class Patsy as a secure person, and I think that came across when she walked out on the stage. And yet she had that feeling that somebody was always trying to get her, get at her. Somebody was gonna take away everything she had.

Gordon wanted to make clear that Patsy was dead serious about her studio work, even when she and studio musicians like Grady Martin would kid around in the middle of a session.

They teased each other a lot. Grady [an A-team guitar player on Nashville sessions] was a very frank person too, and she knew that. So there was a lot of laughs between the two of 'em. I remember, distinctly, a lot of times, walking in when she and Grady would be carrying on. I don't know if they'd told each other a joke or something like that. They'd be havin' themselves a party.

But when the session got going, baby, she was serious. There wasn't much joking between songs or anything. There wasn't much eye contact during the recording. She really paid attention to the heart and soul she was pouring into a song. She was headstrong to the end. Right down to the last session we did with her, she was still Patsy Cline. She'd gone through a lot of pain and suffering, and she was aching to let it all out.

I think her recordings opened a lot of people's ears to country music because of the way she sang it. Every person that listens to a Patsy Cline recording thinks that she's singing it to them. You're the one that she's talking about when she says, "I've got these little things, but she's got you." And they're not dated. Right now, when I get in the car and hear Patsy Cline sing "Faded Love," it's as though she recorded it yesterday.

On March 5, 1963, Patsy, along with her manager Randy Hughes and country singers Cowboy Copas and Hawkshaw Hawkins, died in the crash of Hughes's Piper Comanche airplane near the West Tennessee town of Camden. Gordon had worked with all three singers over the years, and her death left a huge void in the lives of the Jordanaires. Alan Stoker had a special reason to remember the days that followed.

Alan Stoker

The Saturday night following the plane crash, the Jordanaires followed a moment of silence at the Grand Ole Opry with a gospel hymn. Pop always said that was a hard song to get through.

The next day, the Stoker family drove to Pop's hometown of Gleason, which is near Camden. Pop *had* to stop and see the crash site. What I remember as a nine-year-old, after what seemed like a long walk from the road down to the site, is the many people combing the ground, and others just solemnly standing, observing. Others were talking among themselves, in shocked, hushed voices, with a stunned look on their face. There was a large jagged hole in the ground, with tree roots exposed, and rain water in the bottom of the hole. That's a lot for a nine-year-old boy to remember.

After the Jordanaires and Elvis stopped working together, the quartet continued their wearying schedule of two to four sessions per day. Over the decades, Nashville's music industry continued to grow. In addition to the talent agencies, management companies, record labels, record pressers, publishing companies, and record promoters, there were some really good studios servicing the labels and the independent producers, and most of them, sooner or later, needed the Jordanaires. The Jordanaires watched as the studios got better, and artists of all the popular music genres were coming to Nashville because the studios were great, the musicians were terrific, and there were lots of good songs to be found here. But studio life could be extremely hectic. Although studio times were usually 10 a.m. to 1 p.m., 2 to 5 p.m., 6 to 9 p.m., and 10 p.m. to 1 a.m., arranger and musician Bergen White remembers that some sessions were scheduled at odd times in between and beyond. If you were a regular musician on Elvis sessions, did you dare complain? You did not. In fact, Nashville was known as a place where most session players, including the top ones, were tolerant of difficult artist behavior.

Gordon Stoker

By the time we were working with Patsy in the Quonset Hut, the studio sounded real good, thanks largely to studio engineer Mort Thomasson. I remember we cut there with Johnny Ray. His hearing was so bad that he'd take his hearing aids out and get right up to those huge speakers to hear what he was sounding like. That was past his peak success. We did several things with Andy Williams at RCA Studio B. It was after *his* biggest days, but he was still selling albums; so was Perry Como and all those people we worked with there, at RCA Studio B.

In order to keep track of the Jordanaires' busy studio schedule, Gordon, as the group's manager, kept a detailed appointment book.

Brent Stoker

The first week of December 1970, appears to be typical for Pop and the quartet during that time, says Brent. "Over 30 songs recorded with a variety of artists: Three with Bobby Lord, total of nine with Dottie West, eight with Don Gibson, four with Sue Richards, three with Chuck Howard, four with Jean Shepard, and four for Del Reeves. Friday afternoon December 4 at Jack Clement's studio Pop and Hoyt Hawkins along with Bergen White and Herman Harper recorded seven versions of a Miller Beer jingle—'When It's Time to Relax'—that aired on network television and radio for years."

Their schedule never seemed to let up, but I never heard Pop or any of the others complain. They were getting so they weren't kids anymore, but when it came to filling up their appointment books, and racing off to Woodland Studio in East Nashville, or RCA Studio B on Music Row, or all those new studios in the old houses in Berry Hill, or Bradley's Barn out in Mount Juliet, they were ready to go, ready for the next singer, the next setup, ready for the next song. And I know why they continued to fill those appointment books with hour after hour of session work.

I saw them, day after day, and I believe they could do it because that's how much they loved it. That's how natural it came to them.

Perhaps the first promo shot of the Jordanaires with Gordon Stoker as piano player. Circa 1951. Left to right: Bill Matthews (1st tenor), Monty Matthews (2nd tenor and arranger), Culley Holt (bass), Gordon Stoker (piano and 1st tenor), Bob Hubbard (baritone). The Matthews brothers were not related to Neal Matthews Jr., who later joined the quartet. COURTESY OF THE ESTATE OF GORDON STOKER

In-studio 1951 rehearsal for an Armed Forces Radio Service recording date. Note the matching shoes. Left to right: Monty Matthews, Bob Hubbard, Culley Holt, Bill Matthews, with Gordon on piano. COURTESY OF THE ESTATE OF GORDON STOKER

The lineup as of late 1951 was left to right: Culley Holt, Gordon Stoker, Monty Matthews, and Bob Hubbard, with Hoyt Hawkins on piano. Since Gordon had moved to singing 1st tenor, they brought in Hoyt, who'd only recently taken Gordon's place on piano with the John Daniel Quartet. COURTESY OF WSM RADIO

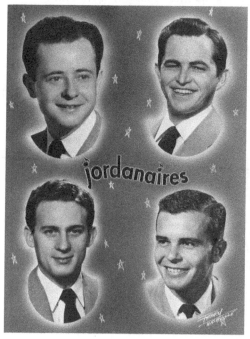

Circa 1953—By now, the Matthews brothers were gone, Bob Hubbard had been drafted, and Hoyt Hawkins had moved from playing piano to singing baritone. Neal Matthews had joined as 2nd tenor, and Culley was still singing bass, but not for long. Top left clockwise: Gordon, Culley Holt, Neal Matthews Jr., and Hoyt. COURTESY OF THE ESTATE OF GORDON STOKER

A scene from one of the Eddy Arnold Time *TV shows, filmed in Chicago in 1954. Working this show four days a week for six months, the quartet learned many new songs, in many varied styles. Left to right: Neal, Hugh, Betty Johnson, Gordon, and Hoyt.* COURTESY OF THE ESTATE OF GORDON STOKER

The finale of an episode of a Purina Grand Ole Opry *TV program, on the stage of the Ryman Auditorium in September of 1956. Left to right: Chet Atkins, Marion Worth, Judge George D. Hay, Martha Carson, Carl Smith, Arlene Francis, Marty Robbins, June Carter, Gordon, Neal, Hoyt, and Hugh.* PHOTO BY GORDON GILLING-HAM/COURTESY OF THE GRAND OLE OPRY ARCHIVES

Appearance contract for the Jordanaires on the Arthur Godfrey Time *radio program from April 1956. After one of the quartet's gospel performances, Godfrey said that he didn't know what kind of music that was, but it sure was happy.* COURTESY OF THE ESTATE OF GORDON STOKER

April 14, 1956—The second recording session Gordon did with Elvis Presley. "I Want You, I Need You, I Love You" was the song being recorded here. Note Elvis in his sock feet and Ben and Brock Speer singing with Gordon. Elvis was none too pleased that Chet Atkins hadn't booked the full Jordanaires for the session. From this point on until 1973, Elvis insisted on it. PHOTO BY DON CRAVENS/ GETTY IMAGES

Elvis, the band, and the Jordanaires rehearse at Presley's home on Audubon Drive in Memphis for an appearance at the Mississippi/ Alabama State Fair in September 1956. Left to right: Hugh Jarrett in profile, Hoyt, guitarist Scotty Moore, Neal (sitting on the floor), drummer D. J. Fontana, and Elvis. Bassist Bill Black is behind Elvis. Gordon's taking the picture. COURTESY OF THE ESTATE OF GORDON STOKER

Hanging out with actor Nick Adams and actress Natalie Wood. Somewhere in 1956. Left to right standing: Neal, Nick Adams, Gordon, Natalie Wood, Hoyt, and Hugh. Drummer D. J. Fontana down front. COURTESY OF THE ESTATE OF GORDON STOKER

Elvis and the Jordanaires appearing together in Daytona Beach, Florida, at the Peabody Auditorium, August 9, 1956. One night later in Jacksonville, Judge Marion Gooding was in the audience and the next day, threatens legal action if Elvis doesn't tone down his act. Left to right: Neal, Gordon, Hoyt, and Hugh Jarrett with Presley. COURTESY THE *DAYTONA BEACH NEWS-JOURNAL*

In studio working on Elvis's second RCA album in September of 1956 at Radio Recorders, Hollywood, California. Left to right: Gordon, Elvis, and Hugh. COURTESY OF THE ESTATE OF GORDON STOKER

Elvis working on a song for his second RCA album. September of 1956 at Radio Recorders, Hollywood, California. COURTESY OF THE ESTATE OF GORDON STOKER

At Radio Recorders, Hollywood in September of 1956, recording Elvis's second RCA album. Elvis with his original hair color. Left to right: Neal, Hoyt, Elvis, Gordon, and Hugh. COURTESY OF THE ESTATE OF GORDON STOKER

Rehearsal for their second appearance on the Ed Sullivan Show, *taken October 27, 1956. The week following the next night's broadcast, Elvis was reportedly burned in effigy in at least two major cities. Left to right: Neal, Gordon, Elvis, Hoyt, and Hugh. Scotty Moore, Bill Black, and D. J. Fontana are seen in the shadows on the right.* COURTESY VINTAGE KING PICTURES/FASCINATIONSTART.COM

January of 1957 at Radio Recorders, Hollywood. The Jordanaires with RCA executive Steve Sholes, the man who signed Elvis to RCA Records. Left to right: Hugh, Hoyt, Sholes, Gordon, and Neal. COURTESY OF THE ESTATE OF GORDON STOKER

*January of 1957 at Radio Recorders, Hollywood.
Elvis warming up singing at the piano while the
quartet is behind him. Left to right behind Elvis:
Hoyt, Neal, Gordon, and Hugh.* COURTESY OF THE
ESTATE OF GORDON STOKER

*Live onstage in Ottawa, Canada, April 3, 1957. Elvis's only
performances outside of the United States. Neal, ever the
perfectionist, giving Hoyt an earful about something. Left to
right: Guitarist Scotty Moore, Elvis, Gordon, Neal, Hoyt, and
Hugh.* EVERY EFFORT HAS BEEN MADE TO IDENTIFY COPYRIGHT
HOLDERS AND OBTAIN THEIR PERMISSION FOR THE USE OF COPY-
RIGHTED MATERIAL

Marquee of the Paramount movie theater in downtown Nashville during the summer of 1957. COURTESY OF THE ESTATE OF GORDON STOKER

In performance at Sick's Stadium, Seattle, Washington, September 1, 1957. Over 16,000 people saw this performance. Elvis in his gold lame jacket with Jordanaire Hoyt Hawkins on piano. Left to right: Gordon, Neal, and Hugh. MOHAI (MUSEUM OF HISTORY & INDUSTRY)

Backstage at the Ryman Auditorium during Elvis's visit to the Grand Ole Opry, December 21, 1957. Elvis in the tuxedo that Gordon helped him be fitted for. Left to right: Hugh, Gordon, Elvis, Hoyt, and Neal. EVERY EFFORT HAS BEEN MADE TO IDENTIFY COPYRIGHT HOLDERS AND OBTAIN THEIR PERMISSION FOR THE USE OF COPYRIGHTED MATERIAL

With 17-year-old Ricky Nelson on April 28, 1958, at Master Recording Studio in Hollywood, California. An overdub session for many songs on Nelson's second Imperial Records album, including Nelson's number 1 hit, "Poor Little Fool." Ray Walker had just joined the quartet earlier that month. Left to right: Ricky Nelson, Neal (obscured), Gordon, Hoyt, and Ray. COURTESY OF THE ESTATE OF GORDON STOKER

Recording at Master Recording for Ricky Nelson's Song by Ricky *Imperial album, June 1959. Left to right: Gordon, Neal, Ricky Nelson, Hoyt, and Ray.* COURTESY OF THE ESTATE OF GORDON STOKER

With Rick Nelson and band on August 29, 1985, at the Mule Lip Saloon in Colton, California. Left to right: Gordon, bassist Patrick Woodward, Neal, Rick Nelson, Duane West, Louis Nunley, guitarist Bobby Neal. COURTESY OF THE ESTATE OF GORDON STOKER

On a tarmac somewhere with Rick Nelson outside the ill-fated DC-3, August 1985. The quartet joined Rick with his band for many shows together the last years of Rick's life. Left to right: Duane West, Gordon, Rick Nelson, Ray, and Neal. COURTESY OF THE ESTATE OF GORDON STOKER

January 1959—The first recording sessions with Patsy Cline at Bradley's Quonset Hut Studio. Patsy was cool to the quartet at first. Left to right: guitarist Grady Martin, audio engineer Mort Thomasson, Patsy, Neal, Ray, Hoyt, Betty Zane Jacobs, Gordon, and producer Owen Bradley. COURTESY OF PATSY CLINE ENTERPRISES, LLC

September 9, 1960, onstage at the Grand Ole Opry with Johnny Horton,
performing "The Battle of New Orleans," as they did on the hit recording the
previous year. Left to right: guitarist Tommy Tomlinson, Grady Martin on
banjo, Gordon, Neal, Hoyt, Ray, drummer Buddy Harman, and Johnny Hor-
ton. COURTESY OF THE COUNTRY MUSIC HALL OF FAME® AND MUSEUM

July 25, 1961—Faron Young recording session at Bradley
Studio, Nashville, Tennessee. Left to Right: drummer Buddy
Harman, Faron Young with an acoustic guitar, Hank
Garland on ukulele, Floyd "Lightning" Chance on upright
bass, on the far right is Ray Edenton on guitar. Around
the piano with his back to the camera is Ray Walker, then
Neal Matthews Jr. and Hoyt Hawkins. Gordon is talking to
piano player Marvin Hughes. PHOTO BY SID O'BERRY

WORLD VOCAL GROUP

1	BEATLES	8234
2	Beach Boys	5648
3	Monkees	4297
4	Rolling Stones	1626
5	Bee Gees	1508
6	Jordanaires	1367
7	Four Tops	1100
8	Diana Ross/Supremes	965

The Jordanaires ranked high for many years in the New Musical Express readers poll. Here, they show up as number 6, ahead of Diana Ross and The Supremes and the Four Tops. NME was the UK's most well-known music publication. Even as late as 1970, the Jordanaires were rated in the Top 20. There are many Elvis fans in the UK. © NME 2022

Neal working on a vocal arrangement for another George Jones hit recording. Columbia Recording Studio, Nashville, Tennessee. February of 1971. Left to right: Neal, Gordon, Hoyt, soprano Millie Kirkham, Ray, and George Jones. PHOTO BY BILL GOODMAN/COURTESY OF NASHVILLE PUBLIC LIBRARY, SPECIAL COLLECTIONS

— THANKSGIVING EVE 1984 —

BENEFIT FOR

GREENPEACE

DON McLEAN

WITH HIS SPECIAL GUESTS
THE JORDANAIRES
MC: JIM MONAGHAN/WNEW-FM

NOVEMBER 21, 8PM AT CARNEGIE HALL

$15; $12.50; $10 AT CARNEGIE HALL, 57TH ST & 7TH AVE, NYC
— AND ALL METRO-NY-NJ-CONN TICKETRON OUTLETS —
OR CHARGE TICKETS TO CREDIT CARDS BY CALLING 212-247-7800.

A promo handbill for the November 21, 1984, Thanksgiving Eve concert with Don McLean at New York City's Carnegie Hall. The quartet and McLean worked together in studio and onstage for many years, and did many Thanksgiving Eve concerts together. Left to right: Gordon, Neal, Don McLean, Duane West, and Ray. PHOTO BY DAVID GAHR/ROCK NEGATIVES

Chapter 9

MUSIC ROW: A GORDON POINT OF VIEW

Back in the 1960s and 1970s, Nashville's Music Row was a big small town, filled with characters worth gossiping about. It seemed like almost every week, there was another story about someone everybody knew, something funny or something sad, or something mystifying but always something human, about the people they knew in this place they called the Nashville music business. And because the Jordanaires were doing so many sessions with so many artists, they must have heard them all and maybe told a few themselves. Here's Gordon, with interviewer Douglas Green, starting with one on Loretta Lynn when she was boarding a plane headed back to the United States from London, then on to Gordon and Ray on a TV interview.

Gordon Stoker

Some guy came up, introduced himself, and he was so proud to meet Loretta and all that kind of carrying on. Loretta turned around and she said, "I have never seen the strange names everyone's named here in London. Everyone is either named Larry, or Harvey or Peter." She said, "I have never seen so many Peters in my life." And everyone within hearing distance of her nearly died laughing at what had come out of her. She said, "What did I say? Did I say something wrong? I just said I'd never seen so many Peters. What did I say wrong?"

This is the way her mind runs, which is great. She is the normal one, we're the ones whose minds wander into strange places. You know, she does a lot of canning. . . . Like she told my wife she'd been puttin' up poke salad, a wild weed that has to be cooked and cooked just to get the poison out of it. My wife said, "I didn't know you could even do that!"

Loretta said, "Yeah." She said, "I put up poke salad." She's making about two million a year and she's gatherin' poke salad growin' wild and puttin' it up like it was precious garden greens. And she says, "I've been cannin' some berries too. "I tell you what I'll do. On the session tomorrow I'll bring you guys some strawberry preserves." Which she did. She brought each one of us a jar of preserves about this big. "But I want them there jars back!" And that Mason food jar must have cost a quarter in those days. So I brought home my preserves, and my wife Jean poured the preserves into something else and we all brought back those Mason food jars the next day.

Now, Mason food jars is an expression I haven't heard since I was a kid. And here is a gal, like I say, that makes all that money, and she's concerned about three Mason food jars. That's not because she's stingy. I think it's because she grew up so poor that she still can't bear to waste a perfectly good Mason jar. They were cheap then. They're not cheap now. She was just ahead of her time.

Ray Walker

Loretta, she's just one of my favorite human beings in this whole wide world. She never realized how big [famous] she got, you know? NBC, I believe it was, was gonna do a special on her and they wanted to come out to her ranch where her mansion was, a beautiful colonial place. She had just gotten back from being on the road, and she looked at the pillars on the house and the kids' handprints were all over them—and she was out there paintin' over those pillars as high as she could reach. Well, these men in suits had gotten there early and they came up the walkway and Loretta says, "Looka here, we got some people coming here to do a show on me and these kids got their dirty hands all over these posts. Get them brushes and help me paint them before they get here. So here are these suited up executives of NBC, painting Loretta's pillars!"

Gordon Stoker

I remember, they were doing etchings instead of a picture on the front cover of some albums [this was the 1970s]. On one of her albums this guy came in from New York and pulled off the onion-skin paper and showed her the etching he had drawn for her next album. Loretta took one look at it and she said, "Hmm, I could have drawed it better myself. Just make a picture of me with my plain old cowboy suit on." She said, "That's what the public likes to see me in, so just make a plain old picture of me in my cowboy suit."

Loretta during sessions is very concerned about time. She's always pushing on sessions. I mean, she pushes Owen Bradley all the time. The things she'd say are so funny. You know, that big wide [recording] tape when it first came out. She couldn't get their attention in the control room, 'cause they had her mic turned off—and she'd go up and beat on the window [between the studio and control room] and say, "Hey y'all in there get that two-inch tape rolling." She's very concerned. Of course, a lot of times, the instrumental part is not quite worked out, or maybe the voices haven't quite got their part on some of the deal, or Grady Martin, who's playing guitar, hasn't got his lead-in, you know. A lot of times, the red light will come on, and Loretta will look around [into the control room] to see if the tape is rolling. If it is, but the music hasn't started, she'll say, "That two-inch tape is costing me money." She's very concerned about wasting time and tape on sessions, as if she had anything to worry about with all the money she's got coming from the record label.

Ray Walker

You know, I wanna say one other thing she said on a session that was so sweet. We were working with her over in RCA Studio B for some reason. She had had some people visiting out in Hawaii. She had a condominium out there, an extra one. And I said to her, "You know, Loretta, it's just wonderful to be in a place where you can do that for your friends, invite them to see you, and they don't have to be crowded around your family." She says, "Looka here, the way I feel is, the dime is the same as the dollar. If you need a dime and I've got it you can have it and if you need a dollar or a thousand dollars, I've got it, you can have it." And that really endeared her to me all these years.

Alan Stoker

During the early days playing piano with the Jordanaires, Pop found work as a session pianist on country recordings. Columbia producer Don Law hired him as early as 1951 to play piano on numerous Carl Smith recordings. These sessions were recorded at Castle Studio, which was on the second floor of the Tulane Hotel in downtown Nashville, four years before Owen built his first studio on Music Row, or before there was an "A Team" working sessions there. The first number 1 record that my dad was ever on was Carl Smith's "Let Old Mother Nature Have Her Way," which topped the country-and-western charts for eight weeks in 1951. Another number 1 recorded that year with him on piano was for Carl Smith's "Are You Teasing Me," which also reached number 1.

Two years later in 1953, he played piano on Smith's recording of "Hey Joe" (number 1 for eight weeks) and in 1954 on Smith's recording of "Go Boy Go," which reached number 4. By this time, he found less and less time available to play piano on sessions, as the quartet was getting too busy. Pop's friend "Papa" John Gordy took over for him on Carl Smith's sessions. For all the number 1 songs he sang on with the Jordanaires over his lifetime, the first number 1 recordings he can be heard on, he was playing piano.

In the early days of recording in Nashville, the record labels frequently used studios at local radio stations. Or their acts headed out of town to studios in Chicago or Cincinnati. In the late 1940s, a number of studios opened in Nashville, most notably the Castle Recording Laboratory, located downtown in the Tulane Hotel, the brainchild of Aaron Shelton, Carl Jenkins, and George Reynolds, three engineers for WSM radio, owner of the Grand Ole Opry, a company that hated the thought of their employees doing music business on their own. The studio hung around for several years and had some success, then shut down. Nashville needed a good studio bad, or it would lose its nascent recording industry. Along came Owen Bradley and his brother Harold, with plenty of experience as musicians but little or none in studio architecture. Owen was determined to create a competitive studio in Nashville, and the two men, aided by Mort Thomasson, started by renting a lodge hall at Second and Lindsley downtown and experimenting with equipment, acoustics, and instruments. "At the end of the year, the landlord came around and tripled the rent," Harold Bradley later recalled, so they moved their studio uptown to 21st Avenue South in an area known as Hillsboro Village. Harold described this second attempt in the book How Nashville Became Music City, U.S.A.

Harold Bradley

We actually built the concrete block walls ourselves. We made some industrial films there for Genesco and Springfield Woolen Mills. The problem was that when you put the flats in that studio for a session, it changed the sound. The low ceiling was also a problem.

Gordon Stoker

Yeah, Hillsboro Village behind McClure's Department Store. As a matter of fact, I played piano on a lot of records there. Ray Price, Jimmy Dickens, Carl Smith. I played piano on all those. I remember the last session I did in Owen's studio out there was with Johnny Horton.

The studio in Hillsboro Village was not going to solve the Bradleys' problems. So after a couple of years there, they thought they might try again elsewhere.

Owen had decided to build a real studio. He bought an old house up here on 16th Avenue South. The house had a basement. This was a run-down area. It wasn't dirty, but just run-down houses, and some of them might have had chickens. Owen bought this old house, and it had a basement, and he built a studio in the basement of that old house. They called it the Bradley Studios. This is where we did "Young Love" with Sonny James. We did "Gone," with Ferlin Husky, which was a *huge* record. "Gone" was the first recording where we used echo.

The Jordanaires had been working with Ken Nelson at Capitol Records in Hollywood for quite some time. One day he called me and said he wanted to record a guy by the name of Ferlin Husky, and he wanted a choir sound on one of the numbers. He said, "I want to make the group sound bigger. I'd like to use a girl with you guys."

I said, "Well, we've never used a girl, but, you know, that'd be fine with me."

He said, "Well, do you know who you can use?"

I said, "I've got some ideas. I'll call around and see." I called Millie Kirkham.

Millie was a native Tennessean who grew up in Donelson, just outside of Nashville. After she graduated from high school, she began to appear on a popular WSM radio show called Sunday Down South, *which led to studio work with the Anita Kerr Singers.*

I called Millie, and I told her, "Ken Nelson wants the Jordanaires to use a girl singer next week on a session."

And she said, "Do you mean you want me to sing with you guys?"

I said, "That's what we're going to try."

She said, "Well, if you want me, I'll be there." I said, "Be there." And I gave her the time and place.

"Gone" was a tour de force for Millie, who sang her part with such power and emotion that many of the important labels began to use her on their sessions. The song was a number 1 country hit and a number 4 pop smash in 1957. All of a sudden, Millie was the go-to soprano in Nashville, and her voice would soon be familiar to many millions of Americans who would never know her name but would hear her voice on records by Patsy Cline, Roy Orbison, Brenda Lee, Eddy Arnold, George Jones, and many more artists. The Jordanaires would use her again and again over the years, including their classic version of "Blue Christmas," mentioned earlier in this book.

Before we go any farther, it's important to understand that Owen and Harold Bradley and the people they worked with were learning as they put together their studios. Soon, RCA, Columbia, and others were building real studios in buildings constructed for that purpose. The Bradleys were music people converting houses and small commercial buildings into makeshift studios that had their flaws, yet they worked well enough to compete over the airwaves and in the record shops with studios created by studio architects in New York and Los Angeles. Sonny James's "Young Love" crossed over to become a number 1 national pop hit. Gene Vincent recorded "Be-bop-a-lula" in that tiny house on 16th Avenue South. Right from the beginning, Bradley Recording Studios was a success, and to hear people like Gordon Stoker and Harold Bradley tell it, it was created by trial, error, and instinct. The year was 1955.

This "new" studio was considerably better than the Hillsboro Village place, according to Gordon.

They had a bit more room because they had three floors. They had a basement and then the main floor and an upstairs. They had a bit of room in the house to do what Owen wanted to do.

What they didn't have room for was space to accommodate more musicians and equipment. Still, Bradley Recording Studios would be a vast improvement over the vaunted Castle Studio, which had decent acoustics but did not have an echo chamber.

We always said that the Jordanaires came at about the same time echo did. Later, of course, the German echo chambers came on the scene. They were invented, and really revolutionized the entire echo idea. But Bradley Recording Studios could boast of one of the first echo chambers in Nashville by just planting a microphone and a speaker in a tiny concrete room. Mort Thomasson set it up. He put a speaker under the steps coming down, and it was closed in, kind of under the front porch where he had just a concrete room. It was a concrete floor, and he concreted the walls and the overhead. It was about a five-by-five height of the room, and he had a microphone in there with a speaker, and this was the echo chamber. The sound, see, hit those concrete walls and bounced off them back into that mic, and they could give you as much of that sound as they wanted. And what we did was we recorded in the studio, and they fed it through that speaker into that microphone and back into the tape machine. That's how you got that echo sound.

A lot of times, someone would be in that room looking for something. They had a few tapes stored in there. Owen would holler, "Get the hell out of the echo room! Someone's in the echo room! Get out of there!" Because they were making noise in the echo room. This would be a lot of sound. Bad noise on the tape. This was our first idea of an echo chamber.

So, to finish the story, "Gone" was really the first recording we did that had a huge echo sound. If you listen to the recording, it sounds like—you know, we almost sound like a choir. Ken Nelson said we sound like the Norman Goof-off Choir [a pun on a famous recording group of the time called the Norman Luboff Choir].

Alan Stoker

On October 30, 1956, Sonny James along with the Jordanaires recorded "Young Love" at the Bradley Recording Studios. Hailed as the first teenage country crossover single, it hit the number 1 spot on the *Billboard* Country chart beginning on February 2, 1957, and was there for nine weeks. It peaked at number 11 in the UK Singles Chart and it sold well over a million records worldwide.

It climbed to number 1 on the *Billboard* Pop chart and probably would have stayed number 1 longer if Capitol Records had been better prepared to meet the growing demand for it. Initially they had only pressed enough copies of the record to satisfy the anticipated country-music demand. Sonny James was quoted as saying "'Young Love' caught Capitol off guard, it hit so fast and was such a big hit. They told me they couldn't press them fast enough." Because of that, Tab Hunter quickly covered the song for Randy Wood's Dot Records using the same arrangement.

The popularity of "Young Love" has lasted through the years. It's been covered by artists as diverse as Leslie Gore and Celtic Thunder and by Mary Hopkin for her Postcard *album, which was produced by Paul McCartney.*

Gordon Stoker

That studio was small but they kept it for a long time. They did many many hits in there. They were busy all the time, six days a week.

But Owen Bradley had just gotten started. For $7,500, he and Harold bought a Quonset hut kit and had it assembled directly behind the studio/house on 16th Avenue South. A Quonset hut is a prefabricated metal building with a curved roof, not what one would dream of to house a sound studio, and the original use was supposed to be the production of music videos somewhat similar to the videos that would dominate the pop music world decades later.

But the cramped basement studio in the house was proving to be a pain in the butt for musicians, artists, and producers, so gradually, the Bradleys morphed the Quonset hut into a sound studio so popular that it dominated Nashville hitmaking during the 1960s and 1970s. Marty Robbins, George Jones, Tammy Wynette, Tanya Tucker, Charlie Rich, and dozens more would build their recording careers around hits recorded in that big tin can.

Among the first sessions *we* did there was with Patsy Cline, I'm sure. We did many, many sessions there, way too many to remember. I think they got the best sound in that studio of any studio in the city of Nashville. In 1962, Owen sold the Quonset Hut and the house with the little studio in the basement to CBS, and they, in turn, tore down the house and built their offices on that site. But one of their decisions was that Studio B, which was the Quonset Hut studio, would remain the same. They said, "We don't want to change one thing. As a matter of fact, we don't even want to clean the rugs."

I thought it was a joke, but if you'll go up there and look, you'll see what I mean. It isn't a joke. They haven't cleaned the rugs. This has been years, and we still have worn-out rugs on the floor. They said they didn't want to do anything at all to change the sound in there. The only thing they've ever done in that studio was, they put in a new control board. Of course, as new equipment comes out, your 16-track and your 32-track and all these various things, then they get the more expensive boards.

Stoker said all this in 1975, and much has changed since then. First, CBS turned the Quonset Hut into their art department and a more modern (if less beloved) studio they had built called Studio A into office space. By then, Studio A had achieved fame as the place where Bob Dylan recorded three very successful albums: Nashville Skyline, Blonde on Blonde, *and* John Wesley Harding. *Later, they renovated the office building, which had housed Studio*

A. Eventually, record mogul Mike Curb bought the whole shebang for Belmont University, which turned the Quonset Hut back into a recording studio and now uses the entire complex as part of its highly regarded music industry program. Owen no longer owned a studio on Music Row, but he still had a future in the studio business. According to Gordon:

I think CBS and Owen had made a deal, because CBS was afraid that Owen would go a block up the street, buy another house, and start another studio, and give them competition. So I believe they had some sort of agreement that if CBS bought the studio for the agreed price, Owen would not build a studio within a certain radius of miles of them. It must have been probably 25 miles.

Owen had a farm in Mount Juliet, with a barn on it. It had a real nice barn, and he thought that it might make a nice studio—really, what he told us, he just more or less started for kicks, because Owen is very genius-minded in electronics and boards. He gets his kicks out of playing with control boards, and this, that, and the other, sound and what have you.

So Owen had this barn out there, and it was a big barn. He concreted the floors and really left it more or less as a barn, then he put a control board in there, and echo chambers and the whole works, probably $250,000 worth of equipment and, believe it or not, got a fantastic sound. The next thing we knew, he took all the MCA sessions to Bradley's Barn. So these days the Jordanaires go to Bradley's Barn several times a week.

Now a lot of times we'll still do three or four sessions a day, and we're at RCA at 10 in the morning, and at Bradley's Barn at two o'clock in the afternoon, and back at Columbia [back in Nashville] at six o'clock at night, and maybe back at the Barn at 10 p.m. at night. Believe me, that isn't a pleasure at all, because it's really a rat race to travel Nashville's interstates during rush hour. In good weather, it is a pleasure to drive out there. A lot of times, ice and snow, it's not a pleasure, I assure you, but we get a great sound at

The Barn. A lot of people would rather work out there than in the city, because they say it's a relaxed atmosphere.

Many people in the industry believe that the mainstays of the Nash-ville recording industry are the session musicians, and they have a point. The Jordanaires worked very much like the musicians, except that their instruments happened to be their vocal chords. Nashville studio musicians and backup vocalists have a major role in creat-ing the parts they play, and for many years, the ones who were very good at their jobs got all the session work they could handle. One of the legendary guitar players in the early years of Music Row was Hank Garland. The Jordanaires did many sessions with Garland and like all the other session performers were in awe of his skills. Back in his 1975 interview with Doug Green, Gordon told the Hank Garland story.

Hank Garland was one of the greatest—Hank had more to do, I think, with the sound of country music so far as fantastic guitar picking than any other person. We all grew up together [in the business]. He worked on *Eddy Arnold Time* with us. He did most all the records, all the earlies, way back then.

He came from South Carolina. He never had many lessons or anything like that. It was just more or less a gift. He and steel guitar maestro Roy Wiggins played with Eddy Arnold for years. It was just Eddy Arnold, Roy Wiggins and Hank Garland. That was the act. He worked some with Red Foley, and he had a big record on a tune called "Sugarfoot Rag," after which everyone called Hank "Sugarfoot" Garland. He was a very sensitive type of guy, very tal-ented and he did most—well, he was the number one guitar picker in Nashville.

The many artists Garland recorded with included Elvis, Patsy Cline, the Everly Brothers, Brenda Lee, Roy Orbison, Don Gibson, Boots Randolph, Conway Twitty, and a whole lot more. Later in his career, he played jazz with George Shearing and Charlie Parker and recorded a jazz album for Columbia titled Jazz Winds from a New Direction. *At the time Gordon is telling this story, Garland still had nearly 30 years to live, but his career as a top-tier session player was over.*

Very interesting person. Clean cut. He drove off one day after a session, reportedly chasing after his wife, lost control of his car and ran off the interstate, ran off the highway, and he was unconscious for three months in Vandy [Vanderbilt] Hospital. They really didn't think he'd live at all. All of a sudden, one day, he came to enough to say, "Hey, where is everybody?" That's the first thing he said. They thought he'd be all right but his mind is—he doesn't play much at all. They say if you put his hand on the guitar he can pick but he doesn't know what key he's in.

His mind is getting some better, but at first they said he had the mind of about an eight- to ten-year-old boy. He knows who you are, and he'll kid with you. He liked to kid with people, and he'd always pick at you, so to speak. Everybody loved Hank Garland, but he had this serious accident and he's real pathetic. A lot of people will say that he would have been better off if he had not lived, because he was never able to do sessions anymore. Jim Vienneau [head of MGM Records in Nashville for many years] was just so sure that Hank could still play on the sessions that he brought him into a session one day and let him sit down and play. He sat for about 30 minutes and then just got up and walked off. His mind is not coordinated with what's going on.

He loved jazz so much. Before the accident, you should have heard Anita Kerr [on piano] and Hank, and Bob Moore on bass. Man, I don't think anybody in the United States would have much more than touched them if they had wanted to make a career out of that particular type of music. But that's really one of country music's big losses, was Hank Garland. He was the greatest, and all the other musicians thought he was the greatest too.

Garland passed away in 2004 at his brother's home in Florida, where he had been living for many years.

Brenda Lee recorded more often with the Anita Kerr Singers than with the Jordanaires, but during her long career as one of Music Row's greatest pop singers, then later as a successful country recording act, she took a whole lot of interest in the recording industry, and she can tell us plenty about the way it was in Nashville, during the great days of the Jordanaires.

Brenda Lee

Their easy-going, attitude was indicative of that time period. With the Jordanaires, the Anita Kerrs, the A-team, as we called our top musicians, it wasn't like work on their part, it was more of a joy that they felt to be there, to be a part of something, and to be in at the start of something. I think we all had that mindset. There were no stars. We were all there trying to be the best we could be and learn from each other to put out the best product that we could. It wasn't just about the lead vocalist, it was about all of us.

Success for Brenda, like Elvis, went well beyond country. Throughout the 1960s, she had one pop smash after another, and she saw Elvis and the Jordanaires follow a similar career path.

Bear in mind, I don't believe the Jordanaires stopped to think, Oh, this is a country song or oh, this is a pop song. I think they created much like the Anita Kerrs did, much like the musicians did as they went along. We didn't come in with arrangements all written, except maybe for the string parts. And they heard those demos just like I did. You walked in and you listened to the song and then you started tinkering till you got it. Of course, I'd hear my songs in advance, but not very much in advance. When session time was coming close, I'd listen to songs with Owen. We'd go through the songs that had been submitted, and listen and choose, and he'd tinkle at the piano. We hardly *ever* did any of the songs like we heard them on the demo. Of course, we kept the melody, we kept the thought, we kept the words and all. But the licks would change. Everybody on the session would feel it *their* way. And that was the great thing about Owen. As far as the musicians and the background singers went, he just let them do it! He didn't come out and tell them, "Okay, I want you to play that run here, that lick there." He let them create it themselves.

You were working with highly intelligent musicians. Talented musicians. And they thought about what they were gonna play. And they absolutely gave you the best licks they had in them. And most amazing about that, you didn't hear those licks again [on their other sessions]. They never seemed to run out of ways to make a song sound great. They never had to go back into their past and find an old used lick to fill in because they'd run out of ideas. They *never* ran out of ideas.

And the songs! There was always a new hit to be heard. "That's All You Gotta Do" was a Jerry Reed song. I met him on the Tarmac at the Atlanta airport. He had just gotten out of the service and he introduced himself and he said, "I wrote this song. Would you take it and listen to it?" and I did and loved it. And I cut it. "That's All You Gotta Do." It was on the back side of "I'm Sorry." "I'm Sorry" was a number 1 pop hit and "That's All You Gotta Do" was number 4.

Imagine a time when a guy you'd never met could hand you a hit song on the tarmac of an airport, and, of course, you'd listen because you never know where the next hit song may be lurking.

I had great people who trusted me with their creativity. I make the argument that sometimes less is more, and sometimes just give somebody their head, and don't write it on paper. Just let them create it, and nine times out of ten it'll be exactly what you want. I love that era, when I grew up and made records. I just wish the kids of today could learn from those people. It's a different world.

I get that. But talent is talent. And you gotta respect that. You got to learn from it. You savor it.

Stan Hitchcock has enjoyed successful careers as a country singer and TV executive, and one of many people in the music business who holds a special place in his heart for Gordon's kindness and generosity. Back in 2019, Stan explained why Gordon meant so much to him.

Stan Hitchcock

Gordon Stoker died six years ago, this week (March 30, 2019). In my mind, my flag is at half mast, I wear a black ribbon around my heart for this man was the centerpiece of the old 16th Avenue, Music Row, Music City and all the other terminology that goes to define what Nashville, Tennessee, has meant to the world of American music. He was the stalwart, the innovator, the strength to so many in the making of music. I loved him and always shall credit him with so much of the sound of my records, recorded in the old Quonset Hut Studio that became Columbia Records Studio. As head of the Jordanaires, and high tenor of the group, his sound was unmistakable, once you heard it. But he was far more than just a voice. He was a presence, a role model, and encourager.

I remember one day, in 1962, I was 25 years old, greener than a gourd, and shortly after I had moved to Nashville. I was walking down Music Row, when a car slowed down and Gordon Stoker told me he wanted me to get in, he wanted to talk to me. I guess I had been in town about six months, and the Jordanaires had backed me up on some of my early recording sessions, so I knew Gordon pretty well.

Gordon said, "Stan, I been watching you pretty close, and I believe you are a good guy, but I want to warn you about all the temptations that this business holds for people like us. There's gonna be women offering you pleasures that you probably have not even heard of. You're gonna be right in the middle of drinking and drugs all the time, and there are some things that can just wipe a man and his career out. I really hope that doesn't happen to you. I just want you to know that I am pulling for you, and I hope you make it."

Well, Gordon, no one ever offered me any better advice, and those words echoed in my mind, on many a long driving night, coming or going to a gig to some stage or honky-tonk in some town somewhere. You always held a special place in my heart, for you cared enough to try to give some good words of wisdom, to a kid who didn't even suspect what the real world was like. Thank you Gordon Stoker, and I'm glad I got to tell you that, in person, a few years ago. You were a man of integrity, a man of wisdom and I love you for what you were to so many.

The Jordanaires are now gone, put to rest with Gordon, and that sound will never be duplicated. Not in this world. Perhaps in the one to come, when we all sing around the throne, and your high tenor soars above all the rest.

Alan Stoker

Dad was involved in working on a Little Richard Gospel record, I don't know if he was the producer, or what, he was certainly there, he loved Little Richard. And they were running down one of the songs, and Dad thought it was in the wrong key, that it was a little too high for Richard, say it was G, Dad walked up to Richard and said, "It's a little bit high, why don't you try it in F?" Little Richard stroked his chin and said "F, hmmm." Dad reached around him and played F on the piano. Once he showed him, that's all he had to do, he knew the inversions, he knew the fingering, but he didn't know the names of the chords.

I have "Little Richard's Greatest Hits," on Specialty Records, and he signed it, "To Alan, please read your Bible, Little Richard." You know, he lived his last 20 years here in Nashville. He lived in the penthouse at the Hilton, across from the Hall of Fame.

Another music professional respected by vocalists and musicians alike was Hargus "Pig" Robbins, the man who succeeded Floyd Cramer as the go-to A-team pianist in Nashville recording studios. Robbins hails from tiny Spring City in the mountains of East Tennessee. He lost his vision at the age of three, and when he was six, he was sent to the Tennessee School for the Blind in Nashville. There he learned a lot of piano, but he also went to school himself on the recordings of many piano players, including Owen Bradley, Ray Charles, and the aforementioned Cramer.

"After I graduated from high school I just stayed in Nashville because I knew there was nothing for a blind man to do up in them mountains, you know," he told me not long before this book was written. Out on his own, he started cowriting songs and demoing them, hoping to get them recorded and make a living that way. Soon he was writing with friends at Tree Publishing Company, and there Buddy Killen, who would become one of the most powerful and productive figures on Music Row, started using Pig on the company demos.

Hargus "Pig" Robbins
Buddy got me on a George Jones session and out of that session come "White Lightnin'," George's first number 1, back in 1959.

That was more like it. Playin' sessions was immediate money, or as immediate as you can get in the music business. Might take you six months to get paid but that was better than the year or more it might take you writing songs—*if* you can get 'em cut.

Pig became the top piano player on Nashville sessions. Over a period of more than two decades, his tasteful riffs were seemingly everywhere. In 1978, he won a Grammy as country instrumentalist of the year.

We talked about how records were made in Music City. The way he explained it, it couldn't be simpler.

It was according to who the producer was. If it was Owen Bradley, he might play the demo, then he'd usually gather everybody around the piano, and Owen would sit down at the piano and kind of mold the arrangement, according to what style he would build behind the particular artist.

Soon the musicians and their producer would be sitting with their chord charts, taking Owen's ideas, adding their own, and listening to each other, each musician a sort of assistant producer to the great Owen Bradley. Meanwhile, Neal Matthews was listening, perhaps taking his cues from the musical ideas he was hearing, and then coming up with his own idea for the Jordanaires' vocals. Neal would show them to Gordon, Hoyt, and Ray, and they might respond with their own thoughts, or, more likely, they might run directly with what had come out of Neal's head, all this going on at once, developing themes that would mesh with what they were hearing, with plenty of listening and interacting when appropriate, and soon came those amazing, solidly accurate four-part harmonies and percussive syllables.

Ol' Neal was a master at doing those sh-boom sh-boom, or do-wop, badda-wadda, those vocal versions of instrumental riffs, you know. Neal just had a feel for the right background phrases, and the right syllables. You know, they did all that stuff with Elvis, and Elvis was so popular, and all the fans, and all the rock and roll artists heard all his records, and all the Jordanaires arrangements, and I'd have to say that the Jordanaires had a very strong influence on how people were making their rock and roll records back in those years. They were masters at filling in, you know, the little holes and little swells and things to complement the song.

Pig had great respect for the Jordanaires, particularly Gordon. He soon learned that Gordon was quite successful in the business world other than music. Like many successful studio musicians, Pig lived in a suburban community south of Nashville called Brentwood.

When I first moved to Brentwood, Gordon told me, "You know, I own part of the waterworks down there." Well, I come home and said to my wife, "Did you know Gordon Stoker owns the water we're drinkin'?"

In January 2022, Hargus "Pig" Robbins passed away. Many who worked with him thought he was the perfect session player. And they miss him as a human being.

Over the years, the Nashville session musicians evolved their own way of making records. Musicians on their first sessions, trying to impress the producers and the other musicians, would often play too much, and it was up to the studio veterans to set them straight. In 1969, Ron Oates arrived in Nashville and quickly established himself as one of Music Row's up-and-coming keyboard players. He tells a story about one of his early sessions, and that story tells us plenty about Gordon's role in the Nashville recording industry.

Ron Oates

My first memory of Gordon Stoker was in very early 1970. Larry Butler had brought me to Nashville October 27, 1969, to be a recording session piano/keyboard player. Larry introduced me to all his producer and publisher-friends and, the next week after moving here, some of those people began using me in the studios on their recording sessions. I had no idea what having Larry Butler bringing me to town would mean to my new career. Thank you, Larry.

January or February 1970. I had a two o'clock session at Music City Recorders with [outstanding steel guitar player] Pete Drake producing. I had never been there before, and I did not know what to expect. In fact, I cannot recall the artist we were recording with that day. But I walked into the studio and, sitting over in the corner tuning his guitar, was Billy Grammer! Billy Grammer of the hit record, "Gotta Travel On," fame! I'm not known for being shy. I went over immediately and introduced myself to Billy. We chatted for a minute or two and then I headed toward the piano. As I passed by the background vocal booth, I glanced in and, OMG, The Jordanaires! I'm thinking, come on, Ron. You've got to be great today. That's the most famous background group you've ever known about! So, I walked over to the piano and sat down. All the musicians were getting settled and tuning up. I didn't have to tune up, but I got settled—nervous as heck!

Pete played the first demo for us so that we could all write our charts. We ran it down a couple of times and then we recorded the first take. In that studio, we had to go back in the control room to listen to the playback. So, I thought I would keep my seat on the piano bench and wait for the background vocalists to go on by and I would follow them in. Everybody was smiling at me, but Gordon Stoker stopped by my side and put his hand on my shoulder. Gordon said, "Ron, you're doing great!" I'm thinking I've got it made!

Then, Gordon said, "Now, when we come back out here to record the second take . . . try not to play so many notes." Pfffffr-rrrttt! Instant deflation. But not for long. We listened to the playback and while listening, I suddenly realized that I had received a lesson from a master. Gordon Stoker. Gordon had begun his 60-year career with the Jordanaires as their piano player. And, after that meeting and working on that session together, Gordon and I remained friends for the next 40 years.

The Jordanaires, along with the Anita Kerr Singers, brought background singing into the country mainstream. Before them, there were plenty of harmonies in country music, but mostly they were word harmonies along with the lead singer, on the choruses, or to put some power behind an important line in the verses. Here's what Gordon had to say about the Jordanaire influence that Pig mentioned.

Gordon Stoker

The fact that Elvis used background voices on his records, all the other artists thought that they must have background voices on theirs. There were no groups in New York or Hollywood or Nashville making big livings doing background until then. The fact that we were fortunate enough to be with Elvis, this left us open to record with all the other big names . . . even in the pop end of it. I remember so well [Nashville music executive] Hubert Long saying to me, when we were doing all the background singing with Elvis, "Well, I'll tell you what, you'd better get all the money you can get right now, baby, because these background voices ain't going to be around very long." Now this was in the fifties when Hubert told me that. And I'm so thankful that Hubert did not tell me right, because there are many groups in New York and Hollywood and Nashville, all three, that are making big livings doing nothing but background voices on records and transcriptions.

Now, a lot of times we'd get hired from the A&R man, you see, and not from the artist. When we got there, the artist would say, "Well, I don't want you guys to be heard very much now, because the records don't sound the same as I do when I'm on the road. I can't take the Jordanaires with me when I go on the road, so I don't want you to do too much in the studio."

Really, we *complement* the singer. We have tried, if the artist is a real hard country singer we try—I don't mean we try to sing corny, but we try to blend our voice to whatever way his or her voice might be. See how country we sound on "I Ain't Never," with Webb Pierce. We try to complement him and make him sound better. We've been fortunate that we've been able to do that. And remember, our record with Webb on "I Ain't Never" was a big pop hit as well as a country hit, corny country sound and all.

I invite the reader to take a break, move right over to the internet, type in "Webb Pierce, 'I Ain't Never,'" and hear what Gordon is talking about. Some of you will get it quickly, others will marvel at just how subtle the Jordanaires can be in tailoring their sound to the individual artist. When you're finished reading this book, you might want to pick out some of your favorite old recordings to get a feel for the artistry of the Jordanaires. Hear why they believe their work on "Hound Dog" might have been the worst they ever did. Try to understand why they thought they did some of their best work with Patsy Cline. Bring up their recording of "Dig a Little Deeper" and some of their other gospel records. You'll hear most of it on YouTube or Spotify. And you just might become a Jordanaire fan forever.

These days, many country fans do not feel that today's country music sounds like real country music. There's nothing new about those feelings. Here's Gordon in 1975 replying to the constant complaint that "you guys are diluting country music":

A lot of the biggies in country music use background voices, as well as drums. Remember how they fought drums? And how they fought other instruments [most notably, electric guitars, electronic keyboards, violins, and horns]. The very earlies didn't want electrical instruments at all, but you see, they didn't win out. For years and years they didn't allow drums on the Opry, then, remember, they had Harold Weakley playing a snare drum and high hat. Now they allow a full drum kit, right?

Well, you know, you must go along with the times. You must go along with what the public wants and what the public demands. It's worked out. I think Elvis proved that background voices should be on a lot of records. They expect the record to sound better than what they do in person. I think the public expects that.

Many country fans expect their favorite artists to have the same view of their music as they do. Two of the greatest artists in country music, Eddy Arnold and Ray Price, stayed faithful to traditional country music during much of the 1950s, and they enjoyed a lot of success doing it. Then in the 1960s, both of them tilted toward pop-sounding ballads. They knew their music, they recorded good songs, and their string section and vocal group–flavored records continued their long caravan of succesess. Many fans complained that Arnold and Price had deserted country, but many more must have liked their new music. Fans need to know that most successful country singers love their careers and will do what they must to stay on the charts and continue their lucrative roadwork. For them, business is business, and they must make correct decisions if they are to remain in business. In their long career, Gordon Stoker and the Jordanaires learned a lot about the business, and they stood ready to give the artists the vocal support they needed. That was their *business.*

Chapter 10
DAY BY DAY WITH THE JORDANAIRES

During their four decades as America's number 1 vocal backup group, the Jordanaires worked with more artists and recorded more songs than you or I could imagine. Many of these songs we still remember today. The recording sessions were almost all "head" sessions, with the songs learned and arranged on the spot, in the studio, and usually recorded within an hour of the first time the Jordanaires heard the songs. These sessions feature many of our most successful singers (pop and country), our best session musicians, the most successful producers and studio engineers, and, of course, the Jordanaires. Put all this talent together in two rooms, and they create not only first-class recordings but also first-class memories. Here, you'll get an idea of how the Jordanaires made their living, three hours at a time.

If you watch them work—the Jordanaires, the pickers, or whoever else is on the session—you'll hear a lot of creativity going on, some joking, and a whole lot of fellowship. These people have been making music this way for years, and they are confident that they know their job. With very few exceptions, the people on these sessions are easygoing, and they don't mind somebody else suggesting a lick for them. Again, with very few exceptions, they leave their egos at home. And when the song is good and the musicians and background vocalists are good, great music can happen.

California-born Johnny Horton found some recording success in the mid-1950s, and toward the end of that decade, his career exploded with two movie theme hits: "Sink the Bismarck" and "North to Alaska." The song that really put him at the top of his profession was "The Battle of New Orleans," and the Jordanaires were indispensable for creating the mood of that record. Gordon recalled:

Gordon Stoker

That was Neal's arrangement. We spent two and a half hours working on a song I no longer remember and a half hour on "The Battle
Of New Orleans," and thanks to the "The Battle of New Orleans,"
the record must have sold five or six million copies.

"The Battle of New Orleans" reached number 1 on the Billboard *Hot
100, the first "country" record to achieve that honor. As Alan Stoker
puts it, the Jordanaires "sing in unison" with Horton and then
"march" in harmony. Listen to the record, and you'll find that somehow that's exactly what they do. Alan tells us that "when you're a
backup group you sing what best fits the song that'll make fans want
to pay money for the recording. That's your job." As usual, the quartet's arranger, Neal Matthews, must have done something right.*

We did almost all [Johnny's] hits. Now, "North to Alaska," that was
quite a long drawn out recording. We were on the first part of it,
but we didn't get to finish our part. We had another session scheduled. So later on the Anita Kerr Singers finished it.

One of the best arrangements that Neal ever did was "Big Bad
John," with Jimmy Dean. Jimmy had written the words to "Big Bad
John" down on a piece of paper, a recitation—you know, "At the
bottom of the mine lies a big *big* man," and all that kind of stuff,
talking about coal mining. He'd come down from New York, I
think, flew into Nashville. It was the last session he was to do at
Columbia with Don Law and Frank Jones as his producers. We did
most all of the Columbia sessions, and Don called for us to be on
the session.

The story goes that they had already recorded the usual three
songs during what could have been Dean's last session for Columbia. Having 30 minutes left over, Dean said he had written a poem
and he wondered if anything could have been made out of it. They
say he brought the poem over to Neal Matthews, who looked at

it and quickly wrote a head arrangement for the quartet to sing behind Dean's recitation.

He had the verses all end with, "Big John, big Joh-on, Big Bad John, Big John." The drummer and the bass player fell into Neal's vocal quartet arrangement, and Floyd Cramer had the idea to hit a steel bar with a hammer instead of playing the piano. The song is Jimmy Dean's recitation and Neal Matthews' minimal music arrangement, which is mostly the Jordanaires quartet.

"Big Bad John" won Dean a Grammy in 1962, in the Country and Western recording category and it was number 1 on the *Billboard* charts for five weeks. Once, when asked directly by Ralph Emory on the TV show *Nashville Now* about the Jordanaires being involved in the recording of "Big Bad John," Dean said something like, "Yeah, they might have been there."

So goes life in the world of studio sessions.

We mentioned earlier Neal and his Nashville numbering system. Neal gets the credit for introducing to Music Row a system of communicating chords that today is known in studios all over America as the Nashville Number System. Back in the old pop days, the labels in New York and Los Angeles generally hired someone to write the arrangements for the musicians before the session. The musicians read the music and played the notes as they were written. But rhythm-and-blues and country sessions were often led by producers and musicians who created the arrangements on the spot, one song at a time. Someone would play the song, either live or on a demo recording, and then the musicians would listen and write down the chord structure of the song, using the names of the chords, like C, F#, or G minor.

But suppose the producer decided the key was wrong for the singer. The musicians would have to rewrite their notation with a whole new set of chords. When Neal was taking notation for the group, he'd use numbers. Then, if the key had to be changed, the numbering would stay the same, and the actual chords would change in the musicians' heads.

We used the number system for some two years before anybody else would use it. Then one day, Charlie McCoy walked over to Neal and said, "Hey, Neal, explain that to me." And so Neal explained it: "If you were playing in the key of C, C is 1. F, that's your 4 chord. E minor would be 3 minor."

Suppose you were invited to a session in Nashville (or a lot of other places). You find a seat, and you watch and listen as the studio musicians hear a song for their first time. Listen to the individual players as they quickly catch on to what the song is trying to say and how it is trying to say it. As they try out their licks and runs, at first, it may sound like noise, but these musicians are doing more than playing: they're listening to everything else going on in that room—percussion, guitars, and keyboards. They hear it all, and soon, good things begin to happen. If you are not a studio musician, you will likely leave that studio asking yourself, "How do they do that?"

And one of the reasons they do that is because the system demands that they do that. To be sure, there were head sessions before Neal Matthews created a system for writing them down. And, to be sure, many musicians use their own variant of the system. Over time, Neal added an idea here and an idea there, put it all together, and published it in a book with the Hal Leonard Corporation, and that system is well known enough for musicians, singers, producers, and studio engineers to use it as a universal means of communication.

Alan Stoker

I remember Pop telling me that in the 1990s while they were doing some personal appearances overseas, the quartet was also booked to do some background vocals on a recording session. When the musicians and vocalist began listening to the demonstration recording and started learning the song, Neal was surprised when he saw that the musicians on the other side of the world were using the Nashville number system—the head arrangement system that he had created for the Jordanaires to use decades before. By that time, it had traveled all over the world. I'm sure that it's still being used in recording sessions around the world today.

I mentioned earlier that the studio musicians mostly tend to be good-natured and easygoing. The same is not always true about the artists on the sessions. Jim Reeves was a popular country crooner in the late 1950s and early 1960s with major crossover hits like "Four Walls" and "He'll Have to Go." Like Patsy Cline, Reeves benefited greatly from the new pop radio format called Top 40. Top 40 was a wonderful, inclusive bit of programming that succeeded in attracting huge listening audiences by continually playing Dean Martin, Dion DiMucci, Patsy Cline, and Dinah Washington back to back. Reeves made a number of journeys high up the pop charts with his country hits, and maybe it was the pressure of continuing that run of success that made him feel a bit stressed on his sessions.

Gordon Stoker

Jim looked at the clock and he wanted to get at least three numbers for every three hours. Well, you know it just don't fall that way a lot of times. Most of the time he'd push for *four* numbers and he didn't want anybody to make jokes. He couldn't stand it if you said something funny and everybody laughed—you know, you're not giving your 100% attention.

Jim was extremely nice, but he always pushed, and most of the time he'd record at ten o'clock at night, and we'd have done two or three sessions before we got to him. I remember the last session we did with him. Buddy Harman, who was one of the most sought-after drummers of all times, had done two or three sessions already that day, and he had an hour to relax between sessions, and he laid down on the floor and was resting his back. Jim walked in at like 9:50 p.m. He took one look at Buddy lying on his back and said,

"Yeah, it's always this way. I get a bunch of broken-down musicians to do my sessions." Buddy said, "You're getting your money's worth, you're getting about two hits a session." And I'm so glad Buddy Harman told him that. Jim was a guy that needed to be told. Like I said, he was a schoolteacher, and I mean no disrespect to schoolteachers.

Alan Stoker had this to say about Jim Reeves and his megahit "Four Walls," which Reeves recorded at the new RCA Studio on February 7, 1957:

Alan Stoker
Pop has been quoted as saying that Reeves wanted him up on a high note at the end of "Four Walls."

Gordon Stoker
He wanted the tenor out in front of the other voices, which, I am out front a lot; at the end of it he wanted me to go up *higher*, which I did. And he was pleased with that. Jim was a former disc jockey and really knew how to work a microphone. So did all of us. This was one of the first times that Reeves was able to use this new preferred vocal microphone technique during a recording session. He would get in very close to the mic and sing softly. This was something that Reeves came up with himself. In their usual background style, the quartet sang with him in the same soft, intimate manner, alternating unison oo's and harmony during the verses, while always singing the words to the chorus in harmony.

It was the first of five songs recorded during a 7:00 to 11:30 p.m. session. The record reached number 1 on the country *Billboard* chart, and number 12 on the pop chart on February 7, 1957.

Take a listen to "Four Walls" when you get the chance. These days, you rarely get an opportunity to hear a soft and warm ballad like this one.

Jim Reeves and Marty Robbins were both a bit tight on sessions. In the studio Marty would do anything he could do to break you up. And then if you laughed, he'd get mad at you. Marty Robbins was a character, believe me. We did most of his recordings, and he would want us to ooh and aah from start to finish. His last great hit record before he died was, "Some Memories Just Won't Die" and he would dance around the studio on the turnaround, and he'd stick his finger in your butt or just anywhere—he'd stick it in your mouth, just anything, to break you up, and then if you laughed, it would bother him. He'd say, "Hey! We're gonna have to do that over because you laughed." Now, if he told a joke or something, and you did a forced laugh, he knew it. You know, some [big shot] guy tells something, and everybody goes hahahahah [to please the big shot]. Well, he'd say, "Hey, don't give me that horse shit laugh." But Don Law was the right guy to produce him. Don Law was what he needed. He was very patient with Marty and he seemed to know exactly what to say to him at the right time.

One of Marty Robbins's biggest hits was a song released in 1961 called "Don't Worry." Sometimes you just get lucky in the studio. "Don't Worry" was a good, serviceable country song with some wonderful bluesy touches that suited Marty's vocal skills, and Marty, the Jordanaires, and the musicians were working hard to make this song the best it could be, when the electronic gremlins struck.

We were there, had to ooh and aah most of the way through that song, and Grady Martin was playing six-string bass guitar, when all of a sudden his amp began to growl. He later said that there was a tube blown out in his amplifier. I know that the speaker made a weird sound. Grady wanted to get a different amp, and Don Law said, "Oh, man, I like the way it sounded, old boy," you know that's the way he talked [he was a Brit]. "Leave it like it is," he said, something to that effect.

So Grady played a soulful solo with growling bass notes through that amplifier with the misbehaving tube.

And they later said, "That was the reason the song became a big hit."

But was the problem really a faulty tube in Grady Martin's amplifier? Jimmy Lockhart, a studio engineer, told his version to Harold Bradley.

Jimmy Lockhart

Everybody thinks it was a tube [in Grady's amp] but it was in the studio *console*! [Engineer] Glen Snoddy said it was the transformer they used in the Langevin amps, shorted out from the high input level. "Grady was playing electric guitar [with a miked amplifier], and then he was gonna play the [bass guitar]," said Snoddy. "So I wired him up direct and said, 'don't hit it,' meaning, 'Whatever you do, don't touch your strings.' I needed to go pad it down in the control room [to control the input so it wouldn't blow up the equipment]. He waited while I walked across the studio and got in the control room, and just as I was about to pull down the control, he barely ticked a string."

That tick of the string blew out the transformer of the preamp, but Don Law liked the sound, so he kept it, thus the birth of a fuzz-tone sound and another Marty Robbins hit record.

Harold Bradley

But then the distinctive fuzz vanished. It wouldn't do it anymore. And they tried everything to get it back. It didn't heal. It just quit.

Gordon Stoker

Different people have different stories on it but we were standing there. We were right there on that session when that happened, and I know it was right there in the amp, 'cause I remember that Grady was disturbed about the way it sounded. Now, it could have happened through the board, but it had something to do with the way that amp fed into the board. You know, those boards are built pretty solid. I don't think the board would have made that kind of error.

To this day, there are two very strong conflicting opinions of how the fuzz tone arrived in Nashville. Glen Snoddy designed a circuit that would make that fuzz sound on purpose and eventually sold it to Gibson, which created the Maestro FZ-1 effects pedal, which, they say, showed up in 1966 on the intro to the Rolling Stones' classic hit "(I Can't Get No) Satisfaction." But there are two versions of how and why it happened, both vouched for by credible sources, and scholars will be arguing which was the true version long after we've all turned to dust.

Marty was one of the few country acts that I went to see in Vegas. Not that many country acts appeared in Vegas. When my wife and I went to check out, the bill had already been paid. That was the way Marty thought about you. He never ever told you, "Thank you for what you've done," but he'd give you a little extra pay here and there, and he'd pick up your tab.

You know, they told Marty that he shouldn't drink so much cholesterol. Milk and things like that. He would order three eggs, slightly scrambled—if they did it right, he'd say, "could you bring me three more." He would drink a quart of milk at one sitting. The doctors told him to quit doin' it, but he was kinda like Elvis, he didn't want authority to tell him what to do. He eventually had heart issues, which cost him his life.

The Jordanaires loved Don Gibson, who wrote "Sweet Dreams" and "I Can't Stop Loving You" and had a huge crossover hit on his self-penned "Oh, Lonesome Me."

Don Gibson was a very sincere person. He played great guitar. He sat on a stool and—now I have heard stories that his wife was largely responsible—with him, of course—for most of those songs. Wesley Rose [son of Fred Rose and longtime head of Acuff-Rose Publishing] told me that she even came in to see him and said, "I'm the one that's been writin' those great songs," and he said, "That's very good. We'll make the same financial deal with you that we have with Don. You just continue to write 'em, and bring 'em in."

But it is kind of strange that Don never wrote another hit after he got a divorce from her. He was crazy about Ray [Walker] and me. He was actually my neighbor. He was one of the few people that I saw get in a fight in the studio. He said it's this way, and Chet [Atkins] said it's *this* way, and back and forth and back and forth until, boy, next thing we knew they was fist-fightin', and Neal, the closest to them, had to pull them apart.

We sang on all his hits except "Sea Of Heartbreak." We were out of town and the Anita Kerr Singers did that one with him, which was one of his greatest hits, I think. He was very shy and had to be pushed. We took a huge interest in him and encouraged him. When he first came to Nashville he sounded like Jim Reeves. And RCA turned him down. They said, "We've already got one Jim Reeves, we don't need another one. You go back to Knoxville and come back here and sing like Don Gibson, and we'll sign you."

So Gibson came up with a distinctive style and carved out an impressive singing career.

Country songs are well known for their two-part harmonies, and Gordon was sometimes called on to do those "duets." His best-known duet performance might have been the high harmony on Waylon Jennings's "Only Daddy That'll Walk the Line." Here is Alan Stoker passing along a recollection from his dad.

Alan Stoker

Pop had a great story about the 1968 record session that produced "Only Daddy That'll Walk the Line" with Waylon Jennings. The quartet only sang ooh's and ahh's on this, except for Pop. He sings the title line with Waylon.

Gordon Stoker

Waylon wanted someone to sing the tenor part with him on that one line, which gets repeated several times. They tried several band members, two or three people on it and nobody could do it. So I said, well I think I can do it if nobody'll look at me. 'Cause I did it like this, put my fingers up to my throat and vibrated it to match Waylon's vibrato and that's the only way I could do it. And they gave me an award for it.

Alan Stoker

Since it was "punched in and out" after the main track was recorded, Pop didn't want anyone watching him because they would laugh when he used his hand to vibrate his throat, and if they laughed, that would make him laugh. So Dad tugged at his throat, and Waylon had his hit.

Gordon did three duets with Elvis: "Good Luck Charm," "Easy Come, Easy Go," and "All Shook Up." Alan talked about one of them.

The most well known of the duets Pop did with Elvis was "All Shook Up." They recorded it at Radio Recorders in Hollywood on January 12, 1957, less than a week after Elvis and the Jordanaires made their final TV appearance on the *Ed Sullivan Show* in New York City, and just four days after Elvis's 22nd birthday. According to Pop, he and Elvis sang into the same microphone looking directly across the mic at each other. It wasn't easy because Elvis kept picking at him, trying to get him to crack up during the recording of the song. When someone asked him what he meant, Pop said,

"You know, picking at me. Like putting his finger in his mouth and then sticking it in my ear."

It took 10 takes before Elvis was satisfied with it. Pop missed the phrasing with Elvis on the last "yea-yea," and told him so. Elvis said not to worry about it. If it hadn't caught the people's ear by then, it wasn't going to be a hit, anyway. You can hear that glitch at 01:53. I don't think it was a great song, as songs go. But it was released in early 1957 and by the middle of April it was at number 1 on the pop charts. It stayed at number 1 for eight weeks, climbed to number 3 on the country charts and was also number 1 on the R&B charts, becoming his second record to reach the top of the R&B chart.

"All Shook Up" is co-credited to Elvis as a songwriter, along with Otis Blackwell, who also wrote "Don't Be Cruel" (also co-credited to Elvis) and cowrote "Return To Sender" with Winfield Scott. Other Blackwell compositions included "Fever," a hit for both Little Willie John and Peggy Lee, and the huge Jerry Lee Lewis smashes, "Great Balls of Fire," and "Breathless." Otis Blackwell is buried in Nashville's Woodlawn Memorial Mausoleum, within a few feet of Pop's resting place.

One day in the summer of 1977, Pop got a phone call from Prissy Hubbard. Prissy was a singer that the Jordanaires used as a background vocalist from time to time, especially when she, her husband and two daughters first moved to Nashville and they were having a tough time making it. Prissy told Pop that her husband Jerry had just recorded a song he had written and was trying to sing the tenor part on it by himself. After he had tried it numerous times with no success, Prissy kept telling him to "Just call Gordon." After hours more of trying unsuccessfully to sing the part, he finally relented and told Prissy to call him. Pop went to the studio and sang to the track that was already recorded. About two takes later, they had it in the can and Pop went home.

The recording that Pop sang the high tenor on is "East Bound and Down." The song stayed on the *Billboard* charts for 16 weeks and peaked at number 2 on the country charts. More importantly, it ended up being the theme song for the hit film, "Smokey and the Bandit." Prissy Hubbard's husband, Jerry R. Hubbard, is better known as Jerry Reed, who had a long career as a recording artist, songwriter, guitar player, and movie actor.

Pop had the ability to closely mimic the lead singer on recordings, and you sure can hear it here. One small note: if you ever visit Pop's resting place at Woodlawn mausoleum in Nashville, you'll find that Jerry Reed Hubbard and his wife Priscilla are, like Otis Blackwell, interred close by.

In another interview, Ray Walker remembered another Jerry Reed story.

Ray Walker

We were doing an Elvis session, and Elvis wanted to record "Guitar Man," another Jerry Reed song, so he said, "Do you think we could get Jerry to come in and play the guitar?" They called his home, and Jerry was fishing, but somehow they found him, so he got right down to the studio, which was RCA Studio B and I never will forget, they pulled up a chair right close to the control room there, and he sat down with his guitar. Elvis, he could be a huge fan of a star that he really did love and appreciate. Well, he loved Jerry Reed's guitar playing, and while Jerry was playin', Elvis was standing there about a foot and a half away watching Jerry's fingers. Jerry would do this riff, and he'd flub it, he'd miss it, and he got kind of frustrated, you know, he's sittin' there, playin', and from a fishin' pole to a guitar is a big change, and he flubbed it again. Finally he just laid his guitar down, stared into Elvis's eyes and he said, as only Jerry Reed could, "God, you're handsome!"

Gordon Stoker

Elvis was kind of timid about his looks. He didn't want people to say nothin' about his looks, and he was embarrassed when Jerry said that to him.

Ray Walker

Yeah, he was. He also was told that the eyes are what make you stand out. Like Rudolph Valentino. He was also told that blonds wouldn't stay stars, so that's why he started dying his hair black.

And then Ray had this to say about a moment with Patsy Cline that could stop you in your tracks if you were thinking of walking somewhere:

I was the last one to speak to Patsy at the Grand Ole Opry before she was killed. We had worked with her on the show that night, and she had just had her second car wreck, and somebody had stolen her full-length black mink, and the insurance company had just replaced that mink coat, and she had it on that night, it was all the way down to the top of her shoes. It was *that* long and it was all mink, baby, wasn't no plastic there. And she had a broken tooth, from the car wreck. And she had come on the Opry in a wheelchair, and people just loved her for it, but at this time, she was standing and she was walking, and so I followed her to the back, behind the stage, and she was going out the back door to the alley, to the car, and I said, "Patsy Honey, be careful, we love you." She had one foot down on the first step. And she *turned* that head around and showed that broken tooth and she cocked that head and turned up that mink collar and she said, "Honey, I've had two bad ones. The third one'll be a charm, or it'll kill me. I'll see you guys later." And we never saw her again.

Gordon Stoker

The Jordanaires were a major force as a backup group from 1955 into the '80s. That's a long run. Of course, you know, we still do recording sessions, but we couldn't, and we wouldn't wanna do four sessions a day or three sessions, like we used to. Occasionally we do two sessions. One day I think last week we did two sessions. But the recording scene in Nashville has completely changed. These days it's me and Ray and Curtis (Young) and Louis Nunley. Louis Nunley was the Anita Kerr Singers' bass singer. He now sings baritone with the Jordanaires. He took Hoyt Hawkins's place. Hoyt died in '82 and between him, Duane West, who later died, and Louis, they did the baritone singing from 1952 all the way up to now.

We just did something for Walmart, we did a new album we got out, it's a Bluegrass gospel album, and you wouldn't believe some of the *bass* singing that Louis Nunley does on it.

Alan recalls one day in early 1957, another important day in the history of the Jordanaires:

Alan Stoker

Pop and the Jordanaires were in Hollywood, working on a soundtrack for, and making an appearance in, the Elvis movie, "Loving You." Back in those days, they always stayed in a suite at the Hollywood Knickerbocker Hotel.

During a day when they weren't needed on the soundstage, there was a knock on the suite door. Pop opened the door to, "Hi, I'm Ricky Nelson."

"I know," Pop replied.

"You know who I am?" Ricky asked, a bit amazed. Everybody, including Pop, watched *The Adventures of Ozzie and Harriet* on TV. Ricky was the most popular teenager on one of the most popular TV shows at the time. Ricky was pleased that they knew him and commented that the last vacation the Nelsons took up East, lots of people there knew him too. Pop thought that was funny. They invited the young man in.

Over the course of the next few days, Ricky and the quartet became good friends. Jordanaire Neal Matthews even taught Ricky some guitar chords. After almost a year, Ricky had talked his father Ozzie into hiring the Jordanaires to sing on his recordings. Ozzie Nelson had many contacts in the music field in California, and had been using Barney Kessel and his orchestra on Ricky's records, but Ricky wanted a smaller rockin' band sound, and he also wanted the Jordanaires.

Gordon Stoker

Well, you know, we did almost all of Ricky Nelson's hits. We did that out on the coast, we'd go out there to work with Elvis and we'd go to Sound Studio at night and record with Ricky. Ozzie was a smart businessman. He knew that Elvis paid our way out to California, so he would only have to pay our session fees. We sang on all of Ricky Nelson's hits except "Garden Party." "Lonesome Town," "Poor Little Fool," "Travelin' Man," we did all those records, and more.

The Jordanaires worked with Ricky in the 1950s and 1960s. Eventually, he changed his musical direction and his life. A few years before his death, Rick and the Jordanaires started working together again. They shared the stage on many live shows in his later years. The Jordanaires worked a whole lot of studio sessions with Nelson, and together, they recorded some of the most memorable pop hits of their time.

Alan Stoker

According to published reports, producer Jimmie Haskell wanted "Lonesome Town" to have a Calypso feel, with a conga drum and a piano melody. After a few takes, one of the Jordanaires, I'm not sure which one, suggested a more minimal approach, with just acoustic guitar, Ricky's mournful lead vocal, and echo drenched haunting backing vocals. Haskell was hesitant and uncomfortable with that approach. He thought it was unthinkable to put out a record that didn't have a rhythm track on it. Once he heard it, I guess he changed his mind. The result was a record that heightened the sense of isolation and solitude, as if, somewhere, there existed a *real* place called Lonesome Town.

By the time he died, Ricky was known as "Rick." His death when his airplane crashed on New Year's Eve of 1985 hit Pop very hard. He sat at home, depressed, looking out the window for days afterward, tears rolling down his cheeks. He told the family that working with Rick and his band, especially guitarist Bobby Neal and drummer Rick Intveld, made him feel young again. Pop was only 61 himself when that plane went down, a plane that Pop and the quartet had flown on with Rick and his band earlier in 1985.

Rick's family requested that the Jordanaires sing at his funeral, and of course, they did. In the years before Pop's passing, he became friends with Rick's twin boys, Gunnar and Matthew. Two of the last recording sessions Pop did were for Jimmy Webb and Sam Nelson, Rick's youngest son. Sam covered 10 of Rick's songs with the vocal backing of the Jordanaires. That project is still unreleased, to the best of my knowledge.

Songs like "Travelin' Man," "Believe What You Say," "Lonesome Town," "It's Late," and "Poor Little Fool" are just some of the great recordings they made together in the studio. I think they still sound great today. A side note: one of Pop's favorite plants in his sunroom at home, was one that he'd gotten from Rick and Helen Blair (Rick's girlfriend) while he was in the hospital when he was first diagnosed with diabetes in the early 1980s. Pop and our family have taken special pride in keeping that plant alive. It's still flourishing today, at my house.

One of country music's greatest hitmakers was Conway Twitty. The Jordanaires were in the studio with him the day he recorded his first hit, "It's Only Make Believe." Conway had wondered what he would do with his life once he was discharged from the army in 1956. He had been invited to attend the Philadelphia Phillies' spring training camp for possible assignment to one of their farm clubs. But he had also been doing a lot of music in his young life, and one day, in his army barracks in San Francisco, one of his bunkmates turned on his portable radio, and the sound that came out of it transformed Conway's life.

His name was Harold Jenkins at the time, and the song he heard was "Mystery Train," the very same song the Jordanaires heard on a car radio, the first time they heard an Elvis Presley record. "I can do that!" he told himself. And he did.

Gordon Stoker

"It's Only Make Believe" was a surprising hit that we did with Conway. Jim Vienneau produced it for MGM. Conway wasn't a country act at the time. He'd been in the rock field, you know. The record was produced in the Bradley Recording Studio on 16th Avenue South, and we were there with our ooh's and aahs.

Months later, we were out working with Elvis at a studio in California and we had an early morning call at Paramount Studios, about seven o'clock. We were on our way out there, we had the radio on and we heard this record. And we said, "Hey, that sounds like us!" And then we drive a little bit further and we said, "Hey! That *really* sounds like us, who could that be?" And at the end the DJ said, "That's Conway Twitty and his new record, 'Only Make Believe.'" And of course it *was* us. MGM was about six months releasing that record, and during that period of time we had done so many recordings, that we had forgot that session. So we were on Conway's first big hit. We did several more hits with him, then he later started using his own group.

Buddy Holly was another performer who sought out the Jordanaires.

Just a short time before he died, Buddy Holly came to Nashville with Norman Petty (his producer) to see about the possibility of getting the Jordanaires to overdub on a gospel album that Buddy and Norman were going to record. At that time overdubbing was something new and he wanted to know if there was a system whereby he could send his recordings into Nashville and get us to overdub our voices on it. We told him we were sure that Mort Thomasson could arrange that. Buddy and Norman Petty and I went down to a restaurant downtown on Capitol Boulevard, Cross-Keys, to eat, and then, I took him over to WSM radio station and introduced him to noted Nashville radio personality Ralph Emery. Ralph wrote in his book, that, "I would have never gotten to meet Buddy Holly if Gordon Stoker hadn't brought him up to meet me." Ralph interviewed Buddy on the air, but couldn't play his records, because WSM didn't have any.

Years later, Don McLean wrote and recorded his classic "American Pie" about the plane crash that killed Buddy Holly, the Big Bopper, and Richie Valens.

Alan Stoker

Don McLean's recording of "American Pie" is the definitive tribute to Buddy and the tragic night that he died. In a later era, Pop and the Jordanaires worked with Don in concert and on records. They performed together a number of years on Thanksgiving night at Carnegie Hall in New York City. Don was one of the few people the family called on the day Pop passed away. He is still a treasured friend of the family.

Not surprisingly, McLean took a great interest in the musical era ushered in by Elvis and the Jordanaires.

Don McLean

Elvis Presley was the most important artist that ever was. And every important hit record Elvis ever had was him and the Jordanaires. That sound [Elvis and the Jordanaires] was the most revolutionary sound ever. All those songs. So you had those four guys and Elvis singing. Five people made that sound. And not a lot of instrumentation.

I mean, Scotty Moore would play the guitar that Super 400, and that big low note on "Don't Be Cruel" and Elvis is beating the back of his guitar, and then the Jordanaires would pump that thing. The Jordanaires as a group—this is interesting what I'll tell you now, when they would do those things, where they would "whop! Whop!" those kind of things, those were like horn stabs, so they would operate almost like an orchestra, and then when they would sing those long phrases, those four-part harmonies, that's almost like a string section, or a horn section where everybody is breathing at different times. There are these long phrases, so they could fill in so much, they would accentuate the rhythm tremendously, and then they would build this wall of sound just like an orchestra. Really, a four-man orchestra is what they were. Because they would do all the functions of an orchestra.

Simply put, they were an integral part of the most important music of the 20th century. Just for the stuff they did with Elvis, and then you can't forget they were on everybody else's sessions; they were on Kenny Rogers' records, they were on Dolly's records, they were on Kitty Wells's records, Patsy Cline—Jim Reeves, Don Gibson, Ricky Nelson, all those hits, Loretta Lynn—through Elvis and those records, they established this commercial sound that [almost] everybody wanted. Chet Atkins really *didn't* want the Jordanaires and Elvis didn't like Chet Atkins. He thought Chet didn't respect him and that was Chet's way, he was a kind of a cool customer, you know. And he didn't fall all over himself for anybody, you know.

Look at the great records they made. The Jordanaires didn't get with Elvis until after the Sun period. The Sun period was just the real rockabilly stuff with Bill Black, Scotty Moore, and then they had the Jordanaires when Elvis moved to RCA and that gave them that commercial lift. And they changed the whole world with that music.

And it's gorgeous music, you know, the thing about it is, this is the funny thing, is that Elvis was seen as such a dangerous person to humanity, and yet his songs are all about love, and tenderness and sweetness and kindness, all these sweet thoughts, never anything mean, not like today, all the stuff people say in these songs, awful. He was just sweetness and yet it *seems* like "Don't Be Cruel" is coming at you like a freight train, but it isn't, it's just a gentle record, and it's this magic, in the music and in the performing.

All this coming from the man who wrote the forever definitive song about the day rock-and-roll music died!

I was pretty good friends with Chet Atkins. And Chet Atkins said something interesting to me—he said Elvis had about 20 different voices. The "Jailhouse Rock" voice is not the "Love Me Tender" voice, "Love Me Tender" voice is not the "Don't Be Cruel" voice, and then he had that almost girl voice that he would use.

In the mid-1950s, when the Jordanaires were beginning to make their reputation as a backup group, Nashville had not yet become a dominant recording center, and yet there was already a small core of musicians, vocalists, and others making a meager to major living in the Nashville music industry. Did Gordon feel a sense of future greatness and glory rising in this medium-sized southern town?

Gordon Stoker

Not really, except I knew that the select six or seven musicians, and the handful of background singers worked really well together.

The closeness of the musicians, which as I said was about seven or eight to ten good musicians that we used all the time, the closeness that they had and the closeness that we had, the warmth that we had toward each other is just something that can't be forgotten, as long as we live. At that time we really did feel like when one of our people got successful, it was good for all of us.

The Anita Kerrs, the Jordanaires, we all had college music training. Musical knowledge had an awful lot to do with our success. And some of the new groups that would come in here sounded really good but you see, when they'd go to a session, they couldn't come up with an arrangement fast, and before they knew it, they were blowin' two hours on one number, and the producers couldn't take it. In other words, they couldn't do harmony that quick—and you had to do harmony that quick, or you'd be replaced.

When Elvis wanted us to go into Vegas with him, one week's show and four weeks' rehearsal, that was five weeks out of town, and we had some 30 sessions set during that period of time with Owen Bradley, or RCA or what have you. There was a big part of us that really wanted to find a way to get it done. So I went to Owen and told him what Elvis wanted us to do and he said, "Well, Gordon, we have *got* to have somebody to do our background singing, and if you guys move out, I'm gonna have to bring in another male quartet." He said, "You just make up your mind what you wanna do," and we made up our mind that we'd have to quit Elvis, and I always regretted that we had to quit Elvis. Us and D.J. and Scotty and Millie Kirkham we all quit at the same time, and he kind of felt like he lost his family, but we had no choice, we had to do what we thought financially was best for the quartet, and had we gone to Vegas with Elvis, we would have missed the Coca Cola commercial, (sings) *Coke is, it's the real thing*, [a few days' work] that paid us more money than working two years with Elvis.

I feel like I have to comment here on the Jordanaires' decision to leave Elvis. Music fans often develop a strong loyalty toward their favorite singers and assume that this loyalty is a moral issue that should be shared by their favorite artist's musical associates. But music professionals have only their one career, and their loyalties must be to their careers and to their families that depend on their decisions. A wrong decision can send an artist's career straight down the toilet. Elvis depended on the Jordanaires for many years, and their reliability was an important part of his success, but Owen Bradley relied on the Jordanaires too, and so did Chet Atkins and many other music figures mentioned in this book. The security of the group's career was based on how many times they had proved their worth in studio sessions and live shows. The Jordanaires owed much of their success to their work with Elvis, but their career security was based on their continued success with the many artists they worked with in Nashville and Los Angeles. And as Gordon has pointed out, Elvis said that he owed much of his success to the Jordanaires.

After the Jordanaires and Elvis split, Elvis recorded some very good records. His movie career over, he recorded what he wanted to record. Meanwhile, the Jordanaires continued to do what they did so well, and they had many good years in front of them. The industry was growing, and there were other groups competing for the backup business in Nashville. Gordon recalled one group in particular.

Joe Babcock was working on the road with Marty Robbins, and he got so much work as a substitute with us that he quit the road and he said *he* would form a studio group so he got Hurshel Wiginton to sing bass, and before we knew it, they were on the TV show *Hee Haw* full time, a vocal quartet with two men and two women. They called themselves the Nashville Edition and one of the women who became part of the group was Dolores Dinning Edgin, who had also sang a lot with us. She lived out of town, and I called her one day and told her I needed another girl singer, and I could give her X amount of sessions a week and she said, "Well, for that much work, I'll move back to Nashville," and she did, and [once she became a member of the Nashville Edition] that was the rest of her story. The other girl singers in the Nashville Edition were Ricki Page, and later on, Wendy Suits. Besides being the background vocalists on *Hee Haw*, they were a busy studio backup group for many years.

The pages of this book reveal the tremendous respect Gordon Stoker has for the many artists, producers, songwriters, musicians, and background singers he's worked with over the years. He also under-stands the extraordinary role the Jordanaires have played in the world of country and pop music. This unique mixture of humility, confidence, and competence helps explain the long success of the quartet he led for more than six decades.

I don't think there's any group that's gotten to work with as many great artists and gotten to know as many great people as we've got-ten to know. You know, we got an award for being on more Top 10 recordings than any vocal group in the world. I think the greatest compliment that we've ever received came from Paul McCartney when he and Linda were recording at the Sound Shop not too far from where we're sitting right now. That's the first time I ever met him. We had done an album with Ringo Starr. I knew Paul was working with Buddy Killen, and I told Buddy that I wanted to meet him and Buddy said, "Oh, well, I'm sure he'd want to meet you, I'll arrange it," so, he did. I walked into the control room at the Sound Shop and Paul turned around to me and said, "You one of the Jordanaires?"

I said, "Yeah, I wanted to meet you."

He said, "You kidding? I want to meet you. The Beatles learned to sing harmony by listening to you guys behind Elvis and Ricky Nelson." He said, "When we'd buy a record of Elvis, we didn't listen much to Elvis. We listened to the Jordanaires. We learned so much about harmony by listening to you guys."

A long time ago, Tennessee Ernie Ford tried to get us to move to the West Coast. You know, we did some successful albums with Tennessee Ernie; matter of fact, the first one we did we won a Grammy. He had that daily ABC show and he wanted us to move out there and do that show with him, and we almost did it. But we took Lee Gillette's advice and stayed in Nashville and he was right. The business *has* been good to us. I remember one week we were on eight of the Top 10 records. I don't remember when it was but Ray remembers. See, Ray keeps up with all that stuff. When I hear a record on the radio I know that's us and I know, basically, about the time they did it. But so far as the exact time, I don't remember.

One of the best things about being a Jordanaire was the variety of musical styles they got to work with. Country music after the mid-1950s was constantly changing, and the Jordanaires were able to both react to the changes and influence them. Some of the biggest country stars, like Eddy Arnold, Ray Price, and Jim Reeves, had become country crooners, and the Jordanaires supplied them with some of the sweetest oohs and aahs that any crooner ever enjoyed. Elvis could rock, and so could the Jordanaires, drawing naturally from their gospel side. George Jones and Merle Haggard were modified honky-tonkers. And then of course there were lots of other pop artists and rock and rollers. Sometimes they came to Nashville. Sometimes the Jordanaires came to them. They all wanted the Jordanaires because they all knew that the quartet knew how to make their records sound better.

And through much of that time, there were still the hard-core traditionalists, and one of the most traditional acts was the Louvin Brothers, who combined secular old-timey country with a whole lot of gospel. In fact, their secular side was so traditional that it verged on old mountain folk music. Maybe time should have passed them by, but their harmonies were so good and their songs so good that they remained in demand until they broke up in 1963 because Charlie could no longer deal with Ira's temper.

Gordon told his son Alan about one time when the Jordanaires were called to a Louvin Brothers session, and Alan told us this:

Alan Stoker

In May of 1961, Pop and the quartet were hired by Capitol producer Ken Nelson to provide vocal background on a Christmas album he wanted to record with Charlie and Ira, the Louvin Brothers. Pop was perplexed that Capitol staff producer/A&R man Ken Nelson wanted him there to add high harmony on a Louvin Brothers session, with Ira Louvin's soaring tenor well established as a trademark of the Louvin sound. When he arrived at the session, Pop found that Ira had not warmed to the idea of having another high tenor on the session. Charlie Louvin was cordial as usual, but Ira made it clear as only Ira could that another tenor wasn't needed and certainly wasn't welcomed. At Ken Nelson's insistence, Pop added his voice to Charlie's melody and Ira's harmony on the Louvins' now-classic version of "Joy to the World." Ira was most likely going through a difficult time, at the time. Pop said Ira was so moved by what they had sung that he broke down in sobs when he heard the playback.

From the ultratraditional Louvins, we move on to country's mightiest crossover act, Kenny Rogers. It seemed that Kenny's career as a recording star might be on the wane when Nashville producer Larry Butler took him into the studio to record an unbelievably country tearjerker called "Lucille."

Alan Stoker

In an earlier chapter you learned that my dad had a slight speech impediment all his life. Sort of ironic for someone whose voice is heard on billions of records. You never knew when that impediment would pop up, and pop up it did on the song that would rejuvenate Kenny's career. When the Jordanaires recorded "Lucille" with Kenny, Pop kept exchanging consonants, so the line kept coming out, "You ficked a pine time to leave me Lucille." And Larry Butler, would say, "Gordon, you're singing *ficked* again!" He finally got it right, and Kenny had his big comeback hit.

Gordon was known and venerated by just about everybody in the Nashville music business and plenty of others in the New York and California music worlds. Alan says that his music friendships put him in a position to help some people along the way, and when he could, he did.

In 1960, Pop met and recorded with a young singer/songwriter named John Ramistella. Ramistella was from Baton Rouge, Louisiana, and had been "discovered" in Birmingham, Alabama, in 1959, and brought to Nashville by Hank Williams Sr.'s first wife, Audrey. She was able to get him signed as an artist to the Cub record label.

Ramistella wrote a song titled "I'll Make Believe," that Ricky Nelson recorded in 1960. He started traveling between Nashville and Hollywood in order to work with some California connections he had made through Ricky's guitarist, James Burton. Ramistella had first met Burton by way of Merle Kilgore down in Shreveport. Kilgore had almost a lifetime of connections between Hank Sr. and Hank Jr.

Audrey Williams was known to "adopt" young male songwriters. If they were struggling, as most were, she would let them stay in her home on Franklin Pike in Nashville. One day, Ramistella called Pop and told him he'd had enough of the way he was being treated by Audrey. He asked if Pop could come by and pick him up and take him to the downtown bus station so he could relocate to California. At the time, the Stokers lived only about a mile or so from the Williams home. Pops said he would.

When he arrived at Audrey's place, John was standing at the top of the driveway with his guitar and his suitcase. Pop had to lend him the money for his bus ticket because he didn't have the money for one. John said that he would send the money back as soon as he could when he got to California. Later that night, Audrey phoned Pop and asked him why he had picked Johnny up.

"I felt sorry for him," Pop told her. "He called me and begged me to." She was not happy.

Sometime around 1964, John Ramistella got a house gig at the Whiskey a Go Go in Hollywood. By then he had changed his name from John Ramistella to Johnny Rivers. He has had a long career with many hits including "Secret Agent Man," "Memphis," "The Poor Side of Town," "Midnight Special," "Seventh Son," "Mountain of Love," and others. In 2009, he was inducted into the Louisiana Hall of Fame. Pop had just a small part in Johnny Rivers' career, but was always proud of Johnny's success. And Pop never had to ask. Ramistella sent him the money.

Over the years, the Jordanaires seemed to work well with young artists: a young Elvis, Ricky Nelson, and Barbara Mandrell, to name a few. And then, says Alan, there was this one:

In 1972, Pop and the quartet recorded for the first time with a 13-year-old by the name of Tanya Tucker. That first session produced "Delta Dawn," which reached number 6 on the *Billboard* country chart. With production by Billy Sherrill and engineering by Columbia studio stalwart Lou Bradley, Tanya and the Jordanaires scored two number 1 hits the next year with "What's Your Mama's Name," and "Blood Red and Going Down." In addition to the Jordanaires, the Nashville Edition worked those sessions. Both "Delta Dawn" and "What's Your Mama's Name" begin with a vocal group and Tanya singing *a capella*. Four years younger than Taylor Swift when Taylor started her recording career, Tanya sang with a voice loaded with conviction. Pop loved those records, and 50 years later, Tanya is still out there singing.

We'll close this chapter with a few thoughts by Alan, of the bittersweet quality of Elvis's—and the Jordanaires'—years making movies.

Pop and the Jordanaires provided the vocal backing on all of the Elvis Presley movie soundtracks from 1957's *Loving You* to *Speedway* in 1967. Many of these songs were mediocre to say the least, and not worthy of a singer of Elvis's caliber, but the quartet always tried hard to come up with the best vocal arrangement that they could. They wanted to give all the movie songs, whether good or bad, something that Elvis would be happy with.

In 1955, producer Hal Wallis purchased the rights to the book, "A Stone for Danny Fisher," and planned to give the movie role of Danny Fisher to James Dean, but Dean was killed in an auto accident in the fall of that year. The role was eventually given to Elvis, and he considered the movie made from this book, *King Creole*, to be his best film.

The movie was filmed in the early months of 1958, while Elvis was on a 60-day deferment before starting his military service for Uncle Sam. Elvis was apprehensive that his popularity might fade while he was out of the public eye during his military stint, and he voiced concern that this could very well be his last movie. Because of a dispute with Colonel Parker, the soundtrack recording sessions in January for this film would be the last sessions where the great songwriting team of Leiber and Stoller had a direct collaboration with Elvis.

In addition to recording the *King Creole* soundtrack, the Jordanaires appeared in the movie with Elvis. "King Creole" is the second of three appearances on the big screen with him by the members of the quartet.

With songs like "Jailhouse Rock," "Hound Dog," and "Love Me," Leiber and Stoller were responsible for some of the best songwriting in Elvis's films and records. Many people believe that because of the colonel's disagreements with the two great songwriters, the overall quality of the songs that Elvis sang in the movies after *King Creole* was considerably diminished.

Thanks to Elvis's continued popularity, some hit songs along the way, and the power of his continued movie exposure, Elvis continued to have hit records through much of his movie career.

Chapter 11
LIFE WITHOUT ELVIS

The music business is a tough business, and many of the most successful music executives are hard men and women who have neither the time nor the will to think of the music. Even the ones with a heart will spend only so much time attempting to extend the career of an artist who is obviously on his or her way down. And the really good ones know that they have to fight like tigers for their own artists and that there is little room for sentiment concerning road musicians, songwriters, or anybody whose skills and reliability are necessary to keep their artists on top.

As long as Elvis was turning out successful movies and records, the money poured in. It was all good for the Jordanaires because they were on Elvis's hits year after year. We never got to hear a hit record credited to the Jordanaires, but that might have been a good thing too. The session work usually came in like clockwork. They still did some roadwork, but they didn't have to depend on it. Their studio work in Nashville was the gift that kept on giving.

And these Jordanaires tended to be homebodies. They could well do without the road travel, the groupies, and the fame. Year after year, it was Gordon, Neal, Hoyt, and Ray. When they turned the radio on, there was a good chance that the music they heard featured their voices. And there was a decent chance that the singer on the record had requested that someone take a picture of him or her with the Jordanaires. For many years, they had a nice piece of the action in the worlds of country and pop music.

All things end, but in the music world, it's not always easy to know the end when you hear it. They knew that they were tied to Elvis's career; they just didn't know how tight was the knot. So when the day came that Elvis's movie career was done, they must have wondered.

The next step would be Elvis in Las Vegas. That must have sounded good. Las Vegas was glitzy. Las Vegas was glamorous. Las Vegas was exciting. It was a change. That was good. Maybe. Gordon knew that Elvis would want the Jordanaires. And the Jordanaires wanted Elvis. After all, he'd been a huge part of their success. Who knew if the magic would go on without him? Much of what Gordon has to say here comes from that 1974 interview with Douglas B. Green.

Gordon Stoker

When they called us to go play Vegas with him the first time—this was after the movie deals were over—Tom Diskin, who worked with Tom Parker, Colonel Parker, he said, "Figure out what you guys want for the four weeks." Two shows a day, seven days a week, four weeks of shows, which is a hard way to go—and one week of rehearsal. All right. I went home, and we got together, and we figured we'd have to cancel 30 sessions at home. "Figure up how much you guys want and let me know," he had said. So we figured up what it would cost for us to be out there, and how much it would cost to eat, and this, that, and the other; and we didn't pad it a lot over what we'd have made if we'd stayed in Nashville.

Tom studied the numbers, and he considered. "That's unreal," he said. "We can't even begin to pay it." And he [Elvis] was making 50 grand a week. This is the way it's been. So we had to just say, "Well, we can't do it." Instead, he hired the Imperials, which is a great quartet. He wouldn't pay them much either. Unreal. And they couldn't survive.

So the Imperials had to resign. They worked with him for a while, but they kept their career too. You can only do so much to help your career. Their guy who booked them said of Elvis, "Gordon, we love him. We think the world of him." Like we love him too!

But this was the way Colonel Parker—Colonel Parker's idea was to keep you as low as possible financially so you keep crawling to him. This was his philosophy. He figures to keep everybody's salaries low, and they'll keep crawling to you, they keep working for you. After all, this is Elvis!

I'm so thankful and grateful that the country music business has been so fabulous to us that we haven't needed Elvis. I don't like to really put it that way, but that's the truth. We love him. I think he's been the greatest thing that's ever happened to the music business, but we could not sacrifice our career to stay with him.

Going back to the Imperials, when they quit, the colonel picked up the Stamps Quartet—J.D. Sumner and the Stamps Quartet. They had to pay them more, a little more. J.D. had his boys on salary, but they didn't keep the same personnel, only one or two are the same that started out, because they were just fed up with it. It's a hard way to go. You're on the stage in Vegas at the same time that all the other shows are on the stage. So this means that you don't get to see any other act that's performing in Vegas.

Two shows a day. Believe me, it's not easy. It's true you're free most of the day, but you don't get off until it's like three o'clock in the morning, so your hours are turned around.

But what I was going to say, he was not only a big boost to musicians and background singers, he was the biggest boost in the world to manufacturers of record players. Now, this is an angle you don't even think of. He was the biggest boost in the world to the manufacturer of guitars. Every manufacturer of record players and guitars was absolutely covered up with back orders when Presley came on the scene. Everybody wanted a guitar. Just the funniest thing.

He was the biggest thing that ever happened to the music business, period. He sold almost as many records as the biggest of his time, Bing Crosby, I think. I have my doubts about that, I really do. This is what they say, Bing Crosby's number 1.

The Beatles. [They say] the Beatles are number 3. Of course, the Jordanaires were voted in the Top 10 vocal groups in Europe for some eight to ten years. One year, 1965—I believe it was '65; I can get the charts and show you. I'd have to show you things for you to believe it: We were in the top three. It was the Rolling Stones, The Beatles, and the Jordanaires.

In Douglas Green's interview with Gordon, Doug wanted to know about the guys who lived with Elvis. What was their function in Elvis's life? Since this interview, much has been written about them. Here was a brief story from my book How Nashville Became Music City, U.S.A.: 50 Years of Music Row *that might give you an idea of their collective personality and their role in Elvis's world. The narrator of this story was Charlie McCoy, one of the greatest, most versatile studio musicians to ever bend a harmonica note on Music Row.*

Charlie McCoy

You know, those Memphis Mafia guys hung around all the time. And it was weird. While you were in the studio recording, you didn't see 'em. They were back in the halls, or something, shootin' dice or whatever they did. And the minute a playback started it was like—I mean, we [the musicians] had just finished, and we were walking into the control room to hear the playback and there was hardly any room for us in there because all these guys were— they just appeared out of nowhere.

And they would always stand around and say, "Ah, that's great, Elvis. That's great, Elvis."

They would bring food in at midnight, every night. One time they brought in burgers and fries and all this stuff. There was a big milkshake cup, and it was full of kosher dill slices. Jerry Carrigan was the drummer on this session. He started to reach for one of those pickle slices, and from out of nowhere this hand came and, *slap!* One of Elvis's guys. "Those are Elvis's pickles!" And you know, Elvis would have given you every single slice.

Gordon was very much aware of this mob.

Gordon Stoker

He has eight to ten guys that lived with him for years and years and years, and he gives them things. He gives them cars. He gave Lamar Fike—he gave him a Mercedes not too long ago, I think an $18,000 Mercedes (remember this was many years ago).

He has them as ego-builders. He must be told that his hair looks great, that his eyes look pretty, and that his clothes are pretty, and, "Man I dig that belt buckle you've got on," and, "Boy, I dig those glasses. Those glasses you've got on are great."

His wife's not going to do that, so, you see, he didn't keep her around too long. When the compliments ran out, she went, too. A woman just can't constantly fight this ego deal he has. He's got to have someone who laughs at his jokes. In other words, his life is completely different from what you'd think. He's penned in year in and year out. We had numerous calls the other day wanting to know about this picture that's in the *Enquirer*. He's always had a weight problem. I've seen him go all day long on a hamburger and a bowl of vegetable soup. The only way he could keep his weight down was to starve himself to death—just don't see how he did it, other than he had to take, I imagine, uppers to kick him up enough that he could do his work, because he was always in a good mood and always came on strong when the cameras were turned on. He just knocked everybody out and he still—now, my wife and I went to Vegas to see him last year, and man, when he walked onstage he looked fantastic. But he wasn't out there very long until his hair came down, he got real sweaty, and he got real worn-out looking.

When he'd come into Nashville to record, he'd get to the studio eight o'clock in the evening. Maybe the session was called for six, he wouldn't walk in till eight. We would have been recording during the day and were tired. He'd sit down and play the piano and sing for an hour. Then he'd listen to some demos for another hour and a half. Maybe about twelve or one o'clock, we'd do the first playback. Most of our hits were done with him anywhere from midnight till seven the next morning.

I remember so well, and I sometimes listen at home to "Crying in the Chapel." We sound so tired. That thing was done at three o'clock in the morning, and of course, we had been working all day, and we were worn. The musicians were the same way. And we couldn't schedule an open day before his sessions because he wouldn't give you enough advance notice. So this was bad. He would come into the studio and often he would not know what songs he was going to do. Of course, a lot of times he would, but then there were all those times he wouldn't. And we, as I said, would be worn out by the time we got around to recording the number that he wanted to do.

His guys would listen to the playback. This gives you a pretty good inside story of the entire deal. They'd listen to the playback, and they'd say, "Man"—snap their finger—"ten million. That's a ten-million seller if I ever heard one." Elvis would say, "No, man. I don't like it too much." Another guy would say, "Three million. Three million." All the time they're sitting there all around him jiving and snapping their fingers and all this, that, and the other. Elvis would say, "No, man. I don't believe I even like this song," and throw it out. They'd say, "Well, since you mention it, it's not too good. It's really pathetic." Who couldn't see through it, that they're not sincere, that they laugh at the things that aren't funny? Many times one of his boys might be standing close to me, and Elvis would tell a joke, and the guy would just laugh real big. I'd ask, "What did he say?" "Man, I don't know. I don't know what he said."

Do you get what I'm talking about? But the guy laughed. He just knew he had to laugh. That's what he's getting his salary for, and it's just one of those things. Many people say, "Man, that would drive me nuts in no time." This, I'm afraid is—I'm afraid this is the reason Elvis is a very unhappy person, and I'm afraid he's headed for trouble if he doesn't get a hold of himself soon. I'm very concerned about many things.

Gordon had a right to be concerned. Less than three years after he voiced his concern at this interview, Elvis was dead at the age of 42.

In spite of their mutual regard for gospel music, their lives led in opposite directions. Gordon, Neal, Hoyt, and Ray projected the lifestyle of heartland family men, while Elvis in many ways was a quintessential rock star with the excesses that go with that role. Journalists seem to enjoy the "what-ifs" attached to such relationships, as if the Jordanaires could have somehow driven their influence into the innards of their protégé. Or was he their protégé? Colleague and protégé are two different animals. Their singing styles were compatible but not the same. The Jordanaires were disciplined, conscious, capable of adapting to the singers they were supporting. Elvis's singing style (and performing style) was more extraverted and emotional. The Jordanaires were exactly what they needed to be to succeed as background singers.

As for Elvis's young men? There's plenty of reading and documentary film material describing their role in his career. Gordon has more to say about them.

Listen, man, Elvis's boys kept Man Tan in business. [Man Tan is a commercial product applied to the skin to make it appear suntanned.] They all used that stuff. Lamar had it one day on his face, and it wouldn't take to a greasy complexion too well. It was spotty on his face. All of Elvis's guys had on makeup. They'd all come in, man, looked like a bunch of Indians. They'd all come into the set together see—eight or ten of them—and they all had on weird things.

Freddy Bienstock turned around and looked at them. He's a foreigner, and he has broken English. He said [imitating accent], "Lamar, you look like you have been taking a sunbath through a piece of Swiss cheese."

"Hey I got your Swiss cheese!" That is a comeback they all have. Elvis has the same comeback. They have a bunch of little things that are just hilariously funny to them that aren't funny to anyone else at all. If you make a remark that Elvis doesn't like, he'll say, "Scorched." If it's a real bad remark, he'll say, "Burnt."

But Gordon tried to understand.

These guys are on call 24 hours a day, 7 days a week, never any freedom for themselves. The thing is, he'll have jobs for them to do during the day, and then he wants them up all night when he's awake all night. So they really had a rough way to go. I don't envy their jobs at all, I can assure you.

One man Gordon did not always appreciate was the Dutchman who called himself Colonel Tom Parker.

Colonel Tom, as I told you a while ago, likes to give everybody crawling time. He likes to play jokes on people. He's very blunt. He's an ex-carnival barker, and that tells his tale. Elvis and the colonel have no time for each other at all. They have no negotiation. Tom Diskin is the go-between for them. Elvis doesn't really say anything bad about anybody. He never put people down, other performers or Parker. A lot of times, he'll keep his mouth shut. Fire will maybe fly in his eyes, but he won't say anything. He's beautiful so far as he don't talk about people like I'm sitting here doing.

When you read what Gordon had to say about Elvis, you can feel the warmth, mixed with regret that Elvis could not avoid the terrible things that fame and fortune do to so many people. His feelings about the colonel were an interesting mix of admiration and negativity.

His deal has always been to confuse the public and to mislead the public, and it's paid off. Like when he first picked up Eddy Arnold, he put a big ad in one of the magazines about the biggie, the big-time Eddie Arnold. Eddy Arnold did not have any dates booked at all after the colonel took him over, but he said, "Bookers, contact Colonel Tom Parker immediately for Eddy Arnold open dates. Just a few open dates left this year." He did not have any dates even booked. This pretty well tells the entire tale.

It's like he'll have a booker or maybe a movie producer or something on the wire for Elvis, and he'll say, "Well now, let me tell you, I want a million dollars. If you don't want to give it, I've got another man waiting right now. I can't wait no longer. You've got to tell me right now. I'm not talking about tomorrow. I've got to talk about right now. I've got another man that's gonna pay him a million and a half."

This is the way it would go, and this type of behavior—I'm not putting him down, but that type of—would you call it promotion—conning the public, conning the bookers and conning promoters, is how he's been able to be big. He's a big joker. He likes to set people up to make them look like an ass. He loves that.

He doesn't have friends—very very few. His friends are so few, it's unreal. The officials at RCA don't like him, because of the way he's conned them for years, and the people at the studios, well, as a matter of fact, he made the studio provide him with secretaries and with a real nice office, which he should have, but outside the door they hung a beautiful sign, had a really nice picture of a snowman. It said, "America's #1 snowman, Colonel Tom Parker," and the colonel thought it was funny. "Did you see the sign outside the door? Hal Wallis put that out there. He called me the number one snowman, not number two. I don't want to be number two. As long as I can be the number one snowman in the entire country, that's for me." That's the way he is.

He was a millionaire before he ever found Elvis. So why should he be squabbling over a budget? But he'd bicker with you all day over $150. Isn't that wild? So you often wonder who's going to go to his funeral. Maybe I shouldn't say that. That may be ugly. He's always been kind to me and all that, but he'll bicker with you on money. He'll look at you like you're crazy.

Before you start thinking unkind things about Gordon, you have to remember that at the time of this interview, Hugh Gordon Stoker and Colonel Tom Parker had been bickering about road fees and other fees for many years. As the manager of the quartet, it was up to Gordon to do most of the dealing, and when Gordon had landed his first piano gig with the Jordanaires, he thought he'd signed on as a musician, not as a dealmaker. He explained how his role as quartet rep usually worked out:

Occasionally we talk things over [before negotiations]. Of course, the other Jordanaires always tell me, "Go ahead and make the decision. You always make it anyway."

This was a man who started building his reputation as a child prodigy gospel piano player and made his career as a virtuoso high tenor in a quartet. He didn't join the Jordanaires to be a deal maker. He joined them to make music! But fate made him a deal-making music maker, and nobody has come forward with any evidence that he ever woke up one morning and told the rest of the quartet to find another business guy because he was tired of the gig.

Actually I've got three great guys to work with. They don't give me a hard time on anything. They'll grumble about a lot of things, of course, but even though they grumble, they still go ahead and do what they have to do.

By this time, it was evident to them that their days as Elvis's long-time musical buddies were over.

Neal Matthews
The last time we tried to record with him he threw such a fit in the studio. Who needs that? I don't need that anymore.

Gordon Stoker
Elvis came into the studio about an hour-and-a-half or two hours late, which was all right. We're used to that. And he listened to the playbacks. Anyway, what I'm saying, on behalf of the engineers, they had set their mics up and their cords and all that. Meanwhile, like three or four hours later, those things have gotten kicked around to where their connections aren't quite as good. The Jordanaires are on one mic and three girls are on another mic, and then Elvis is on a mic, and he had on earphones.

The musicians would play the intro, and then he would come in on the da-da-da-da," something maybe like "My Wish Came True" . . . that thing we did with him many years ago. Well, it was similar to that. He had three or four words, and we were supposed to come in and answer him, and then the girls were supposed to answer us. The musicians played their part, he came in, and then we came in, and he couldn't hear us on his earphones. He said, "I can't hear the Jordanaires. Turn them up. Can't hear them."

Well, the boys came out and readjusted the mics and cords and did a few things like that, you know. Earlier though, he had tried to play a demo for us on a record player sitting in the corner, and it wouldn't—you know, in a lot of these studios, you'll have a fantastic studio with like a half a million dollars worth of equipment in the recording room, and out in the studio they'll have a little crummy, a very crummy, the most crummy-assed player in the world sitting out there in front. Maybe a little hundred—or $75 machine sitting there. Elvis put this demo on and wanted to play it for us, and it wouldn't play good. And he threw a fit. He kicked the cabinet. He says, "All that money RCA has, how do they have a machine like this out here!" Just blew his top. Really, I had never seen him blow up quite like that about just a machine that wouldn't play good.

Thirty minutes later he'd cooled down from that. Then he goes over to his mic, puts on his earphones, and he couldn't hear us. That was just more than he could take. We all came into the studio and he said, "I can't hear the group. Turn them up." So they came in and readjusted, and played the intro again. He still couldn't hear us. He couldn't hear the girls either. He took his earphones off, threw them on the floor, and said, "I shouldn't have come in tonight in the first place. See you fellas later." And that's the last time we saw Elvis in the studio. That was our last session with Elvis.

That's the way he can be, sometimes, just very childish. He never has grown up. But now, let me say for this: would you have grown up, if you had been caged up and never been able to go out on your own and maybe go to a movie or go to a—he can't even go to a restaurant or a bar. When you leave here, you can go out and get in your car and go home and act like you ought to. He can't do that. He's been penned in for so long that it's getting to him. He lives a very lonely life. And I'd like to see him overcome that.

Things could be different if he wanted to make them different. By that I mean, when he was at his peak, he came into Nashville and he says, "Hey, uh-h-h-h, if I had something to wear tomorrow night, I'd go down to the Grand Ole Opry," because, you know, he wanted to really be dressed up nice.

I said, "Well, we can take you over to Mallernee's on 6th Avenue downtown, tomorrow. It'll be no problem, man, no problem at all." So I called the store and told them, "I'm bringing in Elvis Presley in the morning." I knew one of the salesmen down there and I said, "I'm going to bring Elvis into your store in the morning around eleven o'clock."

He said, 'Really? Yeah, yeah."

I said, "Well I am." I said, "I'm going to take him to the back, and I want you to fit him with a suit and shoes and a shirt and tie. Don't be overwhelmed with him coming in. Tell your employees not to act any different, because if they act any different, he'll walk out."

Well, we parked at the Andrew Jackson Hotel parking lot. It was up the street from the store. Now, Elvis had on a leather jacket and a leather cap of some kind, and goggles—looking like Elvis. We walked all the way from the Andrew Jackson Hotel down to the store, which I'd say was a good block's distance. Not one person did we pass that recognized Elvis, and this was when he was at his peak.

We went into the store. Nobody said a word, because they'd been told not to. We went all the way to the back, and he'd been in there about twenty minutes before people started milling around looking. So we just walked out the back door, walked all the way back to the parking lot, and again, nobody recognized him.

Now, my point in telling you this is, things could be different. If you're recognized by having those [goggles] on like he wears, and having your hair the way it is, couldn't you change that a little bit and maybe put you on something else a little bit different? Or if you're associated with wearing that shirt with everything you've ever worn, couldn't you've changed that shirt if you didn't want to be recognized? Sure! He *wants* to be recognized. Like when we were in Hawaii doing *Blue Hawaii*, that movie, he wanted to come out on the beach. We said, "If you'll come out on the beach and not have everybody with you, and have on an old hat and sunshades and don't make such a big scene out of it, they won't say one word to you."

But what did he do? He came out on the beach with three or four guys, you see, and he looked like Elvis Presley. So he hadn't been on the beach for but about five or ten minutes when they just swarmed about him like mad, getting his autograph. Older people. There wasn't any kids there. That was at the Hawaiian Village, which is an elite hotel in Hawaii. Mostly older people who said they wanted to get autographs for their kids. These are the people that bugged him to death.

What I'm saying to you is, I think if Elvis had come out and dressed different so as not to make you think it's Elvis Presley, I don't think people would recognize him, because I proved here in town that he could do things if he wanted to. A lot of times, you know, you run into somebody who says, "Hey, I saw Elvis last week in So-And-So-City." No you didn't. It wasn't even Elvis. Maybe somebody who looked like Elvis; a lot of people are trying to imitate him. Especially during the '60s, there was lots of boys that looked a lot like Elvis and combed their hair the same way.

We [the Jordanaires] would tell Elvis, "You get that hair combed different, put you in an old cap, and act just like any other people, they won't recognize you." But you see, it's like Jack Benny said. Jack Benny said, "It really brings me up when I walk down the street here in Nashville, and everybody I pass wants my autograph or, 'Hello, Jack,' this, that and the other. 'How are you?' or, 'Aren't you Jack Benny?' In Europe you can walk in those places and nobody will recognize you, and it sure is a bring-down. It really hurts you. I might be out three hours and nobody has recognized that I am Jack Benny."

It's that curse-blessing that hits some celebrities between the eyes and forces them to recognize that a big reason they became a singer, an actor, or game show host is the need to feed a hungry ego by becoming famous, the need to be greeted by people they don't even know and get that special joy that comes when they gain approval from other celebrities.

But with that fame comes a loss of freedom when those people who recognize you and swear they are your fan for life believe that becoming your fan means that they own a piece of your life. It's a form of involuntary servitude, and many celebrities resent the demands their fans make on them.

But they know they must pretend to love their fans or they may lose them and the popularity, the approval, that feeds their careers. Gordon may have been trying to tell Elvis that if you want more freedom in your life, all you need to do is give up a little bit of that precious fame once in a while, and freedom will come to you—that to grab hold of that freedom, you must, at least temporarily, give up your fame by admitting that if you don't puff out your chest and let your clothes scream, "I am Elvis!" you will be just an ordinary person. The price of freedom is being ordinary—not a terrible price to pay if you live your life as an ordinary person but a terrible price for those who love their fame. Maybe Gordon was thinking back to when the Jordanaires were trying hard to have a hit record with "Sugaree." It was a time when they were reaching out for a taste of fame, and Capitol Record executive Lee Gillette sat him down and said, "Stay in the background and treat the background right, and it'll be good to you."

The Jordanaires took Gillette's advice. They never became country superstars, but they were able to go home to their families after a long, fruitful day in the studios of Music City. They had new songs to learn every day instead of having to sing the same old hits over and over. They had long, prosperous careers. They could take their families out in public without being mobbed for autographs. And over many decades, they could feel a part of hit after hit that rolled out of the studios and onto the airwaves, coast to coast and far beyond, and yet still have some privacy for themselves and their families. Surely, all that was worth missing a few million "Aren't You the Jordanaires?" over the years.

The Jordanaires were famous—among people in the Nashville music industry. They got plenty of respect from their peers. But away from their matching plaid stage jackets, they could live relatively private lives.

When Gordon talks about the Jordanaires' function in the music world, he sounds dry and technical.

We "ooh" and "aah," and pad the singer and try to make him or her sound better. If we feel like it needs to be bigger, we double track it. Often we'll sing along with the artist to bring out a particular line or maybe the title line of the song. So it just goes on and on. It's a beautiful world. We've had a fantastic career, and we've enjoyed every moment of it. Sometimes I wish our boys could follow our footsteps—see, we have 13 kids among the 4 of us. Ray Walker has 6, I have 3, Neal Matthews has 2, and Hoyt Hawkins has 2.

So I've often said I wish that Hoyt's boy, and one of Ray's boys, and one of my boys would get a group up and call it the Jordanaire Juniors, because after all, we're not last spring's chickens. But I think there'll always be an opening for someone who can get the sound that we've been fortunate enough to be able to get.

Chapter 12

OOHING AND AAHING IN THE NEW MILLENNIUM

In 1982, the beloved baritone of the group, Hoyt Hawkins, died. Duane West, a member of Sonny James's vocal group The Southern Gentlemen, joined the Jordanaires that year and stayed with the Jordanaires until his death in 1999. The Jordanaires continued their studio and roadwork.

Then on April 21, 2000, Neal Matthews died suddenly. For many years, Neal had been the lead singer and arranger for the group, designer of more vocal sounds than anybody else in the history of popular or country music. His loss to the group was huge, especially to Gordon and Ray, who had been singing with Neal almost every day over the past four decades.

They had to find a replacement. As previously mentioned, the Jordanaires had a small number of substitutes for when a member of the group was sick, busy on vacation, or otherwise occupied, and one of them was a highly respected vocalist from East Tennessee named Curtis Young. His story is worth knowing because it tells so much about how the Nashville music industry in the 20th century was about friendships, relationships, and experiences.

Curtis Young

These days I live in Seymour, about 12 miles out of Knoxville, 20 minutes from Pigeon Forge. We've got a fairly good view of the mountains from our back porch. When the weather is fit, we can sit out there and have coffee in the morning and look at the mountains.

Early on I worked at Channel 6 in Knoxville for seven and a half years. I was a member of a band there. I was the lead singer in the band and we did live shows. We did three TV shows a week for Jim Clayton, of Clayton Mobile Homes. We did the *Star Time Show* and the *Cathy Hill Show*, and a gospel show. We recorded all those at another TV station and they were syndicated and aired all around, I don't know how far out they went, but we got some pretty good ratings.

Also during this time I worked at the Happy Goodman Family studio in Madisonville, Kentucky, did a lot of sessions up there playing rhythm guitar. I even went on the road with them one time and did a live show, so I knew Rusty and Vestal Goodman—I got to record with Vestal on a George Jones session just before she passed.

For readers not intimate with gospel music, over many years, the Happy Goodman Family was one of the nation's most popular southern gospel groups, known for their joyous, infectious performances.

In '69 I had the opportunity to go to work with Wilma Lee and Stoney Cooper on the Grand Ole Opry. They needed a bass player and a singer, and, I was the singer, but I didn't know how to play bass, can you believe that?

Curtis was not a complete stranger to the Nashville music business before he headed west to Music City.

I had recorded for Monument Records in '61 with a partner from high school, but I never paid any attention to what the bass played because I played rhythm guitar and sang, so I talked to the bass player in our band at Channel 6—we were called the Kountry Kings, and he taught me how to play 1-5-1-5-1-5 in about a week.

So, I met Wilma Lee and Stoney one night at eleven o'clock at the Opry, and we headed out on the road. I had borrowed a bass and a bass amp from a friend of mine here in Knoxville, and, first I had to back up the Glaser Brothers who were really hot at that time. I was lucky that I had heard their songs and knew how they went. I walked out onstage with no fears whatsoever, didn't have any butterflies, nothin'! We got through that and, I called Wilma Lee and Stoney to find out their schedule, and they told me, they said, well, we're gonna leave at such and such a time next week, so, be there, and I was there, so I went out with them two weekends, and they never did say, "You're hired," they'd just say "We're leavin'," so that was kind of weird. "You too," was understood, I guess. I was missing one weekend a month because I was still in the Air National Guard. I came back after that second trip and asked for a leave of absence at Channel 6. The guy said, "Well, if I give you a leave of absence, we're gonna have to hire somebody and when you come back in a year you might not have a job." I said, "Well, okay, I'll just turn in my resignation." I did, and took off with Wilma Lee and Stoney, on faith—the whole thing was just on faith. But it worked out.

Curtis worked with Wilma Lee and Stoney for about three years.

Some nights we would only have one spot at the Opry. I remember when I'd pick up my check at the union, it would be like $9.11, after taxes, so, it wasn't very much and I was renting one room from a lady on Boscobal Street, where a lot of the musicians were living at that time, $10 a week, and I had to go through a guitar player's room to get to my room, which was not cool, but then, things started picking up, I met some friends and started getting a session or two here and there, playing bass and rhythm guitar, and then Carol Lee (daughter of Wilma Lee and Stoney) Cooper was the first person that called me to do a background vocal session.

I said, "Carol Lee, I don't know if I could do that." She said, "Well, you're a quick study, you can just find a part and hang on." So that's what I did, and, you know, word of mouth gets around, and so, I started doing different sessions—mostly demo sessions, not masters—didn't make a *lot* of money, but I got out of that one room and, later on, my bass playing turned into a job with Chet Atkins, on the road. I worked with him for about three, three and a half years, which was a great gig. We'd go out once a month, and five days was the longest trip I ever made. You know, these things happen and it's so gradual you don't really remember how everything falls into place. I was getting more sessions and I decided that I was making enough to stay at home and I really didn't need to work on the road any more. But working with Wilma Lee and Stoney on the Opry led to me working with a bunch of other artists on the Opry. When they would come in and rehearse, in a little room in the back, I would sing along with them if I knew the song, and one of my favorite people was George Morgan. He was singing "My Elusive Dreams" one night and I started harmonizing with him and he said, "Hey, why don't you sing that with me onstage?"

I did, and then I started working with different people on the Opry, Ray Pillow, and Justin Tubb—there were about six artists I was working with, so I was making enough that I could stay off the road.

Here's a good time to point out that working on the road is not fun for anybody with any sense. Country stars have to travel a lot, but road musicians like to become session musicians if they can.

So I was making enough that I could stay home. My session work just kept growing and growing. I'd go into a session and play bass and then I would double and play rhythm guitar and, then I would do the background vocals. You could make a living doing that. And then the Willis Brothers came along. I subbed for them when one of them was sick.

One of the brothers, Guy Willis, passed away, and then Skeeter Willis passed away, so the last brother, Vic, started the Vic Willis trio and I was the lead singer. It was a tragic thing. C. W. Mitchell, the third singer, and Vic were both killed in car crashes, so I had to move on from that. I was just doing a lot of sessions and finally, my master sessions started coming in and I worked with George Strait for about 15 years, singing harmony with him on his records, and Toby Keith and Randy Travis and just a whole bunch of people.

Side comment: For Curtis to get all that demo work meant that people in the business were hearing him and liking him, but when he started getting vocal gigs on master sessions with major country artists, that meant that he was earning a huge reputation and that the best artists and producers in town felt like they could trust their careers to this young fellow, kind of the way it happened with the Jordanaires.

Then in 2000—this was kind of weird, I don't know what happened, probably never will know, there was about five of us doing backup on most of the sessions around town: Dennis Wilson, John Wesley Riles, Cindy Walker, Lisa Silver—and then, all of a sudden, in 2000, everything just kind of stopped. Stopped for *everybody*, or everybody in my circle there. I remember talking to Dennis, and I asked him, have you got any sessions coming up? He said no. What the—my phone quit ringing for a couple of weeks. That had happened before—but we always knew someone that was gearing up for a new album and the phone would start ringing again and we'd be busy, we'd be doin' two or three, sometimes four sessions a day, and working every day of the week. But this time, two weeks went by and nothing happened. And then it was a month, the phone did not ring one time. And then it was two months, the phone did not ring one time. Got to the point where I wondered if it would ever start ringing again.

The phone finally rang. I got a call from Gordon Stoker. The Jordanaires were doing the Patsy Cline tribute in Vegas—they were working the Gold Coast and he said, "Neal and I are thinking about slowing down a little bit. If you want to, come out and pick up a tape, and learn the show, maybe fill in for me from time to time."

I went out to Vegas and picked up the tape, and got back home, and I learned the songs and the parts and all that kind of stuff, and by then I'd had to go to Japan in Gordon's place one time so I had learned a lot of the Elvis things. Just two, three weeks, later, Gordon and Neal—I guess all of them came home for a weekend, and there was a ballgame on, everybody was watching the ballgame at someone's house and Neal went to the bathroom on a break and he had a massive heart attack. Later Gordon called me and said, Neal has passed away, could you fill in his part, we have to finish our tour in Vegas.

I said, "Sure," so I went out there with them, and here again, they'd say, we're gonna do such and such and such and such, and never did say, "You're hired!"

But I *must* have been hired, because I kept working with them and it was just a great experience. We were on the road a lot—Gordon would say, "Oh, man, we've traveled more since you came on board than we ever had." We went everywhere, went to Hawaii, and Ireland—we went over there for a week to do one show. We had the TCB Band, the first time the Jordanaires and the TCB Band [Elvis's later band—the Taking Care of Business Band] was onstage together, and there was about 25 people onstage—it was just a great experience, traveling with the Jordanaires—we would go to each other's house; mostly they would come to my house in Hendersonville. It was funny, Gordon said to me, "We don't buy birthday presents or Christmas presents and we don't go out to eat, we just don't do that, you know we work and we go home and that's it." Well, my wife, Libby, she can change anything and she sure changed that quick. 'Cause we had them all coming to our house for dinner, and we'd go to theirs, and it was just a great camaraderie with all of us.

But they still didn't announce him as a Jordanaire, and on some level, Curtis had to wonder.

Libby is responsible for changing that, too. We were somewhere, I think in a hotel room, it might have been in Tunica, Mississippi. We were working the Gold Coast Hotel and Casino and she said, "Well, what's going on? Are you hired to do this?" I said, "I don't know!"

So she called Ray Walker and she said, "Ray, we're just talking about this, is Curtis really one of the Jordanaires now?" and Ray said, "Why sure he is!" So that cinched that, you know, I said, "Well that's great, I'm glad for that," so that's how I got to know for sure that I was a Jordanaire.

During the early years of Nashville as Music City, so much was done with a handshake, as if artists and managers were too embarrassed to consider that they were actually doing business, most notably Elvis and his handshake deal with Colonel Parker.

Gordon and I became really close; we would hang out together sometimes, and talk and he would tell me things about Elvis that nobody ever knew; of course all that's gone over my head because I don't try to remember things to write 'em down but I do know that Elvis, according to Gordon, was a very nice and humble man, and he stuck to his word, whatever he said he would do.

I stayed with the Jordanaires through 2013 and that was when Gordon passed and the Jordanaires name was dissolved—it's still there, if the kids want to bring it back at any time they can, but as far as anybody else using the Jordanaires' name, they can't do it.

During those later years, the Jordanaires did not show up as often on hit records, but thanks to their legendary reputation, they continued their steady work.

We still did sessions but we were traveling, as Gordon said, more than they ever had. There are so many Elvis impersonators out there—you would just not believe it. And they loved singing on shows with the quartet that actually sang with Elvis for so many years. We went to Laughlin, Nevada one time. There was a two-day

Elvis impersonator contest there, and we sang with 77 Elvises! And once you've done "American Trilogy" about 15 times, and the next Elvis comes up saying, "Well I'm doin' 'American Trilogy,'" then I guess you couldn't blame us if we felt we'd done enough "American Trilogy."

We had a little bitty Elvis, I don't know, about 10 years old, or younger, and old, and thin, and heavy, every Elvis you could imagine. We had one *lady* doing Elvis. And she wasn't bad.

[During this time] *most* of the shows we did were Elvis impersonators and when we weren't traveling, we did sessions. We did some remakes. I remember one of them was "Stand by Your Man," with Tammy Wynette. The original session, I believe, was on a four-track machine. And they had lost the track with the background vocals on it, but they had everything else, so we went in and did the background vocals again, and let me tell you, you might think that was easy. It was not easy, because the notes they were holding were really long, and you had to get a real long breath to hold those notes. Also, we redid a background track for a Patsy Cline. I'm not sure what the song was but it was easy and fun to do.

Most of the sessions were in town but, you know, after a while studios started spreadin' out and we'd go to the Castle, down toward Franklin, and just everywhere, Mount Juliet, Hendersonville, then people started havin' studios in their home or they'd have a house on 16th Avenue and they'd give us an address and we'd show up. With all of this and all the Elvises out there, it was busy, let me tell you.

As children, Alan and Brent Stoker lived a life that lots of kids would die or kill for. They loved the music, and after school, they would often drop by RCA Studio B or the Quonset Hut just to check out what kind of music the Jordanaires were doing that day. Their mom and dad never put pressure on them either to get into the music business or stay out of the music business.

Alan and Brent Stoker

Alan: They were supportive. If we wanted a set of drums, they got us a set of drums. If we wanted guitars we got guitars. They knew that if we asked for them, we were going to use them. They supported us, just like Dad's parents supported him, took him around to Paducah and McKenzie so he could see all the gospel groups in the area play.

In spite of all the Jordanaires' success, Gordon had a very cautious view of the group's career.

Alan: I don't think Dad ever felt that they ever really had made it. They were always looking for the next "what are we gonna do tomorrow?" Will we have sessions next month? Of course, eventually, session work did die, it died out some for everybody: groups, the A-Team. . . . Oh, it's not all gone, not by any means, but those weeks of four sessions a day are just dreams of another era.

Brent: The quartet's sessions went from 25 a week to 3.

Alan: About five years after Elvis died is when all the Elvis tribute things started to happen. And the Jordanaires were heavily involved in all of that.

Brent: And they never said no to any work. It never mattered whether the artists were a name or nobody. And they traveled overseas and did a lot of stuff too. They would go a couple of times a year. Holland, Denmark,

Alan and Brent were trying to stress the point that the Jordanaires considered their career at all times to be a job, that just because they were not backing Elvis and Patsy and Jim Reeves did not mean they had lost their mojo. They were still making musical sounds, the best they could, making their artists sound as good as possible, entertaining audiences when the situation called for it. They still took pride in their arrangements, hit their notes, and gave the audiences a live taste of the artistry they had been hearing on records for decades. Generally, on those shows, there was some guy who would do Elvis numbers, and they would re-create their parts, usually standing behind the guy who was being Elvis but sometimes not.

Alan: And then they got to where they were working with Ricky Nelson, again. The group I was with at the time, we opened a show at the Opryland Hotel. Rick Nelson was the headliner. And Dad came backstage, and said hello to Rick, and I think that's kinda how their relationship started again. I'm not sure if that's true or not, but that's what I think happened. So they started back working with Rick and that band, and Dad loved those guys. They traveled on Rick's plane. Matter of fact that New Year's Eve gig, that ended up [with the crash] Rick had called Dad and asked if the group could do that show with him. Rick asked, "How much money would you need," and when Dad told him, Rick said, "Well, we can't afford that."

Brent: They last appeared with him in September of that year. He died December 31. That death was much more upsetting to Dad than Elvis's death.

Brent: He expected Elvis to die.

Alan: He last saw Elvis a year before Elvis died. He saw him at the quartet convention, at the Nashville Municipal Auditorium downtown. They had a little trailer set off to the side, and Elvis was in the trailer.

Brent: A policeman friend called Dad and said, "You need to come down here," and Dad said, "Why?" The policeman said, "Elvis is down here."

"Elvis is there? I'll be right down."

Alan: They met and they talked, and Dad came home and told Mom, "He's in bad shape. I don't think he'll be around long." And that was the summer before he died, the summer of '76.

Brent: I remember Dad saying, "He hugged me, and held me close to him, which he had never really done before." Dad said, "He didn't have a good look in his eyes."

A few late thoughts on Elvis: Alan and Brent say that the quartet didn't go on the road with him after he came back from the army, though they did join him for a few live dates, and, of course, once he traded the road for the movies, he would see the group only briefly when they'd come out to Hollywood to sing on the movie sound tracks or make their very rare actual movie appearances and when he'd come to Nashville to record with them.

And there was always the colonel. To the Jordanaires and others involved in the world of Elvis, "colonel" Parker was not only the man in charge of Elvis's professional fate. He was a genuine character, always capable of introducing something new into their lives.

Alan: I do remember Dad saying, "The colonel tried to hypnotize me one time. He had me lay back and he said, 'When I snap my fingers, you will awaken and will not remember what'"—forgot what else he said. He snapped his fingers and said something and Dad sat up and said, "Well I remember that, you didn't hypnotize me." And the colonel moved on to somebody else.

Those people who wanted to impress the colonel probably would have acted like they were hypnotized.

Brent: Dad had little time for the so-called Memphis Mafia. He thought they were a distraction, and he never understood what that was all about. Why did Elvis need that? Dad was frustrated with that. What was that insecurity, that he had to have constant support from these guys?

Alan: I went with Dad to one of the Elvis tribute things, at Graceland, summer of '85 or '86, and Dad was doing kind of an interview on the street. There was a guy hanging around by himself, and when Dad came out of the interview, the guy came up to him and said, "Gordon"—he gave him his name and I don't remember what it was—"you probably don't remember me but I used to be one of those guys that hung out with Elvis, and you came up to me and told me, 'You have more on the ball than all these other people. You need to get out of this situation.' And that really stuck with me. And I did. And I'm glad that I did, that was the right thing to do."

They were an odd set of companions, the Jordanaires and Elvis Presley. They were sons of the South with a deep love for gospel music, yet their lifestyles had evolved so differently. But their common goals and their desire to make a good living making good music together resulted in love and respect that may have occasionally bent but did not break.

Alan: Dad thought Elvis could have insisted that he have better songs, but Dad said Elvis just didn't want to fight for better song choices. And Dad said Elvis was the only man he knew that took a makeup kit around with him. If he didn't carry it one of his guys did. If he thought his eyes needed touching up, he would go do it.

Strange? Who says so? We tend to admire successful people who take care of the details that make them successful: the musicians who play their scales again and again until they're fast and smooth as silk, the lecturers who practice their speeches with marbles in their mouth, and the singer who knows the girls love to look at him while he sings.

Earlier in this book, we saw Gordon describe Elvis as "beautiful." It was as if Gordon had found a sculpture to admire, the same sculpture that he also noted had a dirty neck the first time he met him.

Alan: Dad said that Elvis had the best laugh of anybody you ever heard. You hear that laugh and you'd remember it.

Brent: He also felt sorry for him, that he didn't have the guts to stand up for himself like he should have. He would have been better off and his career would have been better off if he had stood up for himself.

The classic quartet stayed together for a long time. We always read about bands, how you can't keep a band together. Even the Beatles, with all their success, broke up after 10 years.

Alan: The Jordanaires main four guys stayed together from '58 till Hoyt died in 1982. Then the other three continued (with Duane and Louis singing baritone) until Neal died in 2000, 42 years after Ray joined.

It's interesting that until the classic four came together, there were many changes that went on in the quartet for one reason or the other. A vocal group might have one singer who wasn't quite as quick or as good as the others, and soon the others are sitting around muttering things like, "We've gotta get a better baritone than old Joe. Did that ever happen during the heyday of the Jordanaires?"

Alan and Brent saw the Jordanaires a lot, together and separately, over a long period of time, and they never heard such talk.

Alan: Dad and Hoyt were friends from the time they were teenagers. Dad was from Gleason, Tennessee, the Hawkinses were from Paducah, Kentucky. That's right close.

Brent: Do you know that Mom took all the calls? She made sure that they got paid correctly. If they needed a substitute singer, she would make sure it got done. The secretaries would call the Jordanaires' office, which was our home. We weren't allowed to answer the phone, because it was considered a business phone. I would have friends over and they would say, "Your phone's ringin'!" And we wouldn't even hear it, because we weren't allowed to answer it. So we just tuned it out. If mom and dad weren't there to get it, it would just go to answering service. But mom would take those calls from the secretaries, and write it in the book, and she handled all that.

Alan and Brent did not feel particularly pressured by their parents to follow in Gordon's footsteps.

Alan: Did they support us? Yes.

> *Brent*: But they never really pressured us to do anything.

But they had dreams nonetheless.

Alan: As we said before, when we wanted a drum set, Dad bought us a drum set. We both had piano lessons. I think we didn't take to it, certainly not as well as he did.

Alan: We were learning out of the wrong book. If we'd been taught to play gospel piano, I probably would have kept playing.

> *Brent*: It was too much like school.

Alan: So we both have a little bit of facility on piano, but nothing like what he had.

> *Brent*: Of course he never thought that he did either. Often he said, when we were growing up, "If I had really practiced, and really worked hard, I could have really been something."

As the main carrier of the Jordanaire institutional memory, Gordon took the history of the Jordanaires seriously, and he wanted it to be right to the best of his ability and memory, a difficult task for anybody but especially as the years of memories multiplied.

Brent: Dad mentioned to me at least once about the pressure that he went through, when Elvis's first RCA recordings came out and it said on the label "Elvis Presley with the Jordanaires." The Jordanaires weren't on RCA. They were on Capitol, and Capitol pushed back and said, "Whoa, now just a minute! You're not gonna have the Jordanaires' name on an RCA record. We didn't give you permission to do that!" I don't know what political gymnastics he had to go through to get Capitol to allow that, but he did it. He was able to convince—I don't know if it was Lee Gillette, or Ken Nelson, over at Capitol—that this was good for Capitol, for the Jordanaires to be mentioned on his records—he's the biggest name in show business! You know, the other side of that is, Elvis didn't *have* to put their name on those records. They didn't sell one extra copy because it said "With the Jordanaires." But he insisted on that credit.

Alan: If the colonel didn't want the Jordanaires' name to be on the records, it wouldn't have been.

Brent: Elvis was so insistent, is how I understood it. The colonel said "Okay."

Readers, make up your own minds. Maybe Elvis loved the idea of being the lead singer of a gospel group. He knew that these four men approved of him and did much to help him create the music he loved, even when he did not like the songs that the movie suits and the colonel demanded that he do. In the studio, they were always there for him. During those 14 years, musically the Jordanaires were an enormous part of his comfort zone. Scotty, Bill, and D.J. were there too, of course, but when Neal created his vocal arrangements and Elvis and the quartet turned those arrangements into great sound, that was where the happiness was.

Alan: By the time he started working with them, they were already established. He knew about them before they really knew about him.

Brent: Unlike almost everybody else he worked with, they didn't approach him as a star because he *wasn't* a star when they started working with him. You hear all those people talking about, "Aw, the first time I worked with Elvis I was so nervous, I couldn't figure out how to act and what do I do, how do I behave?" The Jordanaires knew Elvis before he was a national superstar. He sought *them* out.

Alan: They met him before they heard any of his records.

Brent: So he appreciated that.

And he knew what they were musically before he knew what they were personally. And they didn't know him at all, yet they treated him kindly from the first moment they met him.

Alan: Dad came home one time and told Mom that the songs they were giving Elvis to do "are so terrible!" and I think Mom said—

Brent: Oh, I remember this vividly. I remember Dad complaining that "the material they're giving him to sing is awful! Aw, this is so bad," and Mom asked what the movie they'd just finished recording the soundtrack for was called. And Dad thought for a minute and said, "ohh [painfully] . . . ohhh. Clambake." I was nine and I didn't know what a clambake was, but I remember Dad saying that and them talking about it. A nine-year-old in Tennessee, I didn't know what a clambake was.

But they weren't all like that. Think of "Don't Be Cruel." Great song! "Stuck on You" came off real good.

Alan: Yeah, they did a really good job on it. They knew that he hated it and they did the best they could. They tried to make something good out of it, even though they knew that Elvis didn't think it was good. And they made it work, didn't they?

I heard Dad say that he thought they (the RCA people) made Elvis sing too high. Over all, they wanted him to sing near the upper limits of his range. And Dad said it was very fatiguing for him. He said it would have been better if they had let him do it in a lower key. And Dad said that they wouldn't let him do it in a lower key. You listen to "Jailhouse Rock," you listen to those outtakes, and about the third time through, he's having trouble getting through it. And of course that would have been something they'd already had an arrangement written for, being a movie and all. It wasn't like a Nashville head arrangement where you could just change the key.

I think I was listening to the outtakes of "Jailhouse Rock" with Dad and he said, "He's losing his voice, this is too high for him." He said, "Yeah, they're always making him do something that was too high."

Brent: The guys at RCA thought it was more commercial to do it in a higher key?

Alan: You know, I never saw them rehearse. Like for any of the shows they did at the Band Shell in Centennial Park. Or that show at Percy Priest Lake for the opening of the dam. I don't ever recall them rehearsing.

Brent: They might have rehearsed right before they were supposed to go on. Run through it.

Alan: Well, they sang so much together that it's not as if they had to.

In your memory, did Neal ever come up with an arrangement that was so unusual from what they usually did that they had to really think about it a lot, or did it always seem to be, oh, organic?

Alan: I don't recall anything that gave them a whole lot of trouble.

Brent: The only thing that comes to mind when you ask that is I was always intrigued when they would not repeat what the singer was singing but they would occasionally turn that around and make their repeat third person rather than first person. I always wondered how they made that decision. They did it a few times. "Teddy Bear" is one of them. "Oh let me be (Oh let him be) your Teddy bear."

Alan: I think Neal liked—to me a lot of their vocal parts are horn parts. Like what you might have heard behind '40s vocalists. Bop-bop; bop-bop. Hasenpfeffer; hasenpfeffer—in the song, "G.I. Blues," from the movie of the same name." It's not a great song but man, their background on it—I'm thinkin' *all* the Hollywood sound stage stuff they did were written arrangements. I doubt they'd leave their movie arrangements to hillbillies from Nashville.

Alan: You know I was thinking about this earlier today. Dad started playing piano with the Jordanaires in '51. By '55, just four years later, he was the manager; and singing. Just four years.

Brent: He would have told you he had no experience in either one.

Alan: And he would have said, "I didn't know what I was doing." He'd be the first to tell you, "I shouldn't have been doing any of that. It was God's will that I do it."

Alan: I never saw Dad feel the pressure to continue to perform, continue to be successful. He wanted to be, but he never outwardly showed that pressure. He didn't blow up at us. He didn't blow up at mom.

Brent: No, he always seemed to take it all in stride, the ups and downs of them being the Jordanaires.

When, in your minds, did the business begin to calm down? When did the artists and producers no longer feel the need for the Jordanaires every session?

Brent: Early '80s. I remember Dad saying, "I wish we were still on fire like we were in the '60s."

Alan: Nobody in his generation was on fire like they were in the '60s. All those people, like the A-Team, it had stopped for many of them. They [the quartet] continued to work. They did a Thanksgiving Day with Don McLean at Carnegie Hall for how many years and of course, all the Elvis impersonator shows.

Brent: They worked with B.J. Thomas a lot. They worked a lot still, but things had shifted.

Alan: The producers were getting younger. It wasn't Owen. It wasn't Chet. Tony Brown used them some. Larry Butler. Larry (producer of Johnny Cash and Kenny Rogers hits) was the last of the classic producers to use them a lot. That was in the late '70s or early '80s. That was "Lucille" and "The Gambler."

Brent: Yeah, and the Dottie West and Kenny Rogers duets. They were using younger singers for backup. Instead of a quartet they'd use a pair of voices, retracked.

The Jordanaires never completely went away from gospel music?

Alan: Not completely. One of the last albums they did was a Bluegrass gospel album, which is a double CD. Dad always said that Neal had something against Bluegrass music and he wasn't sure what it was. He said, "We would have never done that album, had Neal still been living. He would never have agreed to do that." But Neal was gone. Dad, of course, loved all that Bluegrass gospel stuff. He loved John Cowan. That kind of soaring tenor. Neal's dad, Neal Matthews Sr., was a guitarist for the Fruit Jar Drinkers (a pioneer hillbilly group that played the Grand Ole Opry for many years). Our Neal was known early on in his career as "Junior Matthews." I've got a Wally Fowler radio show, where Neal plays guitar. *They* call him "Junior Matthews."

Neal didn't want to do anything with Bluegrass. But Dad loved it.

The Jordanaires used to do those gospel quartet conventions. The last time they did it, though, they were appearing with a prominent gospel group. And one of the singers made a comment; he said, "Aw, you gotta love these gospel music women fans. You sing your way into their hearts and then you get into their pants." Dad said, "Neal looked at me, and I looked at him, and he said, 'We'll never go to another one of these.'" And they never did another one.

Brent: That sounds like Dad and Neal.

Alan: Dad told me a couple of times, when I was thinking of playing drums kind of professionally, maybe I'd play with a gospel group, he said, "Gospel groups are not all they appear to be." You know, the Jordanaires didn't do like, southern gospel, they did more Golden Gate Quartet, more black gospel music than they did southern gospel music. They were totally different. And then later when they were doing those albums for Capitol, they had that gospel feel but they had really close harmonies, and sophisticated arrangements, where they were syncopated spirituals. Dad always said, "Jordanaire albums like 'Heavenly Spirit' and 'Gloryland,' are what drew Elvis to us, hand-clappin', syncopated." He said that a gospel song tried to teach a moral, while a spiritual, in most cases told a story right out of the Bible: "Jesus Met the Woman at the Well," "Shadrack," "Joshua," "Ezekial Saw the Wheel," songs that tell stories.

Did the Jordanaires change country and pop, or did they just go along with the changes that were a part of their era?

Alan: The music did change, certainly, from the '50s to the '60s, from the '60s to the '70s. They were part of the change, and they were so adaptable, they could change into whatever you needed, and they were so prevalent, I mean they did so much work, they worked with everybody. On one hand, they did what was asked of them. On the other, the artists and producers wanted that Jordanaire sound. So in the long run, I think without either the Jordanaires, or the artists and producers knowing exactly what was happening, there was a lot of give and take. I don't think they made big changes, maybe just session to session, and then day to day, and week to week, month to month and then before you know it it's year to year, and remember this, everything they did in the studio was in response to the needs of the songs, and the artists, and the producers. Had the songs been different, the changes in the music would have been different. Sometimes Neal got inspirations you could not miss, but often the Jordanaires' contributions were subtle. Then once those records were mixed and the producer or artist could hear what they had done, they wanted the quartet on their next sessions. The influence of the Jordanaires was the force of recording after recording, year after year, song after song, hit after hit.

Brent: But the Jordanaires couldn't have done what they did without all those great songs, and those great musicians, and those Nashville string arrangements that critics love to complain about, and of course, the great artists like Elvis, and Patsy, and Ricky, and Marty Robbins and Loretta Lynn and Jim Reeves and I could go on and on. When talented people come together and collaborate, great music happens.

Alan: The backup groups were largely an attempt by Owen to widen the appeal of the music, to try to take some of the hard edges off it. That's been the age-old complaint about the Nashville sound, you know, took the steel guitars and the fiddles out and put in a vocal group. They [the Jordanaires] were adept at figuring out what the producer wanted, what was needed. They weren't stuck in one bag. If they were it was a *big* bag. They just wanted themselves to be valuable; they wanted to keep working. So they would do whatever it took to keep working, like anybody. You know, they didn't know today if they were gonna have sessions a year from now. But they knew today that they had a session booked tomorrow, and they knew what was coming up and they just continued to evolve, and they were hip enough to be able to do that.

They didn't say we do this and that's what we do and if you don't like it, hire somebody else. They never said that. They'd say, "What do you want?" and they'd do it. You want us to bray like a donkey? We'll do it. And they did. Listen to "The Electrified Donkey," by Johnny Horton. That's what they're doing at the end of it. You can hear Ray at the end of it, braying like a donkey. And I doubt that that was a written arrangement, I'll bet they said, "Can you sound like a donkey here?" "Sure. Sure." "Can you sound like marching men in the Revolutionary War here?" "We can do that!" "There's a raging river, the bridge has washed out. Can you give us something that visualizes that?" Listen to Warner Mack's "The Bridge Washed Out."

They did what they had to do to make the song work. They didn't think it was stupid—well, they might have occasionally thought it was stupid but they did it anyway. And they didn't make a joke out of it unless it was kind of *meant* to be a joke.

Brent: Mom remembers Dad coming home one night and saying, "I've gotta watch TV tonight, we've gotta see this kid, this kid that we sang with, with the long sideburns is gonna be on TV tonight and I wanna see him." Dad said, "I could not remember his name. I knew it was a strange name." This was probably in the late spring or early summer of 1956, probably when Elvis was doing the Dorsey television summer replacement show. Dad knew it was a strange name but he just couldn't remember it. Dad ran into Ed Sullivan in an elevator, years later, and he went over to him and said, "Mr. Sullivan, I'm Gordon Stoker with the Jordanaires."

He said, "I remember you. I remember all you guys."

Brent has a couple more memories of his dad and, for that matter, the industry he served.

Brent: When we were kids, my brother Alan, our sister Venita and I were told not to boast about how Dad made his living. In fact, if we were asked, we were told to say only that he was self-employed. Consequently, none of us are likely to bring it up these days in conversation with those who aren't aware. But if someone mentions his career in music to us, we'll happily discuss it. When people marvel at his success and achievements, I always make sure I tell them, "He did indeed have a great career. But he was also really a wonderful father." I suspect not everyone with a family member in the music business can make such a claim.

Dad was a very enthusiastic music lover, and his enthusiasm rubbed off on his kids. I spent lots of time in my bedroom listening to music when I was growing up. When I was a teenager, sometimes he would knock on my door and come into my room saying something like, "Last night I heard you playing a record and it went like this (he would sing something to me). What was that? Play that for me." I have wonderful memories of us enjoying great records together such as "A Good Feeling to Know" by Poco (he loved the harmony, the drumming and joyous feel of it), the Eagles' "Take It to the Limit" with Randy Meisner's soaring tenor; Paul McCartney's tenor and Ringo Starr's drumming on "Get Back," pretty much anything by Credence Clearwater Revival (he couldn't get over John Fogerty's unique voice), and the purity of Emmylou Harris's take on "Sweet Dreams," which, of course, the Jordanaires had recorded years earlier with Patsy Cline, and also the song's writer Don Gibson. He loved the joy and celebration found in Stephen Stills's "Love the One You're With." Although I was never sure if he realized what the lyrics were really saying in that one!

I asked him a few years before he died if there were any artists he wished they had recorded with. The only two he mentioned to me were Emmylou Harris and Don Williams.

Backstage at a live appearance (it may have been the Grand Ole Opry) he was approached by a woman who asked for an autograph; she proclaimed what a big fan she was. As he began to sign for her, she said that "El Paso" was the kind of record no one else could have recorded. He quickly realized she thought he was Marty Robbins. He tried to set her straight and assure her he wasn't Marty, but she wouldn't have it. She was insistent. So he signed the autograph as "Marty Robbins." She walked away happy. Dad said he told Marty about it later and they shared a laugh; Marty didn't mind at all.

One of the artists the Jordanaires worked with in Nashville in the early '60s was the great Clyde McPhatter, best known as a solo artist and also lead singer of the Drifters early in their history. Clyde wanted all the singers and musicians to go out to eat together after a session. But he found this to be problematic in the segregated South of the '60s. Restaurants were either "all white" or "all black" but virtually none would allow a mixed party. They finally found a mostly "all black" eatery that agreed to serve them in the back room where they couldn't be seen by the other patrons.

Alan: I think Dad is one of the best remembered people in the history of the Nashville music business. He spent his professional life making music in Nashville and just about everywhere else in the United States and overseas, and wherever he made music, he made friends. I never knew a man who had more friends.

Chapter 13

THE JORDANAIRES: WHAT DID THEY LEAVE FOR US?

If you were lucky enough to grow up in the 1950s and 1960s, you and the rest of America went through what might have been the most rapid change in the history of our music culture. In the 1940s and the early 1950s, most American teenagers pretty much listened to the same music as their parents did. Within about six years, that music would split into two different cultures, fragmented by an age rift that has never quite healed.

The Jordanaires were smack in the middle of this big change. And they didn't intend to be. It just happened while they made their living singing the music they were trained to sing and mostly loved what they were doing. You know, you can draw a line from Hank Williams to Elvis to the Beatles, and the Jordanaires were a part of all of it. In the early 1950s, you could have caught them and Hank at the Grand Ole Opry. Then for 14 years starting in 1956, they were the vocal heart and soul of most of Elvis's hits and, according to Paul McCartney, an inspiration for the Beatles' powerful harmonies. Listen to the vocal ending on the early Beatle classic "She Loves You." It's like the sound the Jordanaires sang with Elvis at the end of "Teddy Bear."

The music revolution was built around southern po' folks music, that is, the so-called hillbilly music of poor southern white folks, the blues and rhythm and blues of poor southern black folks, and the religious music of both. A lot of "new" music isn't new music at all but rather a fusion of several older music genres, and the fusion of the 1950s and 1960s was a doozy. Rhythm and blues was, after all, heavily influenced by black gospel music, and early white rock and roll was heavily influenced by country hillbilly music—and black gospel music. The Jordanaires sang a lot of spirituals that came

205

directly from the black traditions, and when the original quartet moved from Springfield, Missouri, to Nashville, they brought their sound with them. Nashville was busy building its reputation as a destination for musical talent, and the exciting sound of the Jordanaires quickly found a place on Nashville radio. Soon, they were singing some backup here, some backup there for country stars like Red Foley and Hank Snow, and appearing on WSM radio shows with Hank Williams and many others. In those days, mainstream country records often contained two-part harmony sections but hardly ever a backup chorus to add power to the production.

The Jordanaires would soon change that. And they freely give credit to Elvis, who believed in the Jordanaires as a prime element of the Elvis sound.

The timing was perfect. By the mid-1950s, white kids were discovering rhythm and blues, and a man named Sam Phillips was on the lookout for a white kid who could sound black. He found a few of those, including a Mississippi natural named Elvis Presley. Elvis became a sensation in the South, and he happened to think that the Jordanaires hung the moon. When RCA signed him, the executives and producers in the company soon learned that he had some definite ideas about what his records should sound like, and one of those ideas was that they should sound something like the Jordanaires' gospel and spiritual records. To a southern Baptist or Pentecostal kid, those gospel-tinged rhythm-and-blues and rock-and-roll records were happy familiar music, but to a lot of the kids outside the South, that music created all sorts of brand-new excitement, made them dance, and made them happy. Of course, it was a little too much for many of their parents, who had been raised on the music of Irving Berlin and Cole Porter.

When Paul McCartney and John Lennon were learning to become rock-and-roll stars, they absorbed all sorts of knowledge of rhythm, phrasing, lyrics, melodies, and harmonies, and those early Elvis RCA records brought the Jordanaires into their lives. Some unhappy readers will say that they heard the Beatles were heavily influenced by the harmonies of the Everly Brothers or maybe even the Beach Boys. Well, heck, who of us wasn't? What made the Beatles the Beatles was their ability to soak up sounds from everywhere, combine them with their own inspirations, and believe in the result. The Jordanaires were one source.

During the recent Disney+ showing of the Peter Jackson Beatles film, Get Back, *there's a conversation in the Apple Studios control room during a discussion on how to end Paul McCartney's song "Let It Be."*

John: Do that old gospel ending . . . that Elvis did

Paul: Sunday morning, Sunday morning church. Sunday morning. Definitely, yeah.

John: We can do that gospel ending, that Elvis did. Be . . . ee . . . eee

Be . . . ee. . . . eee . . . The same ending that Elvis and the quartet used on the end of Elvis's 1956 recording "Any Way You Want Me (That's How I Will Be)." The same ending Monty Matthews came up with six years earlier, and the Jordanaires used on their 1950 DECCA recording of the gospel song "Dig a Little Deeper." Elvis's record was a secular recording, but he wanted to use that gospel ending, and the Beatles recognized it as being a gospel ending. The Beatles used a different ending for "Let It Be," but the fact that John Lennon brought it up as a consideration means that it still was in the musical lexicon many years later.

Did the Jordanaires run into the kinds of changes that eventually put limits on all pop careers? Of course they did. They were fortunate in that the Top 40 radio format grew up close to the time that Elvis broke big and also about the time that Owen and Harold Bradley cobbled together their studio complex on 16th Avenue

South near downtown Nashville. Never before or since was there a radio format as open as Top 40.

All of a sudden, you could hear, on pop radio, Faron Young and Ferlin Husky and Skeeter Davis and Marty Robbins and Patsy Cline. And you heard lots of Elvis. And where there was Elvis (and Ricky, Patsy, and Ferlin) and so much more, there were the Jordanaires. For just a little while, pop fans were exposed to country music without that music being ridiculed or stereotyped by provincial mainstream media. Wherever there was pop music or country music, there were the Jordanaires. Never before or since was a vocal sound as ubiquitous as that of the Jordanaires in the late 1950s and through the 1960s and on and on. For their sound to last as long as it did was astounding considering how much of it we heard every day. The Jordanaires' career lasted from 1948 to 2013, and for much of that period, they set the standard for backup vocal groups. There were other great ones, to be sure, but the Jordanaires set the standard.

The Jordanaires had advantages. They were fast in creating the sounds and fast in getting them down. Their oohs and aahs were sweet and their syllables creative and communicative, and when the record called for a powerful harmonic blend on a chorus, they delivered. In short, they were reliable, and they were good! They were money in the bank. They had Neal. And a lot of listeners liked the sounds that they heard, even if they didn't know who made those sounds.

One reason Elvis loved them so much was that they were likable and lovable. They were good at helping to keep a session relaxed and creative.

They were especially important during the mono and early stereo days of recording, when one clinker out of a guitar or a voice meant you had to start over again. The Jordanaires could get it right the first take. Once again, money in the bank. Then in the 1960s and 1970s, technology changed things. Three tracks. Four tracks. Eight tracks. Sixteen tracks. Twenty-four tracks! With lots of tracks and good separation, when one musician or singer screwed up, you could finish the take and then have the erring performer do his or her part over.

By the 1980s, instead of having four or five voices singing background, the producer might hire two good singers, and they could do all the voices that used to require an entire quartet or, for that matter, an entire choir.

As the years went by, maybe the Jordanaires didn't get quite as many calls for sessions with the hottest artists, but they were not forgotten. With the death of Elvis, a new cottage industry grew up in the music world called the Elvis impersonator, or most recently, Elvis tribute artist (ETA). No longer able to see the King live, there were still huge numbers of Elvis fans willing to see a good Elvis impersonator, and if the Jordanaires were on that show backing him up, why, that was almost like having the King there himself.

There was a singer out in the world who was not *an Elvis impersonator and who never met Elvis but who nevertheless carved out a successful music career closely related to Elvis and the Jordanaires. His name is Ronnie McDowell, and it was only natural that the Jordanaires would be a part of his career for many years.*

One day in 1977, while he was driving from Nashville to Bowling Green, Kentucky, he turned on his car radio and heard the deejay say, "It's official, Elvis Presley has passed away."

Ronnie McDowell

So I tuned in station after station, and heard the same thing. Before I had made it out of Nashville, these words poured out of me:

I was barely six years old when I first heard him sing,
And somehow I knew it would be a lifetime thing.
And I'd stand in front of a mirror day and night
And I repeated every word and note till I finally got it right.

These four lines of verse would transform the life of a struggling singer-songwriter.

The next day I flew down to Memphis 'cause I had never laid eyes on Elvis. I thought, well, I'm gonna see Elvis, alive or dead, so I decided to see him lying in state. I got in line at 8:30 in the morning and, this is God's truth, there was a line five abreast, a mile long, to get into Graceland. It was August, getting hotter and hotter as the day wore on. People were fallin' out, fainting. I got to the gate at five o'clock. How my bladder held up, I'll never know. Ten feet from the gate, I saw them shut it tight. People started rioting. I said, "I don't want no part of this," so I got in my Camaro and headed back to Nashville. Halfway home, I had the radio on and it told me, "Well, they've reopened the gate." And here's how fate'll find you. I did not head back to Memphis, I continued back to Nashville, to the office of the little label I was signed with, Scorpion Records, and there was a guy standing in the office, name of Lee Morgan, and he said, "Hey Ronnie, let's do a tribute to Elvis," and I said, "Hey man, I ain't wearing no jump suit."

"That ain't what I'm talkin' about," he snapped back at me. "Listen to this song I wrote." I listened to him sing it to me, and something inside of me lit up. I said, "Hey man, listen to what *I* wrote," and I recited that verse you read up above. Lee said, "Well, let's put your part on the front and then you sing my song," and so the next day, we walked into a studio with some musicians and just threw this thing together. I walked out that night owing half of a bill of $2,800, 20th century dollars. *I* didn't have any money. Lee Morgan he walked up to me and he said, "You're gonna have to pay for this. I don't have a dime." I said, "Lee, I've got forty dollars to my name." Well, I had my checkbook and I wrote, this is God's truth, $2,800 in hot checks to musicians, the studio, for the tape, whatever we owed, I paid in worthless paper.

The next morning at 8 a.m. I sat on the steps of Monument Studios waiting for someone, anyone. Along comes Gail Pollock, who I'd known for two or three years. "Ronnie, what are you doing here this early?" she asked and I said, "Gail I want some acetates made." Acetates were a sort of coated metal disc, a cheap, quick way to make a copy of a recording that you could play on a record player for somebody. At the time maybe they cost about eight bucks apiece.

She looked at me and the little box I was carrying and said, "Ronnie, what you got?"

"Gail, I think I got a hit song. Of course, I didn't *know*, I just *felt* like I did. So we walked upstairs and they made us eight of those acetates, and this guy walked by while they was makin' one of them, and he stood there for a minute, listening, and he said, "Who is that?"

I said that's me and he said if I gave him one of those he'd take it back to his Indianapolis radio station, where he was the program director. He said his name was Lee Shannon. He asked me for my phone number and told me he would play the record on the air and if he got any reaction he'd call me. Later I told this story to a friend of mine who owns the world's largest comic book distributorship and he reminded me that if I had gone back to Memphis then when I had returned to Nashville Lee Morgan would not have been standing at Scorpion Records, we would have never assembled "The King Is Gone," and of course I never would have recorded it. "So fate plucked you out of those hundreds of thousands of people lined up in Memphis, and sent you back to Nashville. That was your destiny. Fate found you, and picked you to be the voice of the greatest entertainer that ever lived on planet earth."

So here is the rest of the story. I took my acetates and headed straight to an AM station in Madison, just north of Nashville, a little station called WENO. Why I went there I'll never know, maybe because I thought that little station would let me walk in, so I did and I held up an acetate and said to a woman there, "Would you play this song?" She said, "We don't do that off the street, to which I replied, "Well, it's about Elvis Presley."

She said, "Well, hold on a minute."

She went back and handed a copy to the DJ. There was a glass wall or a window between me and his little studio. He pointed at me and said, "Stand right here. I'm gonna play this, see if you get any reaction." Hey, it wasn't even a fourth of the way into the record when the phone lines began to light up. He said, "Damn, something's wrong with my phones!"

He had to play that song for three solid hours back to back, and the phone lines kept lighting up, more and more people wanting to hear the song.

I was on a roll. From WENO I went straight to WLAC, the biggest rock station in Nashville. It was downtown in the Stahlman building, a tougher nut to crack. There I found three guys standing in the hallway and a secretary behind a desk, and I told her what happened at WENO. I don't think she was impressed. She said, "Well, we're the number 1 rock station and we just don't do stuff like that, but hold on a minute." She handed an acetate to one of the guys, who walked through an open doorway, then a bit later walked back out and said, "I'm gonna play this, see if we get any reaction." He came out a few minutes later and said, "Son, you have jammed our phone lines. You've got a monster." That rock deejay was John Conlee, who would later become a star of the Grand Ole Opry and singer of hit country records.

A short time passed. I drove to see my mother who held down three jobs to take care of her younger children. She was mopping the floor of a truck stop up in Franklin, Kentucky, the town where I first saw the Elvis Presley hit movie, "King Creole." And I said, "Mother, take your apron off, you don't ever have to work again." She said, "Son, don't you see I'm workin'?"

And this truck driver, who was listening to what's going on and had apparently been listening to country and pop radio stations as he drove through the South, said, "Georgie May, don't you know what's going on with that boy?" She said no and I said, "Mother, come on out to the car." This is the God's truth. I turned the radio on and twisted the tuning knob, and my song was on just about every station, gospel, country, rock, pop, and my mother never worked again as long as she lived. And that's the reason why I owe a bigger debt of gratitude to Elvis Presley than anybody.

I was in Walker, Louisiana, weeks later, at the Old South Jamboree, and this guy come up and said, "Dick Clark is on the phone for you." I said, "Yeah, right." But I walked to the back of the venue and got on the phone, and Dick Clark said, "Ronnie, there's a private jet for you at the Baton Rouge Airport, get on it, get some rest, you're on American Bandstand tomorrow." I never slept a friggin' wink. Next day they put me in a helicopter, I landed right on the ABC lot, and they come runnin' out and rushed me into makeup. Dick Clark came in. I'm lookin' in the mirror. I said, "Wow, Dick Clark! I can't believe I'm here." He said, "Ronnie, you're number 9. You sold a million records in a week. You deserve to be here." I said, "Mr. Clark, I'm so glad that y'all pantomime," and he said, "Ronnie, we don't do that any more. You gotta sing it live." I said, "Please don't tell me that." He said, "When that red light comes on, Ronnie, you'll have cue cards underneath the camera." That was before a lot of places had monitor speakers. He said, "You'll have cue cards. Millions of people will be watching you." I went, "Oh, my God, *please* don't tell me *that!*"

You know if you Google me, doing my song on American Bandstand, I look like a guy who's in total control but inside, I was petrified. And that's the story of how that went.

"The King Is Gone" almost made it to the Top 10 on the Billboard Hot 100 Singles *chart, sold millions all over the world, and helped establish a prosperous career music for Ronnie McDowell. For a couple of years, he stayed with Scorpion Records. During that time, he started using the Jordanaires as his backup group on his shows, and that led to a special request from Gordon.*

Gordon came to me and said, "Hey, we want to put our name with you on your records."

"What do you mean?" I asked him, and he said, "You know, like Elvis used to do with us."

I said, "Are you kidding me?" That would be a dream for me. I couldn't believe that they wanted to do that. That was one of the biggest thrills of my life. The first record I did with them was a song I had written called "Animal," and from then on I used them on all my records.

I have so many great memories of the Jordanaires because not only did I record with them, but I performed on the road with them over almost as many years as Elvis lived.

Ronnie was different from the Elvis impersonators that the Jordanaires worked with over the years in that he became a well-known country artist with his own span of hit songs. Although his vocal style approached that of Elvis, he could stand in for Elvis without imitating him. When they performed together, Ronnie's voice and the Jordanaires' backup vocals had a stunning effect on the crowds they drew and kept their career going on a high level. Also with them through many of those twilight years were Elvis's guitar player, Scotty Moore, and his drummer, D. J. Fontana. What a show that must have been!

I never will forget, the first time we played at the Horseshoe, in Tupelo. Nobody who played there played two nights, everybody played just one night. We planned to end our show with "American Trilogy," because what we would do, I would sing Elvis songs and the Jordanaires would tell all these unbelievable interesting stories about Elvis, and so the very first night, when we ended with the American Trilogy, the entertainment director came backstage and said, "Well, I'm gonna be honest with you, we don't do this, but you guys have gone over so unbelievable that next time you come here I want you to do Friday *and* Saturday night." And for 10 years that's what we did, we did Friday and Saturday, and sold out, every time we were there. All those people, they weren't coming to see me. They were coming to see Scotty and D.J. and the Jordanaires, all that history, and all the stories they would tell. I never got tired of hearing them. Some of them the crowd liked, and some of the stories they told, the crowd didn't like, because there were some things they didn't want to know.

But you know the Jordanaires, they would just tell them, and the crowd would learn that at the very first "Heartbreak Hotel" session, Sam Phillips told Elvis, "Don't let them change you, they will try to change what you are and what you do." And they'd hear that Chet Atkins was over in the corner telling Scotty how to play the guitar and Elvis walked over to him and said, "Ah, Mr. Atkins, we have our own sound and I'd appreciate it if you just let us do what we do."

And Gordon would tell them, Elvis disliked Chet Atkins until the day he died but, on the other hand, Chet Atkins called his wife during that session and said, "You've gotta come down here. I've never seen or heard anything like this in my life!"

In 2013, Gordon Stoker passed away at the age of 88, and when that happened, the Jordanaires finally closed up shop. There would be no faux Jordanaire groups traveling the country pretending to be something that they were not. And that was good because the Jordanaires were authentic, even when they were replicating a black female trio or a white swing-era foursome, because they knew the music, and they respected it.

Check out the Jordanaires backing up Elvis on "All Shook Up," "Too Much," "Don't Be Cruel," or "Don't" or the Jordanaires doing one of their gospel tracks, "Working on a Building" or "Dig a Little Deeper." Check out their videos backing up Tennessee Ernie Ford, Don Gibson, or Patsy Cline. See the joy on their faces and hear the joy in their voices. Then remember that most of what they did in their 65 years of existence was stand in the background, sing their wonderful harmonies, and help the featured artist on the session be the best that he or she could be. The Jordanaires were the best, ever, at that.

SOURCE LIST

OH179 CMHOF Gordon Stoker 1974-11-22
OH180 CMHOF Gordon Stoker 1975-02-07
OHC282 CMHOF Gordon Stoker 1983-02-28
OHC283 CMHOF Gordon Stoker 1983-08-03
OHC284 CMHOF Gordon Stoker 1985-11-18
OHC014 CMHOF Gordon Stoker 2001-08-06
OHC286 CMHOF Gordon Stoker 1991-06-13
OHC285 CMHOF Gordon Stoker 1988-06-28
N'ville Cats CMHOF Gordon Stoker, Ray Walker, Bill Lloyd
Self-tape Gordon Stoker 2004-03
Interview Gordon Stoker 2005-04-15
Facebook File Alan Stoker, Brent Stoker 2013–2021
Interview Greg Matthews 2021-07
Interview A. Stoker, Brent Stoker 2021-07
Interview Curtis Young 2021-07
Interview Hylton Hawkins 2021-07
Interview Hargus Robbins 2021-08
Interview Brenda Lee, 2021-08
Interview Bergen White 2021-08
Interview Cole 2021-08
Interview Ronnie McDowell 2021-08
E-mail Ron Oates, Alan Stoker 2021-09

SIX DECADES OF GRAMMY-WINNING RECORDINGS FEATURING THE JORDANAIRES

(list does not include Grammy-nominated recordings)

- 1959: Best Country and Western Performance, "The Battle of New Orleans," Johnny Horton
- 1961: Best Country and Western Recording, "Big Bad John," Jimmy Dean
- 1964: Best Gospel or Other Religious Recordings (Musical), *Great Gospel Songs* (Album), Tennessee Ernie Ford
- 1966: Best Country and Western Single, "Almost Persuaded," David Houston
- 1966: Best Country and Western Recording, "Almost Persuaded," David Houston
- 1967: Best Sacred Performance, "How Great Thou Art," Elvis Presley
- 1969: Best Country Vocal Performance, Female, "Stand by Your Man," Tammy Wynette
- 1971: Best Country Vocal Performance by a Duo or Group, "After the Fire Is Gone," Loretta Lynn and Conway Twitty
- 1977: Best Country Vocal Performance, Male, "Lucille," Kenny Rogers
- 1979: Best Country Vocal Performance, Male, "The Gambler," Kenny Rogers
- 1980: Best Country Vocal Performance, Male, "He Stopped Loving Her Today," George Jones
- 1981: Best Gospel Recording, "Amazing Grace," B. J. Thomas
- 1987: Best Polka Recording, "A Polka Just for Me," Jimmy Sturr and his Orchestra
- 1988: Best Polka Recording, "Born to Polka," Jimmy Sturr and his Orchestra
- 1989: Best Polka Recording, "All in My Love for You," Jimmy Sturr and his Orchestra

- 1995: Best Polka Recording, "I Love to Polka," Jimmy Sturr and his Orchestra
- 1996: Best Polka Recording, "Polka! All Night Long," Jimmy Sturr and his Orchestra
- 1997: Best Polka Recording, "Living on Polka Time," Jimmy Sturr and his Orchestra
- 1998: Best Polka Recording, "Dance with Me," Jimmy Sturr and his Orchestra
- 2000: Best Polka Recording, "Touched by a Polka," Jimmy Sturr and his Orchestra
- 2001: Best Polka Recording, "Gone Polka," Jimmy Sturr and his Orchestra
- 2002: Best Polka Recording, "Top of the World," Jimmy Sturr and his Orchestra
- 2002: Best Southern, Country, or Bluegrass Gospel Album, *We Called Him Mr. Gospel Music: James Blackwood Tribute*, the Jordanaires, Larry Ford, and the Light Crust Doughboys
- 2003: Best Country Album, *Livin', Lovin', Losin': Songs of the Louvin Brothers*, various artists
- 2006: Best Polka Recording, "Polka in Paradise," Jimmy Sturr and his Orchestra
- 2007: Best Country Collaboration with Vocals, "Lost Highway," Willie Nelson and Ray Price
- 2008: Best Polka Album, *Let the Whole World Sing*, Jimmy Sturr and his Orchestra

INDEX

Page references for figures are italicized.